FRAGMENTED TIES

FRAGMENTED TIES

*Salvadoran Immigrant Networks
in America*

CECILIA MENJÍVAR

UNIVERSITY OF CALIFORNIA PRESS
BERKELEY   LOS ANGELES   LONDON

University of California Press
Berkeley and Los Angeles, California

University of California Press, Ltd.
London, England

©2000 by the Regents of the University of California

Library of Congress Cataloging-in-Publication Data

Menjívar, Cecilia
    Fragmented ties : Salvadoran immigrant networks in
America / Cecilia Menjívar.
        p.   cm.
    Includes bibliographical references and index.
    ISBN 0-520-22210-5 (cloth : alk. paper). — ISBN 0-520-
22211-3 (pbk. : alk. paper)
    1. Salvadoran Americans — California — San Francisco —
Social networks.   2. Immigrants — California — San Francisco — Social networks.   3. Salvadoran Americans — California — San Francisco — Social conditions.   4. Immigrants —
California — San Francisco — Social conditions.   5. San Francisco (Calif.) — Emigration and immigration.   6. San Francisco (Calif.) — Social conditions.   7. El Salvador — Emigration and immigration.   I. Title.
F869.S39 S155 2000
305.868'7284073 — dc21   00-020171

Manufactured in the United States of America
09 08 07 06 05 04 03 02
10 9 8 7 6 5 4 3 2

For Victor and Sasha

Poema de Amor

Los que ampliaron el Canal de Panamá
(y fueron clasificados como 'silver roll' y no como 'gold roll'),
los que repararon la flota del Pacífico
en las bases de California,
los que se pudrieron en las cárceles de Guatemala,
México, Honduras, Nicaragua,
por ladrones, por contrabandistas, por estafadores,
por hambrientos,
los siempre sospechosos de todo
("me permito remitirle al interfecto
por esquinero sospechoso
y con el agravante de ser salvadoreño"),
las que llenaron los bares y los burdeles
de todos los puertos y las capitales de la zona
("La gruta azul," "El Calzoncito," "Happyland"),
los sembradores de maíz en plena selva extranjera,
los reyes de la página roja,
los que nunca sabe nadie de dónde son,
los mejores artesanos del mundo,
los que fueron cosidos a balazos al cruzar la frontera,
los que murieron de paludismo
o de las picadas del escorpión o la barba amarilla
en el infierno de las bananeras,
los que lloraran borrachos por el himno nacional
bajo el ciclón del Pacífico o la nieve del norte,
los arrimados, los mendigos, los marihuaneros,
los guanacos hijos de la gran puta,
los que apenitas pudieron regresar,
los que tuvieron un poco más de suerte,
los eternos indocumentados,
los hacelotodo, los vendelotodo, los comelotodo,
los primeros en sacar el cuchillo,

los tristes más tristes del mundo,
mis compatriotas,
mis hermanos.

ROQUE DALTON, Salvadoran poet
and writer (1935–1975)
Reprinted with permission
from the Dalton Cañas family

POEM OF LOVE

(English translation)

Those who widened the Panama Canal
(and were on the 'silver roll' not the 'gold roll'),
those who repaired the Pacific fleet
in California bases,
those who rotted in prisons in Guatemala,
Mexico, Honduras, Nicaragua,
for stealing, smuggling, swindling,
for starving,
those always suspected of everything
("Allow me to place him in your custody
for suspicious loitering
aggravated by the fact of being Salvadoran"),
those who pack the bars and whorehouses
in every port and capital
("The Blue Grotto," "The G-String," "Happyland"),
the sowers of corn deep in foreign forests,
the crime barons of the scandal sheets,
those who nobody ever knows where they're from,
the best artisans in the world,
those who were riddled with bullets crossing the border,
those who died from malaria
or scorpion bites or swarming bees
in the hell of banana plantations,
those who got drunk and wept for the national anthem
under a Pacific cyclone or up north in the snow,
the spongers, beggers, pot-heads,
the stupid sons of whores,
those who were barely able to get back,

those who had a little more luck,
the forever undocumented,
those who do anything, sell anything, eat anything,
the first ones to pull a knife,
the wretched the most wretched of the earth,
my compatriots,
my brothers.

ROQUE DALTON
From *Poems* by Roque Dalton,
translated by Richard Schaaf
(Curbstone Press, 1984);
reprinted with permission
from Curbstone Press

Contents

Map on page 60

Tables

Acknowledgments

This project took a long time to complete, and therefore the list of people to whom I am indebted is a long one. First and foremost, I would like to thank the many Salvadorans who took the time to talk with me, for not minding my asking, my probing, and my frequent presence in their day-to-day lives. Unschooled in the theoretical frameworks that are used in attempts to understand their worlds, they knew better how to make sense of their condition and taught me a great deal about the social interactions that make up their lives. In the process I learned about the true meaning of friendships, human relations, the greatness of the heart, and other important things in life. I cannot acknowledge my interlocutors by name because I promised them anonymity, but my debt to them remains irredeemable.

In San Francisco, there were several people who helped greatly to make this project possible. Rosario Anaya, director of the Mission Language and Vocational School, believed in my work and was supportive in a number of ways. At CARECEN, José Cartagena, Ricardo Calderón, Edwin Rodríguez, and Marina Vaquerano were particularly helpful. I especially want to thank Gloria Cañas, who supported this study from the start and was always ready to discuss my views and impressions. Bryan Schmaedick at the "Dolores Shelter" unselfishly shared with me his views and concerns about the lives of Salvadorans in San Francisco, and Carolina Guzmán lent me a most needed hand during fieldwork. And my cousin Emma Perez and her family provided me with a place to stay and many wonderful meals during fieldwork.

I received institutional support from several sources. I conducted fieldwork from 1989 to 1991 as a research assistant in a project on household strategies among immigrants in northern California. Michael P. Smith and Bernadette Tarallo obtained a grant from the California Policy Seminar to undertake this research; I thank them for having included me in their team. From 1992 to 1994 I spent additional time in the field and began writing with support from a Chancellor's Post-doctoral fellowship at the University of California at Berkeley. A Dean's Incentive Grant and a Summer Grant from the Women's Studies Program at Arizona State University (ASU) helped to complete a final draft of this manuscript.

Many people offered me support, advice, and their knowledge during the time I worked on this project, though I did not always heed their suggestions. I am particularly grateful to María Patricia Fernández-Kelly, not only for reading three drafts of the entire manuscript, but also for her mentoring over the years and for being a gracious senior colleague. Her work has influenced me intellectually, and her kind words and steadfast encouragement have been crucial at various points along the way. Gary Hamilton, Michael P. Smith, and Diane Wolf — my dissertation committee at the University of California at Davis — helped me to navigate through the intricacies of doing research and to refine some of the ideas that I would later develop in this book. As a committee member, though not at Davis at that time, Roger Rouse provided some of the most thorough and helpful feedback I have ever received, which has proven invaluable in framing my arguments. Since my undergraduate years at the University of Southern California, Nora Hamilton, whose work with Norma Chinchilla has inspired my own, has never failed to offer me advice and suggestions when I have asked. At Berkeley, my conversations with my mentor Carol Stack helped me immeasurably to sharpen my arguments, and her regular reminders to "finish the book" must have influenced the eventual completion of this work. I also benefited from the presence of Laura Enríquez, who was generous with her advice, and Rafael Alarcón, Abel Valenzuela, Jr., and Richard (Dick) Walker, who offered me their collegiality and stimulating conversation during the lonely stages of writing.

Several friends and colleagues have given me important support along the way. Pierrette Hondagneu-Sotelo shared her experiences in doing research and writing; Rose Weitz provided fine editorial comments and most opportune advice at crucial moments; and Néstor P. Rodríguez (also my *compadre*) has always been ready to offer support and advice. Special thanks go to Bernie Tarallo (also my *comadre*), who has been an unparalleled friend for more than a decade, for her generosity, advice, and wonderful conversations during our "coffee meetings" with Barbara Lerch. I am also grateful to Beverly Lozano, for her comments and guidance and for helping me intellectually more than she knows; to Amanda Noble, for providing good humor along the way; and to my other good friends at Davis, for their friendship; the list is long, but they know who they are. I would also like to thank my friend Lisa Magaña, for being a good listener at critical moments, and my colleagues and most recent friends in the School of Justice Studies at ASU, for providing practical tips and supporting my work.

There are a few people who merit recognition for their assistance during the final stages of this project: Sang-Hea Kil and Mako Fitts, my skillful research assistants, for taking on tedious tasks; Walter Nicholls, my nephew and a graduate student at the University of California at Los Angeles, for promptly looking things up for me at the library; Sandy Batalden, for excellent editorial assistance; and Mary Fran Draisker at the Publications Assistance Center at ASU (who is particularly happy to see this project leave her hands), for preparing the map and the various drafts. I am grateful to Juan José Dalton Cañas for taking time out from his busy schedule to help me in every detail involved in the reproduction of his father's poem *Poema de Amor*. At the University of California Press, I am particularly thankful to Naomi Schneider for her support and valuable suggestions throughout this project; I would like to thank my reviewers for their very thoughtful comments, Sheila Berg for fine editing, and Sue Heinemann for bringing this book to completion.

I would also like to acknowledge my mother, Mercedes, my first and foremost teacher of immigration, and Tía María, an exemplary woman in many ways, for their lifelong support. They both would have been proud to see this book completed.

And then there are those who are closest to me. My friend, colleague, and husband, Victor Agadjanian, has been involved in this project in various ways since its inception. He accompanied me "to the field" many times; has been a sounding board for my ideas; has read the manuscript; has patiently listened to my ramblings and frustrations; and has supported me unflaggingly in many more ways than I can recount. And Alexander (Sasha), our toddler, who has brought into my life distractions and chaos but mostly the countless moments of indescribable joy that sustained me through the tunnel before I saw the light at the end. My life and work are certainly much better because of Victor and Sasha; I dedicate this book to them, if only as a barely adequate expression of gratitude and love.

Introduction

When people ask me where I am from, instead of saying simply, "I am from Poland," I sometimes give them my "narrative" answer. "It's a long story," I begin. . . . Being characters who often feel lost amid various narratives written for us by law, literature, politics, and history, we resort to telling stories when asked where we are from because no simple answer is possible.

> Magdalena J. Zaborowska,
> *How We Found America*

One afternoon, when I was in my office, I received a telephone call from an assistant to an HBO producer who was interested in making a film based on the life of an immigrant. Because of my work in immigrant communities, this person thought that I might have a story for them. He emphasized that they wanted a "success" story, which caused me to pause, since I was not quite sure what he meant by this. As the assistant explained that they were looking for a person whose life had significantly improved as a result of immigration, the images of several faces ran in quick succession through my mind. I disregarded most of them because in each case "improvement" could not be taken as an unqualified outcome of migration. Then I zeroed in on Marcela Q., whose life, in her view, had indeed been dramatically bettered. When the assistant asked me if this immigrant was already a permanent resident, I said no. When he inquired if this person had a stable, well-paid job, I again said no; and when he asked if this person already owned a home in the United States, once again my answer was no.

Marcela Q.'s achievements in the United States obviously did not fit conventional notions of immigrant "success" — even though she had learned to read and write in Spanish, gained knowledge of her own country's history, been able to send small sums of money to her family in El Salvador more or less regularly, encouraged her daughter to attend college, and begun making plans to write a book based on her own story. For Marcela, a former street vendor in El Salvador, life has been radically transformed by her migration to the United States. In her words, "I feel as if I have opened up a window that I didn't even know was there." Marcela cherishes her newly acquired knowledge and everything that comes with it. Although she is aware that her opportunities in the United States are highly constrained and that she faces many obstacles to her long-term goals, she is content that she has been able to "survive and continue to fight" in spite of the unsettling times during which she (like the rest of the informants in this study) arrived in the United States. She is particularly proud, though at times angry, that she has carried on in San Francisco without much help from her family — or from anyone else for that matter.

The aim of this book is to understand the inner workings of informal social networks among Salvadoran immigrants and, in the process, to identify potential reasons for their instability.[1] By social networks I mean the web of family, friends, neighbors, and so on, who can provide material, financial, informational, and emotional assistance on a regular basis (based on my observations and my informants' perceptions). From my conversations with Salvadoran immigrants, it seems that network instability is closely linked to the structure of opportunities that they encounter on arrival. I demonstrate how structural constraints condition the resources these immigrants have available to help family and friends who are in need. This angle, however, does not disregard the centrality of human agency, as macrostructural forces do delimit human action but cannot determine it entirely. Thus, throughout this study, individuals will be treated as active human beings, not as victims or as robots responding mechanically to larger forces. Their actions, aspirations, and frustrations, however, will be situated within the broader context over which they have little, if any, control. The individuals' stories, though at times unsettling, are not meant to sound an alarm about the state of social institutions among these immigrants. The accounts are testimony, however, to the conditions under which impoverished immigrants live, to the potential deleterious effects of poverty on their informal sources of assistance, and to their remarkable capacity to survive, even when they have very little, if anything, going for them.

Marcela Q., a very smart and vivacious young woman who was

forced to drop out of first grade to help her family, left El Salvador weeks before turning twenty-one; she was two months pregnant, and her husband, a government soldier, had apparently been killed in combat. Although she never saw his body, she assumed that he had been killed when they lost contact with each other after an ambush by guerrilla forces. Marcela's business, selling petty merchandise at a bus depot in the city where she was born in central El Salvador, had all but collapsed. She had tried to engage in other activities, mainly selling other items. For instance, on days when she had not made a cent and needed to buy food for her children, she would get a watermelon on credit from a fruit vendor friend, cut it up, and sell it by the piece at the same bus depot, which would bring in at least what she needed to repay the vendor friend and buy dinner. But she, and her children, simply could not subsist on such an inadequate income. So she left for the United States with only 50 *colones* (approximately U.S. $6) that she had borrowed from a friend. She left her older child with her mother and her youngest with her mother-in-law; neither grandmother would have been able to afford to support both children, even temporarily. Marcela made use of an intricate network of "friends of friends" to make the arduous two-month journey through Mexico (she crossed Guatemala quickly and relatively easily), during which she walked at least one-third of the way. After two unsuccessful attempts to cross the border into the United States, she finally entered with a group of Salvadorans she met on the U.S. side just across the border who were headed to Los Angeles. She refused to stay in Los Angeles though, because in her words, "How could I stay there? It's so difficult to come here; I wanted to get inside the United States as much as possible. Los Angeles still seemed too close to the border." But a more powerful reason was that she had cousins in San Francisco.

Hoping that her cousins would let her stay with them, Marcela found someone to take her from Los Angeles to San Francisco by car. But when she arrived, they refused to help her. "Do you know what it feels to be dropped off at 24th and Mission when you don't know anyone in this city and you don't understand the language? Well, that's what my cousins did to me. And they knew I was pregnant. But maybe they thought I'd ask them for too much. Whenever I talk with people I don't even mention that I have family here." About one and a half years later, when Marcela had her daughter Claudia baptized, things had changed radically. By then, not only were the cousins and Marcela on speaking terms, but Marcela finally seemed to have found the family support she had been seeking. Marcela even asked Sonia, one of her cousins, and me to be Claudia's godmothers, an honor that we both accepted gladly. Sonia organized a small party to celebrate the event, during which she took the opportunity to thank me "on behalf of the family" for helping Marcela in the past, when she was in desperate need. To my surprise, however, about one year later Marcela and her cousins had a major falling-out occasioned by gossip they were allegedly spreading about Marcela's ambivalent marital status and her reputation. This time Marcela was sure she would never contact them again and even took steps to erase Sonia's name from Claudia's baptismal certificate, so as to formalize the discord.

Marcela was disheartened that her cousins had let her down, and although she has since received help from friends and acquaintances, she emphasized the temporary, almost ephemeral nature of this assistance. Help from family and friends seems to come sporadically, conditionally, and unevenly; consequently, newcomers like Marcela do not benefit much from having family or friends at the point of arrival.

My objective is to portray informal networks among Salvadoran immigrants as reflecting dynamic processes, for these networks do not exist in a social vacuum; they are simultaneously affected by the context that immigrants encounter and by the social positions of the individuals involved. It is not my aim to quantify help among Salvadorans — how many received and did not receive help — or to generalize from my observations to other groups. I seek to understand how immigrants go about giving and receiving help from others in their everyday lives, so as to uncover factors that may foster or hinder such exchanges. Rather than focus on these social ties as structures, I intend to shed light on the *processes* that lie at the core of informal networks.[2] The overwhelming majority of this study's participants obtained help from their relatives, sometimes from friends too, to leave El Salvador, even though those who provided help often did so with great difficulties. However, on arrival, many soon found themselves with little or no assistance from those on whom they had expected to rely. Without forcing these immigrants' experiences into a dichotomy whereby ties back home seem supportive but become weak in the United States (as we will see in chapters 2 and 5, it is not the case here), I argue that the structural conditions that they face in the new context have profoundly affected the nature of their social ties.

It may be argued that simply moving to a country with a more individualistic cultural ideology, where individuals presumably pull themselves up by their own bootstraps, may influence the weakening of informal networks among some immigrants.[3] Although culture and ideology are central in delimiting human action (as we will see later in this book when I turn to the effects of gender and generation), there are a few points that preclude my adopting an explanation based mostly or solely on culture, normative factors, and/or ideology. First, while my informants mentioned that their friends or family members have learned, or would like to incorporate in their behavior, U.S. cultural practices (this happens particularly with regard to relatively more egalitarian gender relations in the United States), they never brought up such instances in relation to informal exchanges. When they stated that "people change" (as we will see in chapter 5), they attributed the transformation to the new challenges of life in the United States imposed by the material difficulties of their existence. In the qualitative tradition, the framework that I have adopted here was generated from my observations and my informants' own explanations. And, in their own vernacular, they did relate the creation, transformation, and weakening of networks to the material and physical conditions in which they lived, which are shaped by the broader politicoeconomic context.

Second, even if the immigrants have learned and internalized an individualistic ideology — or the idea of its existence — in a way that may affect their everyday lives (and did not discuss it in our conversations), they still did not seem to adopt blindly a new set of cultural and ideological norms that guide informal exchanges. In fact, it became clear to me that it was often tremendously painful for them to have to decide whom and how much to help; given their great material scarcity, they simply could not fulfill their close ones' expectations of assistance. Also, if cultural or ideological factors made a similar impact on these immigrants' networks as do structural forces, we should expect weaker networks among the immigrants who are more familiar, or who have had more contact, with non-Salvadorans or non-Latino groups, since this supposedly would expose them to more individual-oriented ideologies and behaviors. As this study demonstrates, this is not the case, for it is the networks of the more marginalized socioeconomically (who happen to be those with less contact with non-Salvadorans or non-Latinos) that buckle under pressure.

Salvadoran Migration to the United States

According to the 1990 U.S. Census, there were 565,081 Salvadorans in the United States (U.S. Bureau of the Census 1993). The Current Population Survey of March 1997 estimates that there are 607,000 Salvadorans on U.S. soil (Ulloa 1998, 75), but independent estimates place that figure at or above one million (Montes 1987b; Montes and García Vasquez 1988; Ulloa 1998).[4]

During the approximately twelve-year Salvadoran civil war, the Salvadoran population in the United States more than quintupled, from 94,447 in 1980 to 565,081 in 1990 (U.S. Bureau of the Census 1980, 1993). As El Salvador's population is estimated at about six million, it is possible that up to 10 percent of the country's population may now reside in the United States, constituting one of the fastest-growing groups of Latinos in the United States (Leslie and Leitch 1989). But despite this rapid increase, relatively little is known about important social aspects of these immigrants' experience.

The political crisis that began in El Salvador in the late 1970s (along with the upsurge of Salvadoran immigration to the United States during the civil war and to a large extent the internationalization of the Salvadoran conflict) attracted scholarly interest in Salvadoran migration beyond the Central American region, mainly to the United States. The discrepancy between the conditions of war and violence that many Salvadorans left in their homeland and their official reception as economic migrants by the U.S. government shaped the questions in early studies of Salvadoran migration. Thus scholars of Central American migration in general, and of the Salvadoran case in particular, focused on the root causes of these flows and the political forces that shaped them. Researchers concentrated on resolving the apparent paradox of whether this migration was economic (see Jones 1989) or political (see Stanley 1987), or, in fact, a combination of the two (see Hamilton and Chinchilla 1991; Menjívar 1993). Others argued that the political conflict had little, if anything, to do with the surge in these population movements (see Lindstrom 1996). During this period scholars were also concerned with the mental health of this immigrant group; thus several studies focused on the sociopsychological stress involved in the migration and the effect of war trauma on these immigrants' lives (see Aron et al. 1991; Guarnaccia and Farias 1988; Kury 1987; Leslie 1992, 1993; Petuchowski 1988; Ward 1987).

As the presence of Central Americans in the United States became more noticeable, their demographic profile and other socioeconomic aspects were explored, which called attention to the increasing heterogeneity of the Latino immigrant population in the United States (see Rodríguez 1987). Some studies observed that the demographic profile of these Latino immigrants, particularly of Salvadorans before and during the civil war in their home country, differed significantly over time and characterized later arrivals as refugees (see Dorrington, Zambrana, and Sabagh 1991). As more Central Americans arrived in the United States, researchers became concerned with estimating the size of their migration, its potential to increase, and what all this meant in terms of eligibility for benefits (see Ruggles and Fix 1985; Ruggles, Fix, and Thomas 1985).

During the early years knowledge about Central American migration to the United States was disseminated in the voluminous literature on the Sanctuary movement. This literature conveyed heartbreaking accounts of the travails of refugees in their home countries, during the journey, and on arrival in the United States. It also focused, however, on the development of the Sanctuary movement, on the opposition between U.S. law and the humanitarian character of the movement, and on the lives of the movement's founders (see Bau 1985; Coutin 1993; Golden and McConnell 1986).

The rapid increase of Central American immigrants in the United States also prompted scholars to focus on issues relating to aspects of their incorporation into life in the United States. Thus Central Americans' labor force participation became an important emphasis (see Repak 1995), as did issues of settlement, community formation and intraethnic conflict, acculturation, and adaptation (see Chávez 1991, 1994; Córdova 1987; Mahler 1995b; Rodríguez and Urrutia-Rojas 1990). To place this new migration in a larger perspective, comparisons of the Central American and Mexican cases were made (see Chávez, Flores, and López-Garza 1989; Chinchilla, Jamail, and

Rodríguez 1986; Hamilton and Chinchilla 1984; Wallace 1989). And accounts of important factors affecting the daily life of Central Americans also appeared (see Chinchilla and Hamilton 1992).

Most of these early studies did not differentiate among the various nationalities of Central American immigrants (e.g., Guatemalan, Salvadoran, and Nicaraguan). Even though Central Americans share a common history and face similar challenges, there are important social and cultural differences among them that require separate examination. For instance, many Guatemalans who have arrived in the United States in recent years are of Mayan descent and have had different experiences than their non-Mayan compatriots. This is not the case among Salvadorans, who are relatively more ethnically homogeneous. These important differences have been incorporated in a few recent studies that examine social dynamics in Mayan communities and relationships between established residents and these immigrants in Houston (see Hagan 1994; Rodríguez and Hagan 1992). Paralleling new trends in immigration research, scholars of Central American immigration have begun to examine broad issues of transnationalism (see Landolt 1997). They have also begun to focus on "hometown" associations (see Popkin 1995), the potential for "circular migration" (see Bailey and Hane 1995), and the remittances that arguably keep Central American economies — at least the Salvadoran — afloat (see Funkhouser 1992; Menjívar et al. 1998).

In spite of the growing literature on Central American, particularly Salvadoran, migration, there are important gaps that remain to be studied that would undoubtedly contribute to a better understanding and illuminate broader issues common to other groups. Among these is the effect of the context of reception on the immigrants' social worlds, particularly on their social networks. For instance, although studies have recognized the hostile reception to Salvadoran immigrants by the U.S. government, its effects on the social dynamics within the group have only begun to be explored (see Menjívar 1994b, 1997a). The incorporation of Salvadorans into the labor market has been researched, but the impact of restricted economic opportunities on the immigrants' social institutions has been ignored. Community building among Central Americans has been researched, but the effects of limited community resources on informal social networks that lie at the core of community formation have not. And although research has focused on the incorporation of Central American immigrants in the United States, most studies deal with them as a homogeneous entity, without attention to social differentiation.[5]

This study examines the effects of the receiving context on the dynamics of informal networks, taking into account internal social differentiation such as gender and generation to present a more nuanced account of the inner workings of the immigrants' social worlds. My focus is on Salvadoran immigrants — the largest Central American immigrant group in the United States — in San Francisco, the city that has had the longest, yet least studied, history of this migration in the United States. In moving the focus away from the immigrants and what they bring with them to emphasize the structure that receives them — while at the same time examining the relationship of social position to their response to the conditions they face — this study helps to fill an important gap in the study of Salvadoran migration. By focusing on the city that has received Salvadoran immigrants for the longest time, it contributes to dispelling assumptions about immigrant cohesive ties in community building. It conveys the potent effect of both the structural conditions that immigrants face and the immigrants' social positions, even if the results go against conventional notions of immigrant network solidarity.

The Research Site: San Francisco

Central Americans first established a community in the Mission District of San Francisco in the 1940s (Hansen 1980). Before that, the Mission had been an Irish neighborhood. In the aftermath of the Great Earthquake and Fire that devastated the city in 1906, the newly redeveloped Mission District attracted many San Franciscans, including Latinos, but the Irish predominated and continued to do so until after World War II, when the upwardly mobile abandoned their crowded apartments for more spacious places in the foggy Sunset and Richmond districts (Kathleen Coll pers. com.). There still remain some elderly Irish residents and a few commercial establishments reminiscent of their early presence. By the late 1940s Central Americans and Mexicans started to move in, and since then the Mission has attracted Latin Americans to the city. During the mid-1970s, when the real estate boom began, property prices increased and the city and county of San Francisco stopped requiring that city employees live there; thus many working-class and middle-class residents moved out of the Mission and out of the city altogether (Kathleen Coll pers. com.). Although rents are high, the Mission District continues to be the bastion of Latin American life in San Francisco and to attract Latin American immigrants.

The neighborhood has not remained static during the past decade, however; its demographics are clearly changing, which makes local Latino groups fearful that the Mission is losing its traditional Latin flavor (Garcia and Chung 1990). New produce markets — with signs in Chinese, English, and Vietnamese — that sell plantains, tortillas, beans, Mexican cheeses and sweet bread, and Chinese ointments are becoming commonplace. It is customary to find Asian people behind cash registers in small shops selling toys, appliances, clothing, and a host of household items to the Latin clientele. These business owners can comfortably call out prices and make small talk with customers in Spanish, but for more involved transactions a clerk, invariably of Latin American descent, is asked to assist. Other recent transformations in the Mission include the creation of the city's first distinctly lesbian community around Valencia Street and of a "new bohemia," with poets, artists, and writers bringing cafés, poetry readings, and art exhibits to the neighborhood (Garcia and Chung 1990). The gentrification of some areas of the Mission has effected important changes, as poor immigrants find it increasingly difficult to afford the already astronomically high rents. Regardless of these changes, immigrants of Latin American descent still predominate, and Spanish is widely spoken in the streets of the Mission District.

Salvadorans in San Francisco

Salvadoran migration to San Francisco has roots in the commercial trade between San Francisco and Central America. Early in this century San Francisco became the chief processing center for coffee from Central America, fostering ties with the coffee-producing elite in that region. Initially these contacts were limited to coffee growers and business people traveling to and from Central America. Descendants of these early families keep records of their relatives' marriages contracted in the early 1920s, when a few Salvadorans apparently already lived in the city (personal conversations with and genealogy compiled by Margaret Gentry). Later, Salvadorans and other Central Americans — mostly Nicaraguans — who had been recruited to work in the Panama Canal joined shipping lines that were operating there and then continued to San Francisco (Godfrey 1988). These contacts led many Salvadorans to work for the shipping lines in San Francisco, establishing the basis for the emergence of a settlement center for Salvadorans.

The maritime routes between Central America and San Francisco fueled migrations from Central America during and after World War II. Shipyards and wartime industries continued to recruit Central Americans, mainly Nicaraguans and Salvadorans. A significant number of Central Americans entered these labor-scarce industries during this period, which accounted for a significant increase of Central American migration to San Francisco during the 1940s. By 1950 Central Americans outnumbered the Mexican-born (Godfrey 1988). Don Julio A., one of my informants, was part of this migration. He told me that in those days "everyone wanted to come to work painting ships in San Francisco," and although he went back to El Salvador, many of his friends stayed and later brought their families to the city. Don Julio eventually returned to San Francisco, where I met him.

Salvadoran migration to San Francisco continued to increase steadily in the 1980s; 45.7 percent of the Salvadoran-born population in San Francisco arrived between 1980 and 1990 (U.S. Bureau of the Census 1993). Although Salvadorans live and work throughout San Francisco, their concentration in the Mission District has led to a proliferation of Salvadoran restaurants, businesses, and courier services in this area that cater mostly to Salvadorans. In contrast to other U.S. cities with large concentrations of immigrants from Latin America, San Francisco's multinational Latin group does not have a substantial majority from any one country. The fastest-growing Latin American group in the city is Central Americans, who by 1990 accounted for about 35 percent of the city's Latino population (see table 1). Whereas the Mexican population increased by 22.3 percent from 1980 to 1990, the Central American population expanded 43.6 percent, and the Salvadoran population alone grew by 45.7 percent during the same period (U.S. Bureau of the Census 1993).

In comparison to other cities with a large concentration of

TABLE 1   Census Figures for 1990 (Percentages)

	Salvadorans		Central Americans
	San Francisco (Total 17,797)[a]	Los Angeles (Total 253,086)[a]	San Francisco (Total 34,119)[a]
Latino population in area	18.6	7.6	35.3
Arrived 1980–90	45.0	61.1	43.6
Foreign-born	77.6	83.1	77.3

SOURCE: Census of Population and Housing, 1990 (Summary Tape File 4).
[a]These are county-level figures. San Francisco's city and county limits are the same. The number of Salvadorans and Central Americans would increase considerably if other Bay Area counties were included. For instance, there are 14,099 Salvadorans in San Mateo County. But this study was confined to San Francisco, and thus only these figures will be included.

Salvadorans, San Francisco's Salvadoran population is numerically smaller, particularly when compared to that of Los Angeles, which has the largest concentration of Salvadorans in the United States (see table 1). According to the 1990 U.S. Census, 60 percent of the 565,081 Salvadoran-born persons in the United States live in California; of these, 75 percent are in Los Angeles County, of whom 73 percent reside in the city of Los Angeles alone. In contrast, the Salvadoran population in San Francisco — county and city — was estimated at 17,979 in 1990. Thus, even though in absolute terms the Salvadoran population in San Francisco is much smaller than in other cities, it constitutes a higher percentage of the Latino population in the city (see table 1). Importantly, in contrast to any other U.S. city, the significant presence of Salvadorans in San Francisco goes much further back than the events of the late 1970s and 1980s that propelled their massive migration to the United States. Although San Francisco does not currently receive the largest influx of Salvadoran immigrants, it has the longest continuous history of Salvadoran migration to the United States.

Access to the Setting and Data Collection

I conducted the initial research for this study as part of a larger study on survival strategies of immigrant households among five different immigrant groups (see Smith and Tarallo 1992). Thus, from the outset, certain restrictions were placed on who might qualify for inclusion in order to avoid obvious, major sources of variation. Participants had to have recently arrived — that is, they had to be Salvadorans who had been in the United States for not more than five years — and they had to be eighteen years of age or over at the time they left their home country. I retained these initial restrictions for the duration of my study. I gained access to the study participants mainly through "local notables," as Wayne Cornelius (1982, 385) describes the host of contacts in the community that make possible communication with undocumented immigrants.

I came into contact with twenty-two of my informants through a major language school in the Mission District. The director gave me office space and the opportunity to freely speak to students who might be willing to participate in the study. She circulated a memorandum to the instructors informing them that I was going to ask Salvadoran students to take part in what at that time was my dissertation project. The director also asked the school counselor and her staff to assist me in my endeavor. In exchange for helping me to contact potential informants, I gladly agreed to hold office hours at the language school as an "aide," as the director suggested. The director, a Latina of South American origin, mentioned that she was particularly interested in my presence at the school because, as a Salvadoran, I could be resourceful in reaching the students. My duties were to provide students with information they requested about community resources or to direct them to the appropriate staff person at the school. I gathered information from community organizations so that I could be more efficient in helping the students. Their questions ranged from how to get around the city to how to overcome problems they faced in adapting to the new society. Undoubtedly, by helping out in this way I accumulated invaluable information regarding the daily life experiences of my informants. I conducted some interviews in my office at the school; others took place in various locations, for instance, at my informants' homes after I had accompanied them on errands.

I could have contacted all my informants at the language school, but I needed access to different groups to avoid, as much as possible, selectivity bias. I contacted eighteen informants through a community organization in charge of, among other programs, a weekly food distribution. After a few meetings with the director of this organization and with the person in charge of the food program, I was invited to participate in the activities that took place in a neighborhood parish every Friday. During my first visit to the distribution center, the Salvadoran woman in charge warmly introduced me to the participants. In asking for their collaboration, she appealed to our fraternal ties in the following words: "We have a compatriot with us today, a Salvadoran who needs our help with her studies; she is trying to write a book about our experiences." (From this point on my dissertation project or any papers or articles that I wrote became known simply as "the book.") This introduction was particularly significant, because in many instances throughout my fieldwork, my Salvadoran nationality quickly opened doors for me. Some of my informants were grateful that I had taken an interest in their fortunes. Others could not believe that I was "wasting time" trying to learn about Salvadorans instead of learning more about "Americans, which is more helpful if you live in the United States," as some assured me. But the overwhelming majority were pleasantly surprised that a compatriot was a "doctor" and that, although I was apparently able to mingle with Americans and had a different class origin, I was not embarrassed — and even wanted — to spend time with them. I spent many hours at the food distribution program, which served about ninety families per week. Sometimes I would go to chat with people who were there to receive food. Often I would go just to be there and to help in different ways, such as to provide transportation or to fill out various forms, including applications for the Women, Infants, and Children Nutritional Program (WIC). Also, I contacted ten other informants through Salvadorans I met in the community.

In addition to the two main locations where I contacted the majority of my informants, I spent many hours at community organizations, attending meetings to which I was invited by community workers. During this time I had the opportunity to interview and speak informally with social workers, physicians, school counselors and teachers, public notaries, a psychologist, and immigration lawyers. I approached a local priest and an evangelical pastor, who kindly shared with me observations about their Salvadoran congregations. I also conversed with longtime Salvadoran residents in San Francisco, whose views were important, even though (but also because) most of them had little contact with the newcomers. I spoke with employers of Salvadoran immigrants and with an Immigration and Naturalization Service (INS) official. Also, during a trip to Mexico I had the opportunity to discuss issues about the journey from El Salvador with persons who work with Salvadorans in Mexico City and in Guadalajara.

This range of contacts provided me with crucial information regarding the lives of the Salvadorans in this study. Although I conducted a survey of 150 people and interviewed 50 informants, I spoke with many more Salvadoran newcomers during the course of this project. Furthermore, spending time at the school, at the food distribution project, at community organizations, and in the neighborhood gave me the opportunity to gain invaluable information about the quotidian lives of these people. One day, as I got off BART (the Bay Area's rapid transit system), I encountered Carolina and Ileana A., two sisters I had met at the language school. The apartment they shared with their sister and brother was only two blocks away, and they invited me home with them. There we had coffee and *quesadilla* (Salvadoran-style cheesecake) that they had prepared that day, as we went over photographs they had brought from El Salvador. As we carefully inspected the photographs, they recounted important experiences from their lives. This also gave them the opportunity to quiz me about my knowledge of Salvadoran cultural subtleties, local expressions, cuisine, and geography, and as if doubting my "authenticity," they laughed endlessly when I provided accurate and elaborate answers. There I also met the sisters' other siblings. Carolina and Ileana found this to be an appropriate opportunity to ask me about my own experiences as an immigrant and as a student in a foreign land, to comment about their future plans, and to vent their frustrations with life in the United States.

Methods

Because of the study population's high mobility and sometimes clandestine nature, the questions I posed could not be answered using secondary data. The wisest course in trying to understand the experiences of the Salvadoran immigrants was to use interviewing as my basic approach, complementing it with extensive ethnographic observations and a survey. First, I conducted the survey among 150

Salvadoran men and women, 50 of whom I selected for intensive interviews. The survey's purpose was to delineate a profile of the Salvadorans' exit and journey up to their point of entry into the United States. This instrument included questions on general demographic characteristics, motivation to leave, information channels that made the trip possible, conditions during the trip, planning of the trip and cost, from whom help was obtained to travel, and plans to return home. These questionnaires generated data that I arranged descriptively, so as to depict a general portrait of the conditions of exit and the journey. My main data source, however, was the intensive interviews and ethnographic observations that provided me with an in-depth look at social processes in this migration. This method permitted me to meet and converse with my informants' family members, friends, neighbors, and even acquaintances, allowing me to go beyond the viewpoint of my informants and to integrate the accounts of others close to them. With this array of responses I had many levels from which to corroborate a variety of events, providing me with a unique opportunity to trace crucial social processes. I conducted all the intensive interviews in Spanish in a location of my informants' choice, usually their homes,[6] and the interviews lasted an average of two hours. I collected the data in roughly two periods that together lasted from late 1989 to mid-1994. I made an effort to ensure diversity (in terms of class background, gender, and age) in the group of Salvadorans I studied by contacting them in different locations. However, their lives are not meant to be statistically representative of the Salvadoran population of San Francisco, much less of all Salvadorans in the United States. However, in the qualitative tradition, this study serves to illuminate how particular social forces shape the participants' worlds and how they, in turn, respond and make sense of the conditions they face.

Many recently arrived Salvadorans have unstable lives, being forced to move frequently to seek other living arrangements or job conditions. Keeping in touch with them is often a challenge (Ward 1987). Although I was able to maintain contact with many of my informants, I was unable to keep in touch with all of them for the duration of the study. As important additional information regarding the lives of my informants surfaced in conversations following our initial meeting, I undoubtedly missed much information about those whom I did not

see again.[7] However, I was able to follow one-third of the 50 informants for almost three years, which proved crucial for my research.[8]
This longitudinal approach allowed me to learn about tensions among
relatives as they unfolded over time, for only in a couple of cases did
my informants disclose such stories when I first met them. Furthermore, had I used a different method, I would not have been able to
capture the shifting, dynamic nature of informal social networks;
recording observations over an extended period allowed me to grasp
this important feature of social ties. Moreover, with a different
approach I might have been misled to think that the person from
whom my informants obtained assistance was the first one they had
asked for help, when in fact that person was found only after many
denials from relatives or friends.

In addition to the high mobility of the group I studied and the ensu-
ing methodological difficulties, there may be other potential biases in
this study resulting from the setting where the study was conducted.
The situation in San Francisco has been particularly harsh because of
the tightening of the labor market in recent years, coupled with strict
immigration laws. The cases included in this study may represent
extreme conditions for Salvadorans in the United States. This means
that informants in another locale or at a different historical time in the
same place, where the same confluence of factors that my informants
faced in San Francisco is not present, could generate different results.
Such a situation, however, would serve to corroborate my assumption,
which is that contextual forces at the place of reception are critical in
shaping the dynamics of immigrant informal networks and dictate
change in them.

The Study Participants

I do not intend to make crude generalizations from the results of
this study to the entire Salvadoran population in San Francisco, much
less to Salvadorans elsewhere or to other immigrant groups. I do present, however, some comparisons of the sociodemographic profile of
Salvadorans in this study and of those in San Francisco. (These profiles are presented in contrast to those of Salvadorans in Los Angeles
and of Central Americans in San Francisco; see tables 1–4.)[9] These
comparisons should be used only to assess the experiences of the

TABLE 2   Age and Sex Composition

	Central Americans	*Salvadorans*		*Survey Population*
	San Francisco	San Francisco	Los Angeles	
<18 years	23.9%	25.0%	29.5%	—
18–64 years	67.0%	66.6%	68.6%	—
65+ years	9.1%	8.4%	1.8%	—
Median age — male	28.2	27.3	25.2	31.0
Median age — female	33.5	33.3	27.8	33.7
Percentage male	45.8	46.0	49.5	52.0

SOURCE: Census of Population and Housing, 1990 (Summary Tape File 4); study survey.
NOTE: These are general figures for these populations and do not take into account time of arrival.

TABLE 3   Educational Level and English Proficiency (Percentages)

	Central Americans	*Salvadorans*		*Survey Population*
	San Francisco	San Francisco	Los Angeles	
Educational Level				
9–12 years of education	21.8	24.8	27.6	9.8
High school or equivalent	25.4	23.8	15.5	—
Some college or higher	30.0	26.5	13.5	—
English Proficiency				
Speak English very well	63.9	63.2	45.6	0.0
Speak some English	25.3	24.9	34.1	66.0
Do not speak any English	10.8	11.9	20.2	34.0

SOURCE: Census of Population and Housing, 1990 (Summary Tape File 4); study survey.
NOTE: These are general figures for these populations and do not take into account time of arrival.

TABLE 4   Marital Status and Female Heads of Household (Percentages)

	Central Americans	*Salvadorans*		
	San Francisco	San Francisco	Los Angeles	*Intensive Interviews*
Never married	34.8	36.8	44.5	46.0
Married	43.5	42.9	23.0	20.0
Separated/divorced	14.7	13.9	9.6	6.0
Consensual union	—	—	—	24.0
Widowed	7.0	6.3	2.6	4.0
Female head of household	36.9	39.6	29.6	—

SOURCE: Census of Population and Housing, 1990 (Summary Tape File 4); study interviews.
NOTE: These are general figures for these populations and do not take into account time of arrival. These percentages are based on the 50 interviews, as this information was not collected in the survey.

Salvadorans in this study as the absence of any random selection disallows estimating the comparability of these Salvadorans with their compatriots in another city as well as with a comparable Latino population in San Francisco.

The 150 respondents to the survey and the 50 informants in the intensive interviews have similar sociodemographic profiles. In the survey, 52 percent of the respondents were male; the average age was 31.4 years, and the average educational level was 9.8 years. In the intensive interviews, 52 percent were female, their average age was 30.7, and their educational level was 9.4 years. The time in the United States in both the survey and the intensive interviews showed a bimodal distribution, with most people having entered the United States in the periods from 1985 to 1986 and from 1988 to 1989 (for a comparison with census figures, see table 1). Their socioeconomic backgrounds were varied and included people who had been rural poor and small landowners, urban lower-middle class, a couple of middle-class individuals, and one upper-middle-class individual. Before their migration, the occupations of the 150 respondents to the survey and of the 50 informants included students, teachers, soldiers, homemakers, laborers, small business owners, secretaries, nurses, factory operators, electricians, street vendors, one professor, and two housekeepers.

Reflecting the composition of the Salvadoran migration to San Francisco, the study participants originated in all regions of El Salvador — eastern, western, and central; urban and rural. Two-thirds of those in both the survey and the intensive interviews came from large cities; the rest came from medium-sized and small towns in rural areas. A few of those who indicated that they lived in the capital city had migrated to San Salvador a few years before their departure for the United States. More than half of those in both the survey and the intensive interviews said that they had some knowledge of English before coming to the United States, but none spoke English fluently (see table 3 for a comparison with the general Salvadoran population in San Francisco). At the time of the initial interviews, almost half of the 50, but only one-fourth of the respondents to the survey, were attending ESL (English as a second language) classes.[10] At first, all but 11 of my 50 informants lacked documents — 9 were resident aliens (2 had adjusted their status in the United States while the other 7 had come in with U.S. visas) and 2 had political asylum. By the time I left the field, this situation had changed for several. During the time I was conducting fieldwork, Salvadorans were granted Temporary Protected Status, a special dispensation to protect them from deportation and to allow them to work in the United States. Ten of my informants applied for, and to my knowledge were granted, this status; two others resubmitted asylum applications that had been rejected. However, more than half of my respondents remained undocumented, which approximates estimates by the Immigration and Naturalization Service that place the number of undocumented Salvadorans in the United States at close to 60 percent (U.S. Immigration and Naturalization Service 1997a; Warren 1994).

Twenty-three of the 50 informants (I did not ask this question in the survey) were single, 10 were married, and 12 were in consensual unions; 2 were widows, and 3 were divorced (see table 4 for comparisons with the general Salvadoran population in San Francisco).[11] Several have changed their marital status since they arrived in the United States; some have changed partners but have remained in the same marital status — either in a legal marriage or in a consensual union — as when they first immigrated. More than half of these informants lived with family members, both close relatives and extended kin. Most of the rest lived in rented rooms by themselves or with a spouse and/or children; three lived in and out of shelters or in homes run by a refugee program (even though all three have family in San Francisco); and one, a man, identified himself as homeless. Except for those who lived in shelters or on the street, the rest lived in rental housing in and around the Mission District, and overwhelmingly they resided in overcrowded conditions, averaging 6.5 persons per one-bedroom dwelling. None of the newcomers, or the family members who received them in the United States — some of whom had been residents of San Francisco for more than three decades — were home owners, which may be related to the extraordinarily high cost of real estate in San Francisco.

Overview of the Book

This study examines the transformation, reconstitution, or dissolution of Salvadoran immigrants' networks once they arrive in the United States. In chapter 1, I situate this study within different bodies of literature, tracing the development of the concept of a social network from the research of British social anthropologists to its contemporary use in studies of immigration. Chapter 2 is a discussion of the preamble to Salvadoran migration that focuses on the interplay between structural transformations and their effects on sociocultural aspects of Salvadoran society, divided into three important periods of Salvadoran history. Chapter 3 is a brief synopsis of the Salvadorans' journey to the United States. Chapter 4 discusses the context of reception as it shapes the structure of opportunities for these immigrants. This includes the development of U.S. immigration law for Salvadorans, the local labor market for these immigrants in San Francisco, and the organization of the receiving community, with particular attention to the resources it has available for newcomers. Chapter 5 explores the dynamics of informal networks of Salvadorans as conditioned by the structure of opportunities and the consequent resources that these immigrants have available to assist each other. It focuses on reciprocity and exchange, expectations and disappointments, the process of seeking assistance, and the generation of social capital and access to resources. Chapter 6 explores the manner in which gender ideologies and cultural prescriptions subdivide immigrants' participation in informal networks, within the parameters delineated by the resources available to men and women. Network participation according to the immigrants' relative place vis-à-vis different generations, together with cultural dictates based on age, is examined in chapter 7, and chapter 8 features concluding remarks based on the Salvadoran immigrants' experience and the contribution of this examination to our understanding of social networks among immigrants.

Chapter 1

The Structure of Opportunities, Social Networks, and Social Position

One doesn't come here thinking that this place is going to be heaven. No, we're not children. But one also doesn't come prepared for what awaits us here. Of course, don't think that I expected to be received with luxuries and everything put in my mouth. But who would have told me that I would feel so unwanted here, that I would go hungry, that even people I know would turn their backs on me? It's terrible. Normal people who live here, you know, Americans who live comfortably in their nice homes and have good cars, can't imagine — it's impossible for them to conceive what one goes through. For people who don't know what our daily lives are like, this may sound like a lie or a movie. But for us, this is the reality, [and it's] not beautiful.

Alicia N.

As Alicia's words suggest, the Salvadoran immigrants who have been arriving in the United States since the 1980s have faced serious hardships. Even though many were fleeing the political strife in their land, once in the United States they were not accorded refugee status — and concomitant resettlement aid — and only a handful obtained political asylum. However, they continued to enter the United States because they had family and friends who had migrated earlier and had helped them, in various ways, to make the trip north. Networks of friends and family emerged as the most significant organizing factor behind the massive migration of Salvadorans in recent years. So it seemed logical to assume that in the absence of government resettlement aid, these informal social ties would be the Salvadorans' preeminent source of comfort and support, as had been true for other immigrant groups. As I observed and talked with the immigrants in this study, however, I recognized that this assumption held true only when the structure of opportunities they encountered was propitious. Forces beyond my informants' control were vital to understanding the transformation, continuation, or dissolution of these immigrants' social networks.

Early Research
and Theoretical Antecedents

Social networks are central in migratory movements. The recognition of the importance of these ties has a long history, cutting across different disciplines. Early in this century researchers noticed the social element in migratory flows, as it guided movements from particular areas to specific destination points. For instance, the sociologist Harvey Zorbaugh (1929), in his study of neighborhoods in Chicago, noted the importance of "social agency" in the varied immigrant communities. The anthropologist Manuel Gamio (1930), in his research among Mexicans, documented in detail the social aspects of both migration and settlement in the United States. Scholars of the Chicago school of sociology—whose work laid the very foundations of American sociology (Pedraza-Bailey 1990, 45)—focused on social processes, especially social disorganization and anomie, among immigrant communities in the inner city. William Thomas and Florian Znaniecki's (1927) classic study of the adjustment of first-generation Polish immigrants, for instance, examined immigrants' family disorganization and attributed it primarily to a loosening of the normative constraints in the new society.

As the field of immigration studies matured and scholars began theorizing about the causes and consequences of population movements, an early concern with the broader social aspects of migration gave way to an approach rooted in neoclassical economics that took macro- and microlevel expressions. In their macrolevel form, these perspectives posit that migration is caused by geographic differences in the supply of and demand for labor and that population movements lead to equilibrium in these resources. In their microlevel expression, they postulate a wage gap in favor of the receiving societies that prompts individuals to migrate. As rational actors, emigrants base their decisions on cost-benefit calculations that lead them to expect positive returns as a result of a movement (Massey et al. 1993). In both instances, emigration functions as a self-regulating mechanism to restore equilibrium between sending and receiving societies.

A new approach emerged that disputed the neoclassical assumption (mostly in its microlevel form). This approach, labeled "the new economics of migration," postulates that individuals do not migrate to restore wage inequalities and, in fact, individuals alone do not decide to migrate. The decision is "taken" by the household unit, which seeks to maximize economic benefits for everyone in it, to minimize risks, and to loosen constraints associated with a variety of market failures (Stark 1991; Taylor 1986). This perspective can account analytically for findings from recent research that fall outside neoclassical explanations, in particular, the frequent observation that economic development in sending regions does not reduce the pressures for international migration (Massey et al. 1993).

But researchers who based their approaches on historical-structural explanations of migratory movements also challenged the basic tenets of neoclassical theories (mostly in their macrolevel form). There were two problems with neoclassical frameworks that these theorists sought to correct: the treatment of sending and receiving countries as independent entities and the emphasis on conceptualizing movements as a means to reach an economic balance, either at the national or at the individual level, based on cost-benefit calculations. Scholars who adopted the historical-structural stance redirected the focus to the historical and structural causes of migration, stressing the economic — but also the political, cultural, and historical — linkages between receiving and sending countries as well as the international division of labor. This perspective, for instance, helped to explain why some countries send more migrants than other countries in the same conditions, and why certain migration flows end up at particular destinations. Furthermore, this perspective postulates that the penetration of capitalist economic relations into peripheral, noncapitalist societies creates a population that is prone to migrate to the societies where capital originates (Portes and Walton 1981; Sassen 1988). This view, therefore, does not treat migration separate from a historical analysis of broader structural transformations under way in a particular society. From this perspective population movements are usually discussed within theoretical frameworks that examine broader socioeconomic and political change of which migration is part. For instance, proponents of the historical-structural perspective situate movements within "dependency" frameworks (Cardoso and Faletto 1979), "internal colonialism" (Walton 1975), as occurring from the economic "periphery to the core" (Meillassoux 1981), or as logical outcomes of the dislocations of capitalist development that take place not between autonomous entities but within a "world system" (Portes and Walton 1981; Sassen-Koob 1984).

Scholars within the historical-structural tradition have offered novel ways to conceptualize migratory movements, successfully advancing analyses beyond the ahistorical perspective of neoclassical approaches. Explanations for population movements from this perspective have accounted for a wide range of phenomena, including the effects of capitalist and noncapitalist formations on the distribution of the maintenance and reproduction of labor costs (Burawoy 1976), the anticyclical function of migrant labor in lowering labor costs (Castells 1975), and the place of migration in the international division of labor (Sassen-Koob 1984). But in efforts to correct what were perceived to be faults with neoclassical models, the importance of human agency was left out. The historical-structural approach tended to portray migrants as being equally affected by and mechanically reacting to macrostructural forces, as a homogeneous group devoid of agency or social differentiation, not as living, breathing, thinking human beings.[1] As Robert Bach and Lisa Schraml (1982, 324) observed, "The historical-structural literature . . . suffers from excessive repetitions of the functions of labor migration in the development of world capitalism. . . . In a sense, we have developed good political economy but insufficient migration theory." Researchers in the 1960s and 1970s (see MacDonald and MacDonald 1964; Ritchie 1976) had noticed the important place of friends and family in facilitating migration. But it was not until the early 1980s that migration research sought to correct the shortcomings of the historical-structural frameworks by bringing back into the analysis the social aspects of migration, especially household and social networks, a perspective that quickly took hold among immigration scholars.

British Social Anthropology and the Concept of Social Networks

The relevance of social networks for migratory movements was not new in social science. In the 1950s British social anthropologists, somewhat dissatisfied with the limitations of structural-functionalism for the study of complex societies, shifted attention from cultural systems to systems of concrete ties and networks (see Barnes 1971). They

used the analytical concept of a "social network" to explore how actual
ties among people — in contrast to institutional structures — influenced behavior. John A. Barnes (1954), one of the first to use the concept in a systematic way, introduced the notion of a social network to
analyze kinship ties that cut across social class in a Norwegian fishing
village. Although he was mainly concerned with the analysis of social
class, his focus was on interpersonal links. Elizabeth Bott (1957), in
her work on the relationship between social networks and conjugal
role behavior among London families, was one of the first to measure
network density to specify factors that affect role segregation. Some of
these early scholars used the notion of a social network to refer to sets
of links of all kinds; others narrowed it to friendship, kinship, and
neighborliness. But they were all dealing with sets of ties linking
social system members across social categories and bounded groups
(Wellman 1988, 21). These early works undoubtedly brought the idea
of a network to the attention of a broader audience of social scientists
and gave rise to numerous studies on the topic.

Post–World War II anthropological studies of urban life and urbanization in African societies linked the concept of social network and
migratory processes analytically. That was when rural-to-urban migration compelled researchers to pay heed to the ways in which large
streams of migrants from culturally homogeneous villages adapted to
city life. Focusing on the migrants' actual ties, anthropologists found
that these new urban dwellers were establishing supportive bonds and
at the same time retaining loyalties to their ancestral homelands. This
approach is illustrated by Arnold L. Epstein's (1969) study of the
informal networks that new immigrants established in Ndola, Northern Rhodesia, in spite of the "general condition of flux" that seemed
synonymous with rapid urban growth. And Philip Mayer's (1961)
study showed how migrants in a South African town maintained
close-knit social networks that further ensured orientation to their
rural hometowns.

Social Networks as Central in the Theorizing
of International Migratory Movements

When immigration researchers (mainly from the United States) began
to redress the shortcomings of historical-structural approaches, they
did not revert to previous individual-centered approaches but focused

on the intermediate institutions between individuals and broader forces — social networks and households — that shape individual responses to macro processes. In doing so, they brought back the positive aspects of these social institutions and, contrary to the Chicago school's early focus on disorganization and breakdown, emphasized immigrant solidarity and cultural continuity. Many studies pointed to the importance of friendship and kinship networks before, during, and after migration, serving both to perpetuate migration and to assist migrants with settlement. It was assumed that the structure of social networks based on kinship and friendship allows for migrants to draw on obligations implicit in these relationships to obtain assistance — monetary as well as sociopsychological — and information about jobs at the place of destination (Massey and Espinosa 1997; Massey et al. 1987; Taylor 1986). Other researchers conceptualized networks as forming a system that links the sending and receiving communities (see Fawcett 1989). An advantage of focusing on networks was that it permitted the study of migration as a social product, as an outcome of the interaction between decisions made by individual actors and political and economic parameters (Boyd 1989, 642). In doing so, it provided more refined explanations as to why some regions within a country send a large number of migrants abroad while other regions with similar conditions do not; it also emphasized the importance of transnational networks in maintaining migration flows. Placing social networks at the center of the analysis also served to explain the "self-perpetuating" mechanism inherent in migration (Massey et al. 1993).

A significant area of interest based on the conceptualization of networks as integral to the migration process has gained prominence recently. Not unlike Fawcett's formulation — but clearly more critical than most exponents of the "networks" or the "household" perspective — this approach has sought to correct views that treat communities of origin as separate from those of destination. Scholars in this area have conceptually linked the place of origin and of destination through an increasingly dense web of social contacts. This new subfield has been referred to as "transnationalism." From this viewpoint, it is the continuous circulation of goods, services, money, information, and people between the various settlements of a transmigrant population that constitutes a single community spread across a variety of sites (Kearney 1991).

Critique of the "Social Networks" Perspective

Although focusing on intermediate institutions between broader forces and individuals had the virtue of emphasizing the centrality of social elements in migratory processes and of enlarging the analytic space, it did not achieve this without conceptual problems. The two social institutions that formed the cornerstone of this approach — social networks and households — were consistently conceptualized as cohesive, unified collectivities. Based on altruism and consensus, and out of obligations implicit in friendship and kinship, members presumably pooled material (and emotional) resources, enjoyed social solidarity, and often engaged in strategies to maximize economic gains and to adapt to outside forces for the benefit of all equally.

Research informed by feminist scholarship has criticized notions of the immigrant household based on this approach as democratic, altruistic, and compliant, ignoring tensions and conflicting interests; the "household approach" tended to continue to conceal how social differentiation by class, culture, gender, and generation shapes the actions of individuals. Pierrette Hondagneu-Sotelo (1994a) and Nazli Kibria (1993) observe that idealized representations of the household obscure gender and generation as distinctive experiences in immigration and ignore internal fissures of immigrant life. Kibria argues that this may be a result of an emphasis that tends to see immigrant social institutions only as vehicles for adaptation. Hondagneu-Sotelo points out that in many instances, on close examination of the immigrants' own stories, the notions of collective objectives or household strategies that permeate the literature are difficult to sustain. Sherri Grasmuck and Patricia Pessar (1991) also note that households are not indivisible units, for unequal access to power and other valued resources is based on gender and generation, which leads to disagreements as individuals within households attempt to make important decisions. By presenting more nuanced analyses of immigrant households, this new scholarship has enriched our understanding of the diversity of immigrant social patterns and has clarified the way in which social variation affects immigrant life. We can now understand the intermediate processes through which individuals respond to macrostructural transformations; we also know that not everyone responds in the same way.

Although the majority of research that has criticized unqualified portrayals of social institutions in immigrant life has focused on immigrant households, there are some noteworthy studies that have taken a critical look at immigrant ethnic solidarity and social networks. For instance, Sarah Mahler (1995a), in her research on immigrants in suburban New Jersey, far from touting ethnic solidarity within this group, notes that marginalization and poverty undermine ethnic ties as individuals are pressed to produce a surplus, often at the expense of less seasoned co-ethnics. Hondagneu-Sotelo (1994b) also takes issue with the way in which social networks have been conceptualized and notes that studies of networks have masked the consequences of unequal power relations. She observes differences in access to resources through networks along gender lines and finds that, among the Mexican immigrants in her study, the informal regulation that arises from networks to cope with the challenges of immigrant work can be abusive. Julian McAllister Groves and Kimberly Chang (1993) discuss the pernicious aspects of friendships among Filipina maids in Hong Kong. They point out that those very relationships on which the women relied for support also threatened to control them, in some cases jeopardizing their employment in Hong Kong and family relations in the Philippines. In a similar vein, Jacqueline Maria Hagan (1998) shows that gender plays an important role in determining access to benefits through networks among the Maya Guatemalans in her study; immigrant men and women do not benefit equally from informal networks. These new perspectives have added important nuances to our conception of immigrant social institutions. Macrostructural forces enable and constrain the actions of individuals, but internal differentiation such as gender, generation, and social class places an equally powerful delimitation on individual action.

Macrostructural Forces, Social Networks, and Immigrant Life

The idea that broader forces shape the internal dynamics of social networks in important ways is not at all new. At least since British social anthropologists studied social patterns in rural-to-urban migration, scholars have been careful to acknowledge the power of broader forces on social network dynamics. For instance, when Bott (1957) studied role segregation in working-class English families, she conceptualized network relationships as an intervening variable between institutional structures and the conjugal behavior of spouses. The idea that institutional factors impinge on network structure was central. J. Clyde Mitchell's (1987) situational method also acknowledges the effects of wider forces on urban social relationships. For him, a situation is both a "practice of structure" and a "structure of practice"; that is, it is formed in the structural processes that govern a wider political and socioeconomic order. In his view, however, actors have agency; they do not react mechanically or deterministically to broader processes.

From a sociopsychological angle, scholars in the field of "social support" have also acknowledged the power of forces beyond individuals' immediate control on networks of assistance. Deborah Belle (1982) observes that poverty imposes considerable burdens on potential sources of social support and describes "negative networks" that can be highly stressful to poor families. Stephen Kulis (1992) details the determining effects of children's economic mobility on parent-child relationships in adult life. Perhaps because scholarship in this field is either intellectually based or closely linked to "network analysis,"[2] researchers in this area have focused on the form that networks take and on the internal differentiation that affects their content. For instance, in a review of the sociopsychological literature of social support, Robert Milardo (1988) identifies different types of network formations, some enduring and long lasting, others brief and ordinary. Manuel Barrera (1981) developed a support network measure that allows for distinctions of modes of support, examination of the quality of network, and its potential for conflict. And Alan Vaux (1988), noting the link between the internal composition of a network and specific tasks performed, demonstrates that support networks should be distinguished from broader social networks, so as to avoid assuming that all social ties are supportive.

The study of informal support among minority families in the United States is relevant here. The prevalence of informal networks and the propensity for extended families among minorities have been widely studied, broadly speaking, from cultural and structural perspectives (Roschelle 1997b). The cultural argument proposes that the presence of extended families and of elaborate informal networks of support among minorities is related to traditions inherited from specific cultural patterns. The structural perspective links these coping mechanisms to conditions of poverty. This perspective became popular and was often used in political agendas to counteract negative stereotypes of minority families. Although there are several examples of this view, two classics stand out, as they are among the most frequently cited studies that depict the vital place of networks as sources of assistance among the poor.[3] Larissa Lomnitz's (1985) study of a Mexican shantytown demonstrates that ties with others — conceptualized as networks — can and do provide important financial, material, and emotional assistance to those in need.[4] Carol Stack's (1974) research, which came at a time of heated debate over the "pathology" or "disorganization" of poor minority families, noted the resilience of kinship networks among impoverished blacks. Stack extolled those characteristics of the black family that had been portrayed as deviant and emphasized the importance of informal networks for the survival of black families in the midst of poverty. While Lomnitz (1978) depicts the same resourcefulness, she describes factors, such as tension and physical and psychological distance, that may influence the formation or dissolution of networks.

Lately researchers have begun to note the negative effects of broader structural factors on social support, in spite of the popularity of the view of networks among the poor as viable sources of assistance. Perhaps this is not unrelated to the socioeconomic transformations that have contributed to a worsening of the condition of the poor in recent years. Still linking the social organization of minority families to structural factors, this new scholarship contends that the impoverishment of minorities has left them unable to participate actively in networks because they lack the resources to do so. For instance, Lynn White and Agnes Riedmann (1992) and Dennis Hogan, David Eggebeen, and Clifford Clogg (1993) observe that a general lack of socioeconomic resources prevents families, even among groups that are assumed to have strong kinship networks, from exchanging help. In a study that examines the economic determinants of network participation across race and gender, Anne Roschelle (1997b) finds that social support networks have eroded in racial-ethnic communities, which she attributes mainly to an escalation of poverty in low-income communities in the past decade. Even Stack has noted recently that stressful socioeconomic conditions may affect the individual's and the family's ability to perform effectively (Stack and Burton 1993, 166). A common theme that emerges in these studies is that a disadvantageous position, vis-à-vis socioeconomic resources, effectively undermines family networks of support among impoverished groups, regardless of their race or ethnicity. These studies also point out that ideas about family cohesiveness among minority families need to be revised, particularly in light of current conditions among the poor.[5]

Noteworthy in these studies of social support is the recognition that social networks, particularly those based on kinship, are not infallible and can weaken under extreme conditions of poverty, when too many demands are placed on individuals. With few exceptions, this standpoint has been conspicuously absent in studies of immigrant social networks. In general, immigration scholarship is still concentrated on depicting a one-dimensional view of immigrant informal networks that focuses almost exclusively on their positive aspects. Stressing both cultural and structural factors in the maintenance of these ties, this scholarship has conceptualized social networks as strategies that immigrants develop to buffer the effects of migration. In essence, sociocultural traditions presumably have helped immigrants survive economically in the new context. Kibria (1993) observes the almost celebratory rediscovery of the resilience and strength of immigrant ties and institutions, which she suggests may be a reaction to the tendency of assimilationist models to portray these institutions as deviant and dysfunctional (p. 18). The parallels between these views in the field of immigrant social institutions and those that earlier predominated in the area of minority families cannot be overlooked.

Largely absent from portrayals of immigrant social networks is the potential for tension or even dissolution in these ties, which reinforces images of immigrant social ties as excessively cohesive and "organic," in Durkheim's meaning of the term. Because immigrant networks have been widely acknowledged to provide new immigrants with financial, material, and emotional assistance for resettlement, positive aspects have been emphasized. We end up with overly functionalistic arguments regarding the social organization of immigrant institutions, where different aspects of immigrant life serve to contribute to the maintenance of the system. One exception comes from research informed by economic sociology. Alejandro Portes and Julia Sensenbrenner (1993) attend to the "underside" of networks, noting the facilitating component inherent in social networks for individuals to achieve their goals while also unveiling the negative manifestations and their potential for constraining action. Although some scholars have recognized the potentially deleterious effects of poverty for immigrants (see, e.g., Portes and Rumbaut 1996), most have continued to treat the intermediate web of social relations through which individuals respond to structural forces as entities impervious to structural forces. One of the most thorough and heuristic analyses of social networks also comes from economic sociology. M. Patricia Fernández-Kelly (1994, 1995) shows how particular structural conditions affect the inner workings of informal ties and may facilitate or impede the generation of both cultural and social capital. Although her insights are derived from her work among African Americans, by contextualizing the dynamics of social networks, her approach illuminates the analysis of informal ties of assistance among immigrants as well.

The Intersection of Opportunities, Social Networks, and Social Position

An overemphasis on the resilience and strength of immigrant social networks has led to the neglect not only of the potential for conflict and tension in these ties but also of the fact that they may be transformed, or reconstituted, or may even weaken and break down at the destination point. The portrayal of immigrant networks as interminable sources of support that protect their members from the vicissitudes of the wider society tends to ignore the potential for change in these ties. A "Durkheimian quest for consensus and solidarity" (in the words of Mitchell 1974, 285) has permeated the conceptualization of immigrant informal ties to the point where a wide range of immigrant experiences have been forced into a Procrustean bed of functionalist thought, when perhaps Marx or Simmel has been needed to make sense of noncompliance, conflict, and resistance. These social relationships are neither universally viable nor static and cannot be conceptualized as "attributes" of immigrant groups impervious to the structures within which they operate. A common background, constant contact, and shared migration experiences do not automatically breed cohesive and supportive networks. The internal dynamics of these ties are shaped by politicoeconomic forces over which individuals have little or no control. Structural forces, such as policies of reception and dynamics of the local economy, together with the organization of the receiving community, impinge on informal networks. This occurs because, by shaping the structure of opportunities that immigrants encounter, they determine the kinds of resources that immigrants will have available to help one another. But taking into account the formidable effect of broader structures should not lead to a rigid conceptualization of these ties. Networks are fluent and contingent; broader forces are configured dissimilarly at different historical moments, so social networks may operate differently as configurations of time and place fluctuate. The point here is not to imply that immigrant networks are always ridden with friction and conflict and are never supportive. Indeed, the shifting, processual nature of informal networks makes it difficult to define them unambiguously as enduring or frail. The complexities embedded in these ties defy their understanding as static, fixed entities independent of contextual forces. Conceptualizing immigrant social networks from this wider vantage point may reverse the assumption that they represent a buffer to the hardships that immigrants encounter. The structural conditions against which these ties supposedly guard may, in fact, condition the continuity, transformation, or even dissolution of the ties. This study focuses on the effects of broader structures on social networks, not on the networks' "adaptive function" as coping mechanisms to the receiving context.

To approach the study of immigrant social networks recognizing the importance of larger structures does not mean that the analysis will err on the side of determinism. Even though political and economic factors place limits on the possibilities for action, it is individual immigrants who fashion their own responses within these boundaries. Responses are shaped and informed by internal divisions in the immediate context of immigrant life, such as class, gender, and age, which constrain individual action in various ways. These social positions reflect power differentials that are central to understanding the immigrants' responses to broader structures, as well as the cultural repertoire and ideologies that they draw on to interpret the world around them and give meaning to their own actions. Thus the processes by which social networks operate will reflect different interests and the immigrants' potential for participation in networks according to social position. For instance, social class insertion — determined by what immigrants bring and what they encounter — dictates different access to resources that positions immigrants unequally in informal exchanges. Men and women have different interests, culturally expected roles, and access to resources, which "genders" their participation in networks. The young and the old also have dissimilar interests and views, and age-related cultural prescriptions mold their informal exchanges in networks, as different generations of immigrants recast their experiences in reference to their "imaginary country." These multiple contingencies based on cultural and ideological considerations necessarily render the conceptualization of immigrant social networks as contingent and emergent. But if it is assumed that configurations of broader structures fluctuate as time and place change — as this study does — it cannot be expected that the immigrants' cultural baggage and ideologies remain fixed at one point in time either. Cultural expressions and ideologies change both for the immigrants and for those who stay behind; therefore, they are not fixed traits any more than are the conditions in which they are manifested. The task in analyzing immigrant social networks is, then, to consider both the structural parameters that delimit social action and the individual responses to broader forces as informed by social positions and cultural ideologies. But in doing so, the analysis cannot lose sight of the shifting nature of both, to avoid presenting immigrant social networks — pre- and postmigration — as monolithic entities devoid of the potential for change.

Chapter 2

Background to Migration

Some people say that it was a twelve-year war that we suffered through. I say the war lasted at least fifty or even a hundred and fifty years. We have a rich and tragic and even violent, and very sad history — so we can't forget it, it's in all of us, in our veins. If we forget it, I can't remember who said something like this, but we're condemned to repeat it, or something like that.

Armando L.

Well, you see, what has happened to us [in El Salvador] has changed our lives forever. That war has left some scars in us that run very, very deep. I am talking about real scars — yes, physically and mentally. While I was there, of course, like the rest, I suffered the devastation even in the smallest things. Once I was getting a vaccination and our town started to get bombed. The nurse became very nervous and she put the injection in the wrong place, so now look at this huge scar that I have right here [in the arm]. I'm embarrassed because it's ugly and everyone can see it. But I also have another scar inside, which no one can see. It's from all my afflictions and the terror that I lived through there. I was left a very nervous person, even the noise of a motorcycle makes me jump now. I get irritable and little things get me very upset. Sometimes I find that absolutely nothing pleases me. My mother says that with time these things will go away. But I think it's memories I will carry for the rest of my life.

Amparo A.

Armando's eloquent words and Amparo's vivid recollection suggest that to understand the lives and social worlds of the Salvadoran immigrants, one must examine the developments that took place in El Salvador immediately preceding their migration. What follows is not an exhaustive chronicle of Salvadoran history; it is a selective and brief account that highlights the link among structural dislocations, population movements, and social institutions, concentrating on the lives of the less privileged in Salvadoran society, who constitute the great majority of both the country's population and the immigrants in the United States.

The political strife in the 1980s that gave rise to massive population displacements within and emigration from El Salvador cannot be attributed to a sudden crisis fueled by external forces. Rather, it may be conceived as one stage in a long history of protest against social injustice, exacerbated by external support. To gain a deeper understanding of the background of the unprecedented migration of the 1980s, therefore, we must go much further back into the history of El Salvador. The roots of the crisis may in fact be found in the contradictions of a social structure established in the late nineteenth century, when El Salvador was finally consolidated as a republic. This period along with two others that followed corresponded to cycles of solidification of political and economic alliances and rearrangements of power and were accompanied by specific migratory movements.

Historical Antecedents to Migration

The Period of Consolidation: 1860 to 1940s

When El Salvador was still recovering from its struggle for independence and its new leaders were looking for opportunities in the international market in the 1860s,[1] the new government encouraged coffee cultivation to generate wealth. In a relatively short time coffee became the main export crop, covering 34 percent of land under cultivation by 1932 (Montgomery 1982, 46). The cultivation of coffee strengthened the country's ties to the international market, and by solidifying the political power of the economic elite, coffee also became the axis around which the contemporary class structure evolved. As Héctor Lindo-Fuentes (1990, 154) observes, "The new century was born under the sign of coffee."

The new coffee enterprises instigated fundamental reforms in agriculture, the national economy, and society. Radical changes in the pattern of land tenure occurred, as vast areas of communal lands suitable for coffee were privatized. A law passed in 1882 (Browning 1971) abolished all communal lands — a large proportion of them located in the central and western parts of the country. This resulted in social unrest that intensified in 1885 and 1895, when peasants were dispossessed and their land reverted to a small clique of landholders (Menjívar

1980). The prosperity brought by rising coffee prices, which peaked in the 1920s, occurred during a period unparalleled in Salvadoran history. At this time the government allowed a wide range of openness and reform, including relaxed labor policies, such as the creation of a ministerial-level worker's advocate, the right to unionize, and the eight-hour workday. New political parties were formed, including the Communist party, and President Arturo Araujo was voted into office in 1931, in the country's first free presidential election.

But the heavy reliance on coffee caused economic disaster when the price in the international market fell 62 percent between 1928 and 1932 (Dunkerley 1988, 91). As the depression wore on, the newly formed labor movement increased in militancy. There was additional unrest when peasants, reduced to landless or nearly landless seasonal laborers, lost their jobs or suffered reduced wages and small landholders defaulted on their loans. Estimates indicate that 28 percent of all coffee holdings changed hands during the Great Depression (Anderson 1981, 8). The result of this process was an increased concentration of wealth and the pivotal shift in the power structure of the country. The coffee planters — whose interests were law — had been ruling uncontested. From this point on, however, the oligarchy would share power with the military (Lindo-Fuentes 1990).

As the depression hit, the brief experiment in democracy turned disastrous. The Araujo presidency lasted only a few months, ending in a military coup d'état in late 1931. General Maximiliano Hernández Martínez, the vice president, was named the constitutional successor, thus beginning the longest unbroken period of military rule in Latin American history (Montgomery 1982, 50).[2] Conflicts over landownership, evictions, and massive unemployment led in early 1932 to an insurrection in the central and western parts of the country. Students and peasants had been organizing for some time, demanding not only political freedom to associate but also more substantial social and economic reforms that would have threatened the interests of the oligarchy. But the protagonists of this uprising were the indigenous people, whose communities were making attempts to organize in order to gain some autonomy and to reinstitute the system of communal lands.[3] The government saw this, however, as a communist rebellion that had to be contained, and the defense of "order" became the fundamental mission of the state (Alvarenga 1996, 327). The 1932 uprising was suppressed with unprecedented ferocity. The government army set out to annihilate all vestiges of communism, including people who were only suspected of being sympathizers. Some thirty thousand people, the great majority of them indigenous, were killed during approximately a two-month period. This meant that 1.6 percent of the total population of the country died, a figure reaching 28.6 percent in the western regions where the massacre took place (Montes 1987a, 19). This event, known as La Matanza, the Massacre, shook the very foundations of the nation, and its legacy has since shaped Salvadoran social, cultural, and political life.[4] It weakened and then condemned to a clandestine life indigenous social and cultural institutions, terminated peasant unrest in the region where 75 percent of the coffee was cultivated, and had significant social and demographic effects for generations to come (Anderson 1992; Dunkerley 1988; Montes 1987a).

La Matanza ended the most progressive period in Salvadoran history; it allowed the economic elite to solidify its power through the appropriation of communal lands and to secure the employment terms of seasonal labor (Dunkerley 1988). It also led to the consolidation of power by the military. Thus the oligarchy obtained a peaceful environment — free of unions and political organizations — to implement economic policies in their own interests. And although Hernández Martínez was ousted in 1944, his successor instituted only superficial reforms, such as paving streets, building a major bridge, implementing programs in the area of health and hygiene, and drafting a "new" constitution identical to that of 1886 (Montgomery 1982).

Migratory Movements: 1860 to 1940s

Transformations of the land tenure system and the expansion of coffee production in the early years of the republic turned the majority of rural inhabitants into a dispossessed and dependent population. This landless sector felt the immediate effects of fluctuations in the international commodity markets. The eviction of subsistence peasants from communal lands in western El Salvador created a context ripe for migration and led many to seek marginal lands in other parts of the country where they could continue their subsistence farming. Migratory seasonal labor emerged as an integral element for the maintenance of the coffee economy and as an enduring feature of

Salvadoran social life. It became the modus vivendi of a large proportion of rural inhabitants, with important consequences for social institutions. During this period some peasant families migrated to form squatter settlements on the fringes of private estates along the roads and highways, on government lands, and in riverbeds near San Salvador (Hamilton and Chinchilla 1991, 86). The catastrophic economic effects of the drop in coffee prices in the late 1920s and early 1930s sounded the alert that agriculture had to be diversified: cotton and sugarcane provided the solution. This diversification was accompanied by more expulsions of smallholders and tenant farmers from their lands, which further increased land pressures.

The first waves of emigration to Honduras took place during this period. Dispossessed from the land in El Salvador and lured by the attractive wages offered by banana companies in Honduras, many poor Salvadoran campesinos made their way there. It is estimated that by 1929 half of the population of several towns on the north coast of Honduras was Salvadoran (Wilson, cited in Anderson 1981). There are indications that Salvadorans might have also started to migrate to the United States as early as the turn of the century, as shown in records of the Immigration and Naturalization Service (U.S. Immigration and Naturalization Service 1978) and by the presence of fourth- and fifth-generation Salvadorans in San Francisco. But the most substantial Salvadoran emigration during this early period was undoubtedly to Honduras, and it was mainly composed of the poorest social class, landless peasants. The savage repression that followed the 1932 massacre caused major population movements internally from western El Salvador — where the massacre had taken place — to eastern and northern regions and to other countries. In the 1930s approximately 25,000 Salvadorans made their way into Honduras, and by the end of the 1940s there were 100,000 Salvadorans there (LaFeber 1984, 131). The rural exodus that began in the 1890s continued throughout this period. William Durham (1979, 56) estimates that the out-migration rates during the period 1892–1930 increased seven times from 1930 to 1950.

The perennial movement of men in search of wage labor had severe repercussions for the life of the Salvadoran rural poor. Such migration was seasonal in some cases, but it often became permanent or semipermanent. It was financially impossible for entire families to move as the agricultural seasons changed. Thus the marginal conditions of life for these workers and their perpetual pilgrimage gave rise to a high percentage of free unions and an accompanying increase in the number of illegitimate children. Rodolfo Barón-Castro (1978, 565, 574) estimates that in the late 1930s, 60 percent of all births were illegitimate, and the marriage rate was 3.6 per 1,000. The incidence of free unions appears to have been more prevalent in the western region of the country (Anderson 1992, 27). Given a situation in which men had to move temporarily or permanently in search of work, the increased participation of women in public life and in the labor force comes as no surprise. Because of men's extremely low incomes as wage laborers, women were often left in charge of the household and also engaged in paid work in a variety of subsistence activities. Thus it was not uncommon for women to become the sole providers of a household. Women's participation in public life was also noteworthy. For instance, in 1924 market women organized politically, demonstrated, and took over a police station close to the marketplace (Dalton, cited in Thomson 1986, 64).

Migration also affected the institution of *compadrazgo* (coparenthood).[5] With physical distance, there was little opportunity to realize the social functions of compadrazgo. Exchanges between people linked through these bonds diminished, people did not visit or help each other regularly, and the social relationship was no longer permanent (Montes 1987a, 167). The institution did not disappear; it simply weakened when it became physically impossible for migrants to render the social responsibilities embodied in it. Thus compadrazgo is not as central in El Salvador as it is in other countries, notably Mexico.

The Developmentalist Period:
Late 1940s to 1970s

Successive governments from 1950 to 1980 tried to diversify the economy by reinvesting profits from agriculture into industrial development. Import-substitution industrialization and the diversification of agriculture based on regional integration were promoted because the Central American economies by themselves were too small for these enterprises. Thus the Central American Common Market was created. Programs in health, housing, and sanitation were implemented.

These gains were accompanied by another period of growth in the Salvadoran economy. Production rose more than fourfold and per capita GDP increased by 21.2 percent (Dunkerley 1988, 60).

The import-substitution model, however, assumed an expanding domestic consumer market. Economic growth was artificially high because there were no fundamental changes that would have threatened the existing politicoeconomic structure. But the new development policies did alter somewhat the country's social structure. A small middle class arose, along with an urban working class; meanwhile, the numbers of rural landless laborers swelled, and significant masses of impoverished peasants migrated to the cities. But dispossessed migrant peasants found only poverty in the cities. The result was social unrest and repression, shored up by U.S. military aid. The emergent middle class did not expand enough to sustain political changes and to cushion class conflict.

By the early 1960s industrialization had shifted from import substitution to a short-lived period of industry for export. Economic reforms continued to attract North American investment, mainly in manufacturing, though labor-intensive industries were not encouraged. The Alliance for Progress helped to create an aura of success, allocating funds for schools, health, and housing, accompanied by a substantial increase in military aid. As opposition groups became more vocal in their demands for fundamental change, repression grew. But despite increased repression, the government was not effective in controlling political discontent in the cities, as the military had effectively done in the countryside. One of the most important developments of the period was the emergence of a significant and organized revolutionary guerrilla group, with key foreign support.

The economic boom that resulted from the alliance of the military and the oligarchy continued, and by 1965 El Salvador had the largest number of small manufacturing firms in the region. This progress, which was generated by foreign capital and channeled through the Alliance for Progress and the Central American Common Market, was accompanied by a further increase in the wealth of the country. As in previous times, however, this economic progress was not shared, which further reinforced existing trends of inequality. Profits continued to leave the country, more land evictions occurred, and the mechanization of production contributed to an increase in unemployment among rural and urban workers. Commercial agriculture grew at the expense of subsistence agriculture. As Héctor Dada Hirezi (1978) points out, wage labor and capitalist relations of production developed more rapidly and more extensively in El Salvador than elsewhere in Central America.

World coffee prices had again dropped by the mid-1960s, disease affected the cotton crops, and private investment declined as international payment deficits increased (Montgomery 1982). The government instituted budget cuts, and unemployment increased. Deteriorating conditions in the countryside contributed to an increase in the number of urban dwellers. The urban economy, however, could not absorb the swelling workforce, and the new arrivals had to turn to the informal economy, which from 1961 to 1975 grew almost threefold (Brewer 1983, 404). In addition, public spending cuts in basic social services, accompanied by increases in the military budget, contributed to a further deterioration of the condition of the new sectors of the population, such as the urban working and middle classes. In 1970, 33 percent of the population of San Salvador lived in *tugurios* (slums), and an additional 41 percent lived in *mesones*[6] (Montes 1987a, 19). This situation bred popular protest, as people took to the streets to demand changes. The protests were met by government force, and paramilitary networks of informers such as ORDEN (Nationalist Democratic Organization) were created to carry out surveillance operations. These networks of informers penetrated all aspects of life, mostly in rural El Salvador, leaving an indelible mark on informal ties among friends, co-workers, and neighbors, for anyone could become, or be suspected of being, an informer.

By 1971 unemployment claimed 20.2 percent of the country's workforce, compared to 5.1 percent in the census of 1961 (Montes 1987a, 19); another 40 percent were underemployed, working no more than 120 days a year (Anderson 1981, 141). In a country where 60 percent of the people depended on the land for survival, the percentage of landlessness increased from 15.6 to 41 percent of the rural population between 1963 and 1975 (Mason 1992, 68). Rural evictions continued, as landowners responded to the economic crisis by intensifying the production of export crops. The concentration of wealth, especially of land, continued to increase during this period: 57 percent of the arable land was concentrated in 2 percent of the farms (Censo

Nacional Agropecuario 1975, in Menjívar 1987). At the other end of the scale, 96.3 percent of the rural population had access to five hectares or less of marginal land per family, when seven hectares were judged necessary to make a living (Haggerty 1990, 68).[7] Attempts at land reform failed because of fierce opposition by the private sector and large landowners. The repressive character of the government and its failure to institute any reforms contributed to the radicalization of more than one sector of Salvadoran society. In spite of increased repression, thousands began to mobilize. At the same time, extremist groups on the right, opposed to any form of change, also started to organize.

Migratory Movements: Late 1940s to 1970s

Each phase of economic growth was characterized by a continuing displacement of people from their traditional means of livelihood, with inadequate compensation to provide for their welfare. The cornerstones of the developmentalist period — industrialization and the diversification of agriculture — brought about a new pattern of migration and reinforced an existing one. The growth in industry and the expansion of social services in the urban areas in the 1950s made cities attractive for rural dwellers, and uprooted Salvadoran peasants joined the growing numbers of the population in the cities, creating added pressure for jobs and services. Nora Hamilton and Norma Chinchilla (1991, 88) report that between 1950 and 1961, 73 percent of all migrants moved to the cities, and departments (provinces) with major urban centers recorded net migration gains of from 3,000 to 6,000 people. In addition, thousands of small farmers who had been growing basic grains were displaced as a result of the diversification of agriculture in the 1950s. The emphasis on cash-crop production brought about increased mechanization of agriculture, which swelled the number of unemployed rural workers. Areas where the new export crops were being produced attracted seasonal laborers, who in turn continued to join the coffee harvest as well. This pattern of rural-to-rural migration continued throughout the 1950s and 1960s.

Migration to Honduras increased during this period and, as in previous years, was composed mainly of impoverished peasants. According to estimates, the number of Salvadorans in Honduras increased

from 100,000 in 1949 to 350,000 by the mid-1960s (Durham 1979;
LaFeber 1984). These remained the largest and most important emigration movements until the late 1960s. In the early 1960s Salvadorans
already constituted 75 percent of all foreigners in Honduras, and by
1969 they made up approximately 12 percent of the population of that
country (Durham 1979, 2). Don Julio A. is a man in his eighties with
a sixth-grade education who migrated to Honduras in the early 1960s
and to San Francisco in both the late 1940s and the 1980s. In his
words,

In those days it was easy to move around and Honduras was truly the land of
opportunity for those of us who were young and eager. Well, and needy. Yes,
you had to be motivated to leave your own land, and when the situation is
tight, when your country doesn't have much to offer, even if you love your
native land, you must find other ways to survive, right? And Honduras was a
paradise — lots of land, jobs. For those of us who had nothing at home, just
our hands to work [with], it was really paradise.

By the mid-1950s, however, an alarming population growth rate,
coupled with an unfavorable trade balance in the Central American
Common Market and the expansion of export crops, created a crisis in
Honduras. El Salvador and Honduras were at odds over a border dispute that dated back to the days of independence and over trade
within the Common Market that favored El Salvador. The result of
internal problems in Honduras was an increasing xenophobia for
which Salvadorans, as that country's largest foreign population,
became an easy target. The Honduran government passed an agrarian
reform law to redistribute land, leading to the eviction of many
Salvadoran families from lands they were illegally cultivating. By mid-
1969 about 300,000 Salvadorans had been expelled from Honduras.
Both governments began a series of diplomatic accusations that led to
an armed confrontation between El Salvador and Honduras in July.[8]
With El Salvador already having the worst people-to-land ratio in the
hemisphere, the repatriation of Salvadorans from Honduras placed
great socioeconomic pressure on the country. The large number of
landless peasants swelled the ranks of the unemployed and underemployed. Furthermore, the abrupt end of migration to Honduras shut
the safety valve this migration had for many years provided. The
war also contributed to the disintegration of the Central American

Common Market, from which El Salvador had benefited greatly. The lucrative Honduran market for Salvadoran industrial products was gone and the Nicaraguan market for Salvadoran goods was adversely affected as Honduras closed the highway through which El Salvador and Nicaragua communicate.

The population movements during this period continued to exert a great impact on the family and other social institutions in El Salvador. The three interrelated characteristics of poor Salvadoran families — high rates of free unions, out-of-wedlock children, and female headship of the household — kept pace with the large migration flows.[9] In the late 1950s it was estimated that free unions accounted for 50 percent of all unions (Brewer 1983, 405), and one-third of all urban and one-fifth of all rural families were headed by women (Adams 1976). By 1978, according to a survey of the urban poor in San Salvador, 39.5 percent of the households were headed by women (FUNDASAL 1979). Families regularly included children from previous unions and one or two adult relatives, which greatly facilitated child care. As Isabel Nieves (1979) notes in her study of Salvadoran household arrangements, the strength of the consanguineal household was that it freed adult women to become economically active to help support the group, which contributed to a degree of economic stability. Thus, for a high proportion of family units, the most significant connecting relationship was through the woman. It is what Richard Adams (1976, 60–61) calls "matrilocality-by-default."

Poverty required that most urban working-class women work outside their homes, especially when they were left as the sole providers for their families. Women's work in this case was not merely a supplement to the household income but the sole source of income for the family. Also, in rural areas among landless peasants women's work has been vital for the family. While men migrate to seek wage labor, women engage in a variety of subsistence activities, such as gardening, crafts, and raising animals for sale. However, with their partners gone, it is difficult for rural women and children to subsist, because they are less attractive to employers as laborers and are subject to evictions from their rental plots (Mason 1992, 76). Women, therefore, have not engaged in agricultural work, which is the most lucrative form of employment in rural El Salvador.

As a result, women have also migrated from rural areas to the cities.

In fact, women have been migrating to cities in larger numbers than men (Jelin, cited in Mason 1992). Their entry into the urban informal sector provides opportunities to earn a subsistence for their families.[10] The ease of finding work in this sector and the flexible hours allow women to work and care for their children at the same time, though the working conditions are often undesirable. In cities women work mainly as domestics and as street vendors but also in petty commerce and in factories. Of the 43 percent of working-age urban females who were economically active in the 1970s, 74 percent were employed in commerce and services (Ministerio Público 1983). Thus, among the urban poor, it has not been uncommon for both men and women to engage in paid work outside the home.

Context of Exit

The events surrounding large-scale emigration from El Salvador during the 1980s can be seen as the cumulative result of a long history of political decisions and economic dislocations that triggered cycles of social unrest and population movements at different points in Salvadoran history. The political and economic crisis that had been brewing in the country in the previous decades came to the surface in the late 1970s. The oil shocks of the 1970s and the rapid deterioration of the terms of trade exacerbated the problems. By the end of that decade, the two main stabilizing forces that held the Salvadoran economy together — a solid demand for Salvadoran exports in the international market and easy access to foreign credit — had collapsed (Gorostiaga and Marchetti 1988).

Since the early years of industrialization, the government had not taken appropriate measures to restrict the flow of capital out of the country, and industrialists and landowners relied on the state to supply credit for their investments and plantings (Barry and Preusch 1986, 136). In an effort to increase agro-export production so as to alleviate the economic crisis, cuts in subsidies and wages for the poorest urban and rural sectors of the population were implemented. From 1970 to 1980, the index of minimum wages decreased from 107 to 75 in industry and from 100 to 89 in agriculture (PREALC figures, cited in Gorostiaga and Marchetti 1988, 126). Furthermore, the state failed to introduce tax reforms, leaving the industrial sector exempt from taxes, and plunging into debt to save the economy. In the absence of political security for international capital, multinational companies — which had been the basis of the country's industry — left en masse. Private sector investment declined from between 70 and 80 percent in the 1950s to below 50 percent in the 1980s; and foreign investment declined from 30 percent in the 1960s to 8 percent in the 1980s (Gorostiaga and Marchetti 1988). Edelberto Torres-Rivas and Dina Jiménez (1985, 40) estimate that an average of one thousand workers were laid off and nine enterprises failed each month during the 1979–1981 period and that open unemployment in 1983 was 38 percent and underemployment approximately 80 percent. Some of my informants provided their views about the flight of foreign investment and its effect on the lives of the urban poor. The cousin of one of them, a woman who had worked for a multinational company since she was sixteen and was laid off when the company left as a result of the political upheaval, observed, "I worked in this company for several years. But the problems the war brings to business, you know, the usual, bombings, death threats, cross-fires, and unions — yes, bosses don't like unions [laughs] — all these made this company leave. So they laid us off, after many years of hard work. But I understand — they went there to make money, not to provide social security for us, right? Then, of course, we had no means of supporting ourselves. In the same way they left, we left too."

The socioeconomic problems of the country escalated to critical levels, and changes in the political apparatus seemed inevitable. By the late 1970s political parties obviously did not constitute grounds where consensus and legitimacy could be created, and popular organizations replaced political parties. Workers, the urban poor, trade unionists, professionals, students, and peasants organized to press for justice. The country's guerrilla movement became a major force, as the government used the military to respond to demands for social justice. Attempts to restructure the leadership of the country in 1977 failed, and elections were marked once again by fraud. Against a stronger and more organized opposition party, General Carlos Humberto Romero ascended to power in 1977, and the opposition candidate, a retired colonel, went into exile in Costa Rica. A staunch ally of the oligarchy who rejected any political or economic reform, General Romero's only response to protest was increased repression.

He governed under emergency public order legislation (state of siege) from 1977 to 1979, during which time mass demonstrations, protests, strikes, kidnappings, and death squad murders were rampant.

The turbulent Romero administration ended with a coup d'état by a military-civilian junta in October 1979. The junta set out to disband the paramilitary organization ORDEN, to free political prisoners, to nationalize the coffee industry and banking, to establish minimum wages, and, significantly, to initiate a program of land reform. The military and the elite adamantly opposed this agenda, and plans for reform soon collapsed. The leadership of the junta was restructured a few times, but their reforms angered the political extremists of the country. For the extreme right, the leaders of the junta were "communists," and for the left, they were puppets of the military. These events corresponded with changes in Washington. During the Romero years, the Carter administration had cut off all military aid to El Salvador due to widely publicized human rights violations. At this decisive moment, however, the Reagan administration quickly restored military aid to El Salvador. The economic contribution of the United States increased so dramatically that by 1982 Washington was sending approximately $1.5 million a day to keep the Salvadoran economy afloat.

The deeper involvement of the United States in the internal affairs of El Salvador and the opposition to the country's leadership by the right and the left triggered yet a new wave of political conflict, escalating to a generalized armed struggle that lasted for approximately twelve years. Revolutionary movements that had developed since the 1960s joined forces and began military offensives, which were met by increased violence from government troops.[11] The war against the guerrillas included "low-intensity conflict," a new type of warfare. A key aspect of its operation was an attempt to get forces hostile to the government to capitulate by producing civilian casualties and suffering (Lopez and Stohl, cited in Gibney 1991). This resulted in gross levels of human rights abuses, which often translated into an escalation of civilian deaths and ever-increasing refugee flows (Gibney 1991, 90). In addition to generating a large migratory movement, the civil war deeply affected the social fabric of the country.

The low-intensity warfare project in El Salvador involved direct armed confrontation and undercover paramilitary operations against all sectors of society that supported or were suspected of supporting or even sympathizing with the guerrilla combatants. (This strategy was not new; it was used during La Matanza to spot the enemies of the state, e.g., "communists" or their sympathizers.) It also involved terror tactics such as death squad operations and attacks against civilian populations (mainly in rural areas), including massacres of entire villages believed to be sympathetic to the guerrillas. Landless peasants and the unemployed were frequently suspected of involvement with opposition organizations. But potentially anyone who was disliked or had an enemy who could point a finger could be branded a guerrilla sympathizer. Archbishop Arturo Rivera y Damas said in a homily delivered in San Salvador in August 1980, "Many people flee because they are stamped as collaborators with the guerrillas and their life is in danger, because being marked is enough to cause the worst to happen" (Americas Watch 1984, 34). To demand justice in this environment would have meant an act of resistance, and consequently a threat to existence (Aron et al. 1991). But the use of intimidation and violence to retain political and economic power in El Salvador was not novel. What was new, as David Browning (1984) points out, was the use of systematic terrorism based on the organized use of murder, kidnapping, and destructive violence by extremist groups as a means to obstruct the political process. The implacable opposition of the organized left and the extreme right unleashed a spiral of violence that affected, in one way or another, all sectors of Salvadoran society. The report by the United Nations Truth Commission (Naciones Unidas n.d.) attributes culpability to both the government and guerrilla forces for the violence that ravaged the country during the war years.[12]

It is impossible to evaluate the toll that such an environment might have on social relationships, but when just about anyone, including friends, co-workers, or even family members could be suspected of being informers, the effects could not go unnoticed. During this period, families were separated not only by migration but also by death, imprisonment, exile, or one of the most terrifying and omnipresent acts, the disappearance of a loved one. According to the noted social psychologist Ignacio Martín-Baró (1990a), the psychosocial trauma generated by this generalized fear and the militarization of social life contributed to a dehumanization of social relationships, because people perceived the environment and each other as potentially hostile and dangerous. An integral part of low-intensity conflict was psychological warfare, which consisted of systematic threats of harassment and torture with the objective of demonstrating the danger of supporting the opposition (Martín-Baró 1990a, 1990b). The basic mechanism to achieve this objective was the unleashing of personal insecurity about one's beliefs, judgment, and feelings, creating an environment that engendered widespread suspicion and mistrust. The anticipation and anguish of a knock on the door in the middle of the night, of being the next captive, or of being "disappeared" without having been actively involved oneself in the conflict could have devastating effects on a person's psychological well-being. The normal daily occurrences to which Salvadorans were exposed — bombings, village massacres, constant surveillance by *orejas* (lit., ears), or informers, and the sight of mutilated bodies on the streets — might have contributed to produce a "numbing" effect, as one of my informants, Marcela Q., explained:

When the war started, I remember that I used to jump when I heard a bomb. Then, I got used to it. Same thing with watching horrible things. One gets used to things that are unbelievably awful. Look, for instance, people would talk as if they were talking about a plate on the table or about a dress when they would say, ah yes, there was a decapitated man hanging from that bridge yesterday. Or when my cousin was — his skin was taken off, yes, taken off, as one does with a pig when it's killed and ready to be cooked. Yes, that's how they left my cousin. You can't imagine how awful that was, but the people around there would simply say, ah yes, he was found today, maybe he was involved in something. After watching so many horrible things and hearing about thousands more, it's strange, but one doesn't react anymore — it's as if one has anesthesia in the heart; one doesn't have feelings anymore. It's very ugly.[13]

The climate of suspicion also posed potentially detrimental effects for relationships with friends, neighbors, and co-workers, as people avoided associating with those who might have been labeled collaborators or sympathizers — even if they were friends or family. Anyone could turn out to be an oreja. For instance, Don Armando Q., a sixty-year-old teacher by training, was taken out of his house at night and interrogated because someone suspected him of knowing a person who had been identified as a guerrilla sympathizer. His life was spared only because a witness walked by and his assailants could not carry out orders to "disappear" him. But Don Armando had to abandon his house within twenty-four hours and eventually leave the country, because the assailants threatened to return. Even though he never participated — directly or indirectly — in the conflict, the mere fact that he might have had an acquaintance suspected of being a guerrilla sympathizer was enough to create a life-threatening situation for him.[14] Sometimes Don Armando thinks that the entire incident was due to "envies." "You know," he explained, "you have enemies that you don't even know you have. Bad people who don't like what you have. They take advantage of the situation in the country and accuse you of being a subversive."

The case of Alicia N., a woman in her thirties with a ninth-grade education, further exemplifies this point. She and her three children were forced to abandon their house in a working-class suburb of San Salvador, literally overnight, as a result of a tip from a neighbor-informer to the government army. In Alicia's words:

I used to give injections, give medications to people, you know, I was like a nurse. One night two guys knocked on my door, they wanted me to put a bandage on a wounded man, and so I did. You know, one must help everyone, regardless of who they are. But I didn't realize that they left bloodstains like that, outside [on my doorstep]. A neighbor saw the blood and denounced me. Soldiers came by the next day, searching my house and demanding that I tell them if I had helped the wounded man or not, about my connections with the "guys" [guerrillas]. I had no idea that the man I treated was a guerrilla member. The soldiers insisted and said that they were going to come back. But one doesn't wait for soldiers to come back; that means you'll disappear. So we left the next day, with my children, for a friend's house.

By the time the soldiers departed, Alicia was certain she had assisted someone from the opposition, so she needed to move quickly. She contacted her friends from church, who arranged for her and the children to stay at a member's house. But Alicia did not want to endanger the friend by staying with her very long. "By then I was believed to be a guerrilla supporter because I had helped out that man, which meant that my friend, who had nothing to do with anything, would also be implicated." Alicia and her children left for Guatemala, where they stayed with fellow church members for four months before leaving for the United States. "My friend was so nervous, shaking when she would talk to me. We were at her house for three days. The poor thing, she felt great relief when we left," Alicia recalls.

Migratory Movements

The combination of political repression, armed conflict, and the economic crisis in El Salvador contributed to a dramatic increase in Salvadoran emigration. From the late 1970s onward, migration trends within and from El Salvador changed dramatically, not only quantitatively, but also qualitatively. Internally displaced people fled from conflict areas (mostly in eastern El Salvador) to other regions of the country; some fled to adjacent regions such as Honduras or Guatemala, and others crossed two international borders (to Mexico) or three (to the United States). El Salvador and Honduras reestablished diplomatic relations in the early 1980s, bringing a resumption of emigration to Honduras. According to the United Nations High Commissioner for Refugees (UNHCR), by 1983 there were 400,000 internally displaced in El Salvador and 200,000 Salvadoran refugees in Mexico and Central America (cited in Naciones Unidas n.d.). Migration to the United States increased from 45,000 between 1951 and 1960 to more than 100,000 between 1961 and 1970, exceeding 134,000 during the 1970s (U.S. Bureau of the Census 1980). But by 1990 the Salvadoran population in the United States had more than quintupled. These population displacements during the war years strengthened an existing pattern of female-headed households, mostly due to men's (voluntary or involuntary) abandonment of their families (Morales Velado 1994, 252).

The class composition of these migrations was significantly different from earlier ones. Internally displaced persons and those who fled to refugee camps in Honduras came from the ranks of those who had been engaged in these movements for decades — the most destitute sectors of the Salvadoran population, whose situation had worsened as a result of the war. In contrast, those who migrated to the United States represented all sectors of Salvadoran society, including the urban working, lower-middle, and middle classes, who traditionally did not tend to migrate. This new U.S.-bound emigration was also different from previous flows to the United States; in earlier years the upper and middle classes had had the privilege of traveling for business or pleasure. The profile of Salvadorans in the United States differs significantly from that of the Salvadoran population in general. Approximately 50 percent of the Salvadorans in the United States came from urban areas of El Salvador (Montes 1987b, 1988), compared to 43.8 percent urban dwellers for El Salvador as a whole in 1987 (United Nations 1996). Their average educational level in the 1980s was estimated to be nine years, a high figure for a country where only one-eighth of the economically active population had completed six years of school (Montes 1988; Wallace 1986). (The school life expectancy in 1992 was 8.6 years [UNESCO 1995, I–5].)

The more impoverished migrants remained inside the country or in adjacent areas, but those with relatively more material or social resources migrated to the United States; however, they were by no means an affluent group. For instance, the majority lacked the financial means to obtain a visa. But the historical switch in the direction and class composition of migratory flows constitutes a new phenomenon in Salvadoran migration history. Some of my older informants seemed to agree that before the 1970s only a handful of people they knew had left for the United States. Doña Tulita, the aunt of an informant, explained:

Now everyone comes here. Tell me, what Salvadoran, whether he's rich or poor, doesn't have a relative or at least a friend in the United States? No one. The whole world is here. Oh no, before no, only those with money could come here. I remember going to the airport on Sundays just to see airplanes — for fun. And people would say, oh, they're coming from the United States, and oh, that was a big thing, because in those days, traveling to the United States was only done by plane. People traveled elegantly too. Not everyone could afford it. It was a luxury, now it's a need.

The personal motivation for leaving El Salvador for the United States during the conflict mirrors the events that were taking place in this period; that is, they reflect a confluence of political and economic factors. For instance, the responses to my survey of 150 Salvadorans show a high concentration in the category "by force or fear of persecution," but they are also clustered in the "harsh economic conditions" category (Menjívar 1993). My informants in the intensive interviews also explained their reasons for migrating as a combination of economic and political forces, for they were usually unable to separate the two. In the words of Carolina A., a college student from San Salvador in her mid-twenties:

I think I came here because I wanted a better future. But the exact reasons why I came are more complicated. See, I used to work during the daytime and go to the university at night. But because of the conflict, I couldn't continue to go to school at night. Once I almost got killed in a crossfire, and once the bus that I needed to take had been burned down by the guerrillas. It's true I wanted to improve my economic situation, but if it hadn't been for the conflict, I could have stayed there to finish my degree at the university and with that get a good job there. I don't want to say, oh yes, I'm here for political reasons, but when I really have to think about it, I can't separate that from other considerations. So I really don't know if my reasons for leaving El Salvador can be categorized as political or economic. I think — I am inclined to say that it's both. That is possible, right?

However, there were a few exceptions to this pattern: those who had been politically active (or had been suspected of political activity), for whom the motivation had been decisively political. But regardless of personal motivation, Salvadorans would not be able to migrate to the United States if they lacked the vital social, cultural, and historical linkages established over many years of U.S. influence in their country.

Conclusion

Migration is an enduring feature of Salvadoran history. At different times economic policies and political decisions generated particular population movements; these in turn have greatly affected the dynamics of social institutions, such as the family. Family separation as a result of migration has therefore also been a persistent characteristic of Salvadoran society and has produced a high rate of free unions, of out-of-wedlock children, and of female headship of households. In recent years the political upheaval has added a psychosocial strain, as families also have been separated by war-related violence. In addition, the militarization of life and the institutionalization of terror in El Salvador have left profound scars on a wide range of social ties. In contrast to earlier movements, the massive emigration of the 1980s has been significantly more numerous and more inclusive, as it has represented all sectors of Salvadoran society. The upheaval within which this massive emigration unfolded was not the result of a sudden crisis. Rather, it was the outcome of a lengthy history of reluctance (on the part of the elite) to fundamental economic reform, of abuses by a military entrenched in power, and of external intervention that supported this structure.

Chapter 3

The Long Journey through Mexico

My mother told me that my husband left ten days ago to come
here. But I really don't know when he will get here. It may take
one week, one month, or much longer, like in my case. You see,
when people leave El Salvador you hear people say, oh, so and so
left, but that's it. One never knows what may happen, so you can't
say anything else with certainty. No one has any idea of when the
person might arrive here. It's like you gamble with your life,
really. Look, my brother also left, but after spending two months
in Mexico he showed up in El Salvador again. So many things can
happen to you during the trip. You can even die, and sometimes
no one ever finds out what happened to you. Yes, you just disappear. So really, no one, only God, knows when — or even if — my
husband will ever arrive here.

Marcela Q.

Marcela is not alone in her uncertainty about her husband's trip. For
the majority of Salvadorans, events that occur between leaving El
Salvador and entering the United States are often as crucial as the
decision to migrate itself. For most of these migrants, who must travel
by land because they lack a U.S. visa, the U.S.-bound journey entails
a risky undertaking that involves the crossing of three international
borders. Furthermore, the trip to the United States is of special significance for the lives of newcomer Salvadorans because many —
whether they travel by land, air, or a combination of both — incur
great debts to their relatives or friends in the United States to make or
continue the trip. The debts eventually can become the source of tension with relatives.

The importance of help from the United States for the U.S.-bound
journey cannot be overstated. Eighty percent of the 150 respondents
to my survey mentioned that a friend or relative already in the United
States had helped them to make the trip — with financial means or

TABLE 5   Help from U.S. Relatives for the Trip

Response	Percentage of Survey Respondents (N=150)
Received help from U.S. relatives and friends	80.00
Ranked help from U.S. relatives and friends as most important	78.00
Received U.S. help to finance the trip	47.00
Confident that help received previously would continue on arrival	77.00

NOTE: This help included names, telephone numbers of people along the way, tips about the journey, and loans for travel.

with information (see table 5) — and an overwhelming majority of my 50 informants acknowledged this vital resource. This support proved so crucial that more than three-fourths of the survey respondents who obtained assistance from friends and family in the United States ranked it as their most important resource and their own means as secondary in importance (see table 5). Amparo A., an insightful woman from a village in eastern El Salvador who is in her late twenties and has a seventh-grade education, explained that her mother's assistance was the deciding factor in her and her siblings' migration. Without this help they could not have even considered the move. Furthermore, almost one-half, or 47 percent, of the survey respondents mentioned that a relative in the United States — usually a parent, a sister, or a sibling — had actually financed their trip, though in most cases the money had been a loan and not a gift (see table 5). Virginia M., a woman in her fifties with a fifth-grade education, said that her sister in San Francisco had petitioned for her to immigrate and had paid all of her expenses for the trip: "She, my sister, submitted our permanent resident applications and paid for everything — tickets, applications, everything. She even sent us the money for the pictures we had to take to the American embassy in San Salvador. We're so grateful, we owe everything to her." In contrast to Virginia's case, for the great majority of these immigrants, the U.S. relatives were never able to send money from their own resources but had been forced to borrow from other

Map showing one route followed by Salvadoran immigrants. Other, equally traveled ways to get to San Francisco go through Arizona or Texas.

family members, friends, or even employers. Repaying these debts —
so that the receiving relatives could, in turn, repay theirs — placed a
great deal of pressure on the cash-strapped newcomers.

Although the most important form of help from U.S. family and
friends was usually financial, other forms of assistance — information
about the journey, an address, a telephone number, the name of a
contact in Mexico — were often crucial in facilitating the trip. For
instance, Marcela Q. said that she gives the addresses or telephone
numbers of places where people can stay in Mexico to relatives or very
close friends; she considers this information a gift. In addition to personal contacts, obtaining the name of religious organizations or solidarity groups was also of great help. As is the case in the United States,
these groups have actively been providing help to Central Americans
in Mexico.

Exiting is the easiest of all the stages of the journey for Salvadorans
en route to the United States. Under Salvadoran law, any person eighteen years of age or older who desires to leave the country is allowed
to do so. But that is where the easy part of the journey ends. The rest
is often lengthy and arduous, even harrowing. With few exceptions,
Guatemala preferred to ignore many of the Salvadorans who crossed
its border on their way north. There were no formalities or visa
requirements to enter Guatemala (recently it has implemented restrictions on the travel of Salvadorans and other Central Americans so as to
reduce the flow of U.S.-bound migrants). Beginning in the mid-1980s,
as a tactic to stem the flow of Central Americans, Mexico began to
require a visa for Salvadorans (and other Central Americans). In
Mexico ever more aggressive measures affect the Salvadorans' journey, and it is not uncommon to face deportation, incarceration, or
demands for bribes so exorbitant that the journey may have to end
there, or change direction altogether.

The average cost of the trip for the respondents to my survey was
$1,700. Most of that, borrowed money from receiving relatives'
employers, friends, and family, went to pay the coyote — the smug-
gler — and, in most cases, bribes along the way.[1] In fact, when the trip
is arranged, the coyote factors money for bribes into the cost. In most
cases, to ensure safe arrival, the coyotes are not paid the full amount
until they bring their clients to a drop-off point in the United States
(usually Los Angeles for the people in this study). The person travel-

ing makes a "down payment" that covers the costs of the trip, and once in the United States his or her family, as is often the case, pays the balance to secure the person's "release." The coyote can detain his or her client until the entire amount is paid off. Sometimes the coyote allows the person to work to pay off the debt, for the coyote has extensive contacts that put both a job and fake documents within the new arrival's reach to facilitate this enterprise. But these arrangements may become terribly exploitive for the client, and often they are dangerous for the coyotes as well. One of my informants, who for a while smuggled compatriots across the border, explained that she would only bring people she or her family back home knew personally, so as to avoid the complications of obtaining payment in the United States.

Mexico

It is impossible to ascertain how many Salvadorans who arrive in Mexico stay there and how many continue to the United States. The trip through Mexico is treacherous, and people are forced to migrate in stages. Laura O'Dogherty (1989) estimates that most Central Americans spend two to three months in Chiapas, stopping in other states along the way until they reach Mexico City. Almost one-half of the 150 respondents to my survey indicated that they had stayed in Mexico an average of two and one-half months, and slightly more than half mentioned that they had met people who were not able to continue the trip and had to go back (see table 6). My respondents indicated that the reasons these people could not complete their journeys were many. They ranged from having been detained by the Mexican immigration authorities and sent back and/or put in jail to having found a job in Mexico, gotten married there, or simply returned voluntarily to El Salvador because of the hardships encountered. In some instances, because U.S. relatives had failed to send additional money to Mexico, the person was forced to return to El Salvador. In a thorough analysis of this question, Sergio Aguayo (1985, 51–52) indicates that the majority of Central Americans prefer to move on to the United States. There are some important reasons why Salvadorans continue to the United States, and these are related to sociocultural linkages between the United States and El Salvador as well as to structural conditions in Mexico.

TABLE 6   Summary of the Journey

Response	Percentage of Survey Respondents (N=150)
Attempted to enter the United States twice	34.0
Attempted to enter the United States several times	20.0
Attempted to enter Mexico several times	68.0
Traveled with a U.S. visa	20.0
Traveled by land part or all of the way	80.0
By air part or all of the way	33.0
Assaulted once	33.0
Assaulted several times	34.0
Felt life in danger at some point during the trip	70.0
Stayed in Mexico over one month during the trip	55.0
Average stay in Mexico (mos.)	2.5
Met people who could not continue trip and returned to Mexico	54.0
Average stay in another U.S. city (mos.)	1.5
Unsure about living in San Francisco in two years	82.0

The United States has had a long history of social, political, economic, and cultural influence in the Central American region that has resulted in the development of social conduits through which goods, information, and technology have traveled. This, in turn, has created conditions that have allowed Central Americans to migrate to the United States over the years. For instance, the Salvadoran community in San Francisco did not suddenly appear in the 1940s; its creation was intimately tied to U.S. operations in the Panama Canal and to labor recruitment there for wartime industries in San Francisco.[2] In later years, as the U.S. economic, political, and military presence in El Salvador intensified, these linkages became stronger and more widespread, resulting in an ever-expanding web of contacts between people at both ends. As one of my informants' cousins assured me, it has reached the point where, "right now, there isn't even one person left in the entire territory [of El Salvador] who doesn't have a relative or a friend or even an acquaintance in the United States." Thus motivations for *leaving* El Salvador are, almost always, directly or indirectly related to the political conflict, but the reasons for *going* specifically to the United States — rather than to other countries, including Mexico — are linked to the United States' enduring presence in El Salvador.

Mexico's immigration policies play a key role in the migrants' decisions to move on to the United States. Throughout the conflict in El Salvador, Mexico, like the United States, did not officially recognize Salvadoran refugees; but unlike the United States, Mexico allowed the UNHCR to operate in its territory. According to the UNHCR, there were approximately 120,000 Salvadorans in Mexico in the late 1980s, only 5,000 of whom were recognized (Aguayo and Fagen 1988, 7). Mexico's immigration policy vis-à-vis Central Americans has complex roots and has been rather ambiguous, including protection and generosity to the refugees at some points and xenophobia and restrictionist approaches at others. Although the Mexican government allows the UNHCR to recognize some Central Americans as refugees and to protect them, it has concomitantly enforced restrictions on the entry and length of stay of Central Americans. For instance, Mexico has adopted the same visa requirements that the United States uses to grant visas to Central and South Americans, including bank accounts with lofty balances, land or real estate ownership documents, and proof of income. However, these documents are not necessary for entering Mexico if the person already has a U.S. visa. Conceivably these legal obstacles act as the Border Patrol beyond U.S. borders. Also, additional immigration agents were sent to the southern border (Chiapas), fees were increased for renewing immigration documents, and in 1985 there were daily raids on Central Americans in Mexico City (O'Dogherty 1989). In the Chiapas area alone there are at least four well-known immigration checkpoints and many more in other regions of Mexico.

Mexico's long tradition of asylum, characterized by relatively small numbers, has been based on individual selection. At different points during this century, Mexico received certain Central Americans who were fleeing their countries' political crises, but the composition of these early flows was selective, including people who had been politically active, usually intellectuals (Castillo 1994, 189). Thus the refugee (or asylee) numbers were small (and human capital high), which facilitated their reception. But massive Central American migration has been Mexico's first experience as a receiving country of large-scale flight from political strife (Aguayo and Fagen 1988). In the midst of an economic crisis and political turmoil, Mexico has not been able to officially adopt a humanitarian or even a uniform national policy toward Central Americans.

In addition to an ambiguous legal situation, Central Americans have encountered inflation, unemployment, and a generally troubled economy in Mexico. The humanitarian welcome that Central Americans initially received there in the early 1980s had largely eroded by the latter part of the decade, as more Central Americans arrived and the Mexican economy plunged deeper into crisis. By 1988 the Mexican public began to think that assistance provided to Central Americans was unjustifiable; they felt freer to express their opposition to the Central American presence and blamed Central Americans for the many problems that afflicted Mexico (O'Dogherty 1989, 37). Central Americans were portrayed in the media as participating in crime, drugs, and prostitution and were viewed as taking advantage of assistance. In a country profoundly struck by an economic crisis, these images contributed to ferment anti–Central American sentiment.[3]

Given these circumstances and the existence of contacts already in the United States, it is not surprising that so many Salvadorans continued their journeys north, even though, as is widely known, entering the United States is not an easy enterprise. In my survey one-third of the respondents indicated that they had tried to enter the United States twice; another one-fifth had tried multiple times (see table 6). Mireya C., a community worker and organizer, almost did not make it to the other side when she crossed in an underground tunnel that connected Mexico and the United States.

They were telling me, "Please go, you have to continue," but I couldn't. That tunnel was horrible — and they say that it runs right beneath an immigration checkpoint, but no one has ever been able to find it. I think it's closed down now. But at that moment, when I was inside, I thought, this is what people who die of asphyxia must go through. I told my brother, "You go ahead, I'll just stay here." But he said, no, no way, hold on to my belt and I'll pull you to the other side. So that's how I crossed.

Mauricio R., another community worker and organizer, almost lost his life on the U.S. leg of the trip. He was traveling with thirteen others, and although they made it across the border in only two attempts, the group ran out of water in the Arizona desert — in midsummer.[4] They drank any fluids they could find, including aftershave cologne, but when they finished it, they had no other recourse but to drink their own urine. No one should have survived the ordeal, but Mauricio and two others did. In his usually casual and easy manner, Mauricio recounted the following: "It was horrendous, a nightmare. We were leaving — we thought we had left *la muerte* [death] back in El Salvador, but it was death itself that was persecuting us. But it caught up with us and took most of the people in the group." They hallucinated and literally agonized for two days; then the Border Patrol appeared. "It was an irony, but we were saved by the INS. If they hadn't seen us, the rest of us would have died too."

The Salvadorans who traveled through Mexico en route to the United States (*transmigrantes,* as they are referred to in Mexico) and eventually crossed over to the United States surreptitiously did so because they had been denied a U.S. visa. This was mostly because they had not met the increasingly stringent financial requirements — and more often than not, lacked a Mexican visa as well.[5] In this study only 20 percent of the respondents to the survey and only seven of my fifty informants traveled with a U.S. visa, making the trip by plane (table 6). Ironically, the transmigrantes' trip is more costly than a safe and quick airplane trip. For example, the average cost of a one-way trip by land to San Francisco at the time I conducted this research was $1,700, whereas an airplane ticket sold for about $550 round-trip.

One-third of the survey respondents mentioned they had traveled by air at least part of the way (see table 6), usually to Guadalajara or Mexico City. But 80 percent had traveled most of the way, if not the entire way, by land, and a substantial number of them indicated that they walked and hitched rides in trucks or trains for at least part of the trip. Marcela Q., who was in her first trimester of pregnancy when she traveled, walked almost one-third of the approximately three thousand miles from El Salvador to Houston, where she stayed for a week after she entered the United States. Marcela also traveled by bus and took rides in trucks that were transporting cargoes of fruit. On one of those occasions, Marcela and one of the drivers ran out of money for food, so they ate mangoes for two consecutive days. After a failed attempt to enter the United States, she made it across the Rio Grande in an inner tube. Evelyn S., a second-year medical student in her early twenties who was also pregnant when she made the journey from San Salvador, crossed the Suchiate River from Guatemala to Mexico in an inner tube and then rode a bicycle with her group, all of them pretending to be residents of the area on a picnic outing. They then rode a bus to Mexico City, took an airplane from there to Tijuana, and finally walked across the border and traveled well into the United States on foot.

It is alleged that between U.S. and Mexican authorities informal bilateral agreements designed to enlist Mexican assistance have operated in curbing migration from Central America into Mexico. Fieldwork by Sergio Aguayo and Patricia Weiss Fagen (1988) along the Mexican-U.S. border indicates that local immigration authorities of both countries have collaborated in enforcing a restrictive immigration policy. In addition, the authors note that they heard accounts that the INS had carried out espionage in Sonora, Mexico, that led to the arrest of twelve members of the Sanctuary movement in the United States. There have been cases in which Mexican authorities have persecuted travelers without U.S. visas as persistently as U.S. immigration officials would, as two of my informants' stories attest. Marcela Q. said that by early 1993, when she was making a second trip to the United States, there was a new immigration checkpoint on Mexican territory between Hermosillo and Tijuana. This checkpoint, she thought, was meant to target Central Americans, because "Mexicans could not be detained for traveling in their own territory by their own immigration [enforcement] agency."

In addition to the official justifications for questioning Central Americans (e.g., because they were traveling to the United States without documents), low-ranking Mexican immigration authorities in border towns or at checkpoints see the bribes from Central American migrants as attractive supplements to their meager incomes. Therefore, they go out of their way to catch undocumented Central Americans. This situation poses serious and sometimes even life-threatening obstacles for migrants en route to the United States. Also, according to workers I interviewed who assist Salvadorans in Mexico, the Mexican government does not know if the Salvadorans will stay there or continue their journey north, which contributes to an inclination on the part of Mexican officials to deny any responsibility for the Salvadorans. By refusing to acknowledge the presence of these migrants in

Mexico, the government severely restricts funds for those who end up staying there.

For Salvadorans — as well as for other Central Americans or migrants in general — the journey through Mexico is plagued with uncertainties and dangers. I would like to point out, however, that most of the abuse came from those in positions of authority, such as immigration officials or the federal police, or from criminals. Many "common" Mexicans, as my informants explained, either lent them a hand or at least did not harass them. For some, entering the United States has been relatively easy compared to crossing over to Mexico. Of the respondents to my survey, while one-fifth had attempted to enter the United States several times, more than two-thirds had tried to enter Mexico multiple times (see table 6). This does not mean that crossing over to or traveling in the United States is easy, for many migrants have almost lost their lives and others have actually perished doing so (see Eschbach et al. 1999).

In addition to the bureaucratic obstacles enforced by Mexican local authorities and the tactics that these officials use to extract money from the transmigrantes, they are prey to common criminals; this vulnerable group is exposed to robberies, assaults, rapes, murder, death from dehydration, and the like. Estela Z. told me:

Somehow, our coyote miscalculated the amount of water that was needed, and we ran out of water. So we had to tolerate the sun and heat without drinking. It was horrible. But you know what people say? That in those conditions you can't stop to rest, because if you do, you'll just stay there and won't ever get up again. You die. So, we just kept on going. Finally, we saw an old lady who gave us all some water, like this, outside her house, in the garden. I think it was a miracle. We all thought that it was probably the Virgin Mary — or maybe we were seeing things from being so tired and dehydrated [laughs].

More than one-third of my respondents indicated that they had been assaulted or robbed in Mexico at least once; one-third mentioned multiple assaults (see table 6). Estela's cousin María Luisa Z. and her husband traveled with a group of about twelve. The group changed composition a couple of times during the journey because some people simply could not continue the grueling trek and others joined them along the way. They were robbed twice, in both cases by bandits whom María Luisa suspects had bribed the local police because they were never caught, even though everyone seemed to know who they were. Each time they were robbed represented a major setback, as the group had to wait for money — most of it in the form of loans — from U.S. relatives to continue the trip. In all, it took them two and one-half months to arrive in San Francisco from the time they left El Salvador. And most, or more than two-thirds, said they had felt that their lives had been in danger during the journey. Deaths of undocumented immigrants, including Mexicans and Central Americans, along the U.S.-Mexico border have started to be reported systematically (Eschbach et al. 1999). But for many Salvadorans and other Central Americans, life-threatening situations begin long before they reach the northern Mexican border.

For Alicia N. and her children, the trip was harrowing. Alicia's mother-in-law, Conchita F., had lent her $4,000 to travel from Guatemala to San Francisco, but they barely had enough to make it. They were assaulted three times during the trip, once by Mexican policemen. In a matter-of-fact way, Alicia recounted bone-chilling stories about her trip:

We had to jump a few bushes, like this, very high. I sprained my foot, and later I couldn't walk anymore. But fright made me walk. And with my foot swollen my shoe didn't fit anymore. My feet peeled because of walking and walking. Yes, *mis cipotes* [my kids] walked too. They saw a lot — too much. Sometimes I feel guilty for exposing them to so much. But what can one do? Imagine, once we thought there were white branches like that, on the side of the road — yes, human bones, it was human bones. The children got scared. They still have nightmares about that. They scream at night. And the same day, there were people coming behind us, another group. They were assaulted and the women were raped — a fifteen-year-old girl had been gang-raped. Their clothes were all torn and ripped. We asked for help in a house, and we washed the clothes to continue the next day, but the girl couldn't walk. Afterwards, they [the bandits] appeared again — always policemen. I gave them more money so they would not touch the girls anymore.

By the time their coyote brought them to Los Angeles, they had nothing left of the $4,000 Conchita had sent them. Conchita had borrowed some of the money from others in the family, but most of it came from her employers. When Alicia arrived in Los Angeles, Conchita managed once again to send them additional money for the last leg of the trip to San Francisco. When Alicia and the children finally arrived, their debt amounted to almost $5,000.

In addition to taking bribes directly from the migrants, Mexican immigration officials seemed to also participate more intricately in the informal webs through which migrants reach the United States. For instance, José R., a man in his thirties from a city in central El Salvador, told me that the Mexican officials who detained him and his compatriots were actually among the coyotes who transported them across Mexico.

This lady, the one who prepared us for everything there [in El Salvador] — yes, the coyote — had meetings in her house. She told us what to say and all that, and then gave us $60,000 pesos for the trip, but we didn't spend them because they were paying for everything during the trip. So when we got to Tijuana, the guys there — yes, the Mexicans — started asking us where we were from [and] all that. We weren't supposed to talk. We weren't supposed to say that we were coming in a group, but they were looking for the leader. So they started asking questions, and I was answering for the group — it was twenty of us. Then this girl next to me was nervous, and her passport fell. Then they said, "All of you, take out your passports and give them to me, you are Salvadorans, right?" "Yes," I said, "I'm Salvadoran." "Couldn't you have said that before?" they asked. So they asked me, "Listen, you, are they bringing money?" I said, "We all have only 60,000 pesos each." "Ah," he said, "what a coincidence, all of you are bringing the same amount, so you're traveling together." And he insisted on asking questions, to make sure who we were — probably because it turns out that he was the coyote who was going to take us across to San Diego, him and another guy who actually got with us to San Diego. The 60,000 pesos were a clue that we were the group that needed to get across. Can you imagine that? How can someone trust authorities like those [laughs]?

The journey seems to be especially dangerous for women. Three women broke down in tears when they described their experiences during the trip. Amparo A. said that Mexican authorities had threatened her not only with rape.

They told me that they were going to take my clothes off, and they would burn me with cigarette butts all over if I did not give them the money I was carrying. Yes, like torture. I told them that no, I didn't have any money, I'm not going as a tourist to the United States. Do you think I'm going there to shop? No, I'm going there to work, to make the little bit of money that I don't have right now to give you. I'm poor, don't take from me.

They eventually let her go unharmed. Victoria O., a deeply religious person, told me,

This trip was a nightmare. I would think, oh, maybe with this God wants me to prove something to Him. I'm not a young girl anymore, but I felt in as much danger as a young one. I felt as if my hands were tied. I wanted to do something, but I couldn't. I saw things that made me ask God, are these your children too, why do you let them act like this? You know, God forbid, but I sometimes don't feel any pity for Mexicans here because going through their country is hell, it's a test of fire.

When I asked Priscilla F., a lively twenty-year-old who used to be a cheerleader in eastern El Salvador and left the day she finished the ninth grade, about her trip, she said it was all right. But then her contagious smile and easy manner disappeared; her voice began to tremble and tears rolled down her face as she recounted details of her journey. She zeroed in on the awful treatment by the men.

They did many terrible things to women. I can't tell you all the horrors that women go through there [her voice now barely understandable because she was crying]. I have heard that those men do whatever they want to women — you know, [sexually] abuse you. Many women arrive pregnant in the United States from what they go through in Mexico. Other times they [the men] take you to brothels in the area, where you can rot for the rest of your life because no one ever hears from you again.

Although the trip seemed to be particularly difficult for some women, others had a different perspective. Lety R., a widow in her forties who barely finished the fourth grade in her rural town in central El Salvador, always pointed out that the fact that she is a woman had opened some doors for her. She firmly believed that people had been more willing to let her enter their homes than they would have a man because "women are more trustworthy." Along the same lines, but offering a more nuanced explanation, Marcela Q. commented, "If women encounter good people, they will be treated better than the men because people pity women—you know, [laughs] women are believed to be weak. The problem is when women find bad people, then they suffer more than anyone because the first thing that they suffer is, well, that they are [sexually] abused."

Given the dangers of the journey, Salvadorans have prepared themselves in many different ways to cross Mexico. Marcela Q.'s friend decided that instead of attempting to fake a Mexican accent — a common tactic among Central Americans — she would not talk at all, and she made the entire trip pretending she was mute, communicating only by signing. Others have obtained fake Mexican documents, which apparently are easily purchased in Los Angeles. These documents are bought by Salvadorans who need them to go home for a visit, or are sent to relatives in El Salvador to make their journey much easier. The Salvadorans who decided to pass for Mexicans had learned specifics of Mexican life, such as the national anthem, names of politicians and state capitals, and important historical dates. But Mexican authorities soon grew suspicious when these migrants would correctly provide detailed information about Mexican history and politics, something their own nationals would often fail to do. Thus the questions switched to commonplaces of daily life, such as culinary preferences, shoe and clothing sizes (different in Mexico), and weights (kilograms in Mexico, pounds in El Salvador). But communication between these migrants and compatriots and family back home travels quickly, and recent migrants now include such subtleties in the repertoire of knowledge needed to make it across Mexico. Coaching the travelers on these matters is among the services that the coyotes offer.[6] And almost all my informants — the fervently religious and the less so — included a prayer in their preparations for a successful trip. As Priscilla F. said, "It [the trip] makes you remember God, whether you go to church or not. Before I left, my grandmother *me encomendó a San Cristóbal* [placed me in Saint Christopher's care] — you know, they say that he's the patron saint of travel, so that I would arrive safe. That's all my poor *abuelita* [granny] could do for me, but it helped a lot. During that horrible time [in Mexico] I prayed hard to San Cristóbal, and I think that's why I'm still alive now."

Although many of the migrants faced danger and suffered during the journey, several of the study participants also experienced hospitality and remain grateful for the assistance received from Mexicans they met on their journey. As Mireya C. said when we were discussing the experiences of the many Salvadorans who had gone through Mexico: "Don't forget to mention all the great people who have helped us there. Many Mexican brothers and sisters received us in their land with open arms, and we must never forget that. Many Salvadorans owe many Mexicans their lives." During the time they stayed in Mexico, some migrants tried to earn money to continue their trip north. Sometimes a local resident in a town would learn about the situation of a transmigrante and would offer a place to stay — sometimes even her own bedroom — and a hot meal, or even a temporary job. For instance, when Marcela Q. told her host in Veracruz that she was pregnant, the host immediately made sure that Marcela had enough to eat and moved her to a more comfortable room in the house and would address her as *hija* (daughter) or *m'hija* (my daughter). The host — who had never met Marcela before — also put her in touch with relatives in the outskirts of Guadalajara so that Marcela would have a place to stay there on her way to the United States. When Marcela arrived in Guadalajara, her new hosts hired her to work for them picking tomatoes, but this proved too taxing, so instead they gave her a job in their bakery. Marcela met other kind locals in a border town who coached her on when and how to cross the border and even gave her food for the road. An older woman gave Marcela a small medal that bore the image of the Virgin of Guadalupe, which was supposed to guard her during the trip and beyond. Obviously moved, Marcela noted: "I really believe that when I crossed [the Rio Grande] in that inner tube, and it tipped a little, it was the Mexican Virgin that saved me. I'll never forget what all those [Mexican] people did for me."

In addition to such informal, unorganized forms of assistance for Salvadoran migrants, there were two other very important sources of help for them in Mexico — political and religious organizations, which often worked in conjunction with one another. Not unlike the case in the United States, in the absence of a national assistance policy, private groups took the initiative. Some collaborated with counterparts in the United States to help channel resources to Salvadorans, both to those who stayed in Mexico and to those who continued to the United States. For instance, the Sanctuary movement in the United States supported Mexican organizations that helped transport Central Americans through Mexico. Several of my informants had obtained assistance from a church or a solidarity group at some point during their journey. Chentía A.'s nephew worked for a church group to earn money while he waited for a loan from his aunt to continue the journey. Also, a solidarity group gave him a place to stay and often provided him with meals. Don Armando Q. worked in Mexico for a month, selling cereals at a local market. A church group had given him a small loan to buy the cereal to start up his business. This group had also helped him receive needed psychological help. Lolita Q., a college-educated woman in her thirties originally from rural eastern El Salvador and a former union organizer, was extremely grateful for the help she received from "our Mexican brothers who fight for the poor" while she was in a very difficult situation in Mexico. A solidarity organization gave her clothing and food and also provided shelter for a group of Central Americans who had been assaulted during the time she was there. There are various nongovernmental organizations (NGOs), human rights groups, that have been providing legal and judicial protection to the migrants in Mexico as well. These organizations help those who are en route to the United States but also those who stay in Mexico. Their activities include legal assistance, training in various trades, settling disputes with employers, and pressuring the Mexican government to ratify international conventions for the protection of the migrants' rights.

Where Will the Journey End?

For many Salvadorans the journey does not end in San Francisco. Throughout my fieldwork I kept hearing stories of instability, of insecurity, of the need to move to another city or to another apartment or job. It seemed that for many the insecurities of the journey continued even after they entered the United States. Thus I inquired about subsequent moves. First, I asked if they had come directly to San Francisco on reaching the United States. Slightly more than half of the survey respondents mentioned that they had stayed in another U.S. city—usually in Los Angeles, but also Houston, depending on which route they took—an average of one and a half months (see table 6). For instance, Tony, one of my informant's roommates, stayed in Houston for three months and had the opportunity to go to Washington, D.C., but a cousin persuaded him to come to San Francisco. I also asked the survey respondents if they thought they would still be living in San Francisco in two years; more than 80 percent could not give a definitive answer and simply responded "Talvez"—maybe (see table 6). In conversations with my informants, with community workers, and with a Catholic priest, it surfaced that this uncertainty was directly linked to the uncertain legal status of the majority of the Salvadorans in this study and in the United States in general. In fact, Josh Reichert and Douglas Massey (1979) found that undocumented migrants tend to be more mobile than their documented counterparts, both in terms of distances traveled and in terms of frequency of movement. Alejandro M., an army lieutenant in his early thirties, had to drop out of his fifth year of medical school in El Salvador because he was suspected of being a guerrilla supporter. He told me, "I don't know where I'll be even tomorrow. First I was deported from Guatemala, but I couldn't go back to El Salvador, so they put me on the Mexican side. Then the Mexicans wanted to get rid of me. But I bribed everyone — everyone — so they let me go north instead of south. I feel like I am at a bus station, always waiting to go on. This country doesn't like us, so we shouldn't really feel a part of it. Why lie to ourselves?"

Yet for others, the possibility of returning to El Salvador or, more likely, of going back and forth remains a firm plan. Given the increasingly tight immigration measures, this may not prove feasible for the majority who still lack proper documentation. Marcela Q. tried to go back and forth in 1992 and 1993 because two of her three children live in El Salvador. But she said that she would like to remain in the United States for now because as an undocumented person the trip is much more difficult to make and entering the United States is simply a nightmare these days.[7] For those who have been able to procure documents, have financial resources, and have close relatives still back home, however, going back and forth may prove a viable option, and one that seems to be emerging with the vibrant binational ties that this migration has brought about. Manuel, an informant's cousin, arrived in San Francisco in 1980 and was granted amnesty under the Immigration Reform and Control Act (IRCA). Along with his brother-in-law and a few friends, he travels by land now to take electronic appliances and used clothing to sell in El Salvador. From there they bring, among other things, Salvadoran cheese, dried fish, and products such as instant coffee and medicines (which cannot be obtained over-the-counter in the United States) to be sold at local stores. Virginia M.'s niece travels by air every month doing the same thing; stopping in Los Angeles first, she delivers fresh products to a large clientele there. While most of this woman's family lives in El Salvador and most of Manuel's family lives in San Francisco, the two emphasized that for now "they live in both places." But they remarked on their privileged situation: most of their compatriots cannot afford—

legally or financially—to visit their home country. Indeed, it is the impossibility of travel for many—and, of course, the dire condition of the postwar Salvadoran economy—that has proven very lucrative for a relative few to develop a huge industry that serves as a conduit between those who have to stay put and their families back home. But many, even those who lack documents, do seem more oriented to settling in the United States, at least for now, particularly if they have U.S.-born children or youngsters who have been in the United States for most of their lives.

Conclusion

Because the great majority of Salvadorans are unable to secure U.S. visas, they must make an arduous and costly journey through Mexico. They do not depend on friends and family in El Salvador but rather on their friends and family in the United States, who seem to possess a measure of resources to lend them a hand.

Assistance from family and friends in the United States, however, has had unforeseen consequences for both the arriving immigrants and for those who receive them. As assistance usually comes in the form of a loan, the immigrant is immediately confronted with thousands of dollars of debt. As we shall see later, this debt becomes almost impossible to repay. Given the particularities of the context of reception that these new immigrants face, they end up scraping a life off the margins, unable to support themselves, let alone repay their debts. The conditions in which they come to live in the United States are shaped and often reconfigured by broader politicoeconomic forces, a discussion to which I now turn.

Chapter 4

The Context of Reception
in the United States

Who would have told me that here, in the richest country on earth, in the most beautiful city, full of luxuries and wonderful things, I would go hungry, that I wouldn't have a roof over my head? Because it is here that I have learned what it is to go hungry, to have no money even for a bus ride, and yes, to be even homeless, not back there [in El Salvador], a much poorer country. This is truly incredible. Where can I start? I would say it's the papers. Look, we don't have papers and each day the situation [to obtain them] gets worse. This has ramifications in everything else that we do, absolutely everything. From not being able to get jobs, even with a university degree like in my case, to not having a more or less livable place to stay, or health care, everything. It condemns us to live day by day. We [Salvadorans] are very determined and *arrechos* (courageous), and we can survive. But it's a nightmare. When I walk in the street or ride the bus and look at Americans, they look calm, nice, sometimes they even smile at me, and I ask myself, could these be the people who want to get rid of us or is it only their government?

Lolita Q.

For Lolita, as for many Salvadoran immigrants, the context of reception in the United States has been far from hospitable. This context is shaped by broad forces — government policy, the local economy, the organization of the receiving community — within which the immigrants must restructure their lives. These forces matter for a variety of reasons. The reception by the state is critical for the lives of the immigrants: by defining who stands inside or outside the law, it determines whether immigrants qualify as full participants in society or become its most destitute members. An analysis of the local economy is pivotal because labor market opportunities are subject to fluctuations in the economy, which directly affects immigrants' opportunities for work.

77

The community is central because it channels the effects of macrolevel forces to the lives of immigrants and links the microlevel world of everyday life to broader forces. Thus together these factors shape the structure of opportunities for immigrants, condition their access to resources (and to what kind), and ultimately determine the potential for immigrants to informally assist one another.

The State and Refugee Immigrants

Defining a particular group of immigrants as refugees is based not only on whether they fled persecution or unsafe conditions in their country of origin but also, and even more important, on the fact that a receiving state recognizes them as deserving asylum and assistance (Zolberg, Suhrke, and Aguayo 1989, 6). Relations between sending and receiving states determine whether immigrants originating in politically conflictive regions will be admitted as "regular" immigrants or as refugees. In essence, refugee policy turns into an instrument of foreign policy, as the consistent history of the U.S. case attests.[1]

Before 1968 U.S. refugee policy tended to be ad hoc, and it overtly reflected ideological biases, making no pretense that refugee policy should be equitable and based on need. No legislation for asylum existed, and policy was set by the attorney general or the INS. Congress had adopted an ideologically based definition of "refugee," institutionalizing the practice of admitting refugees according to cold war standards. As the cold war intensified in the 1950s and early 1960s, ideology became the principal determinant of merit. Thus refugee legislation singled out those fleeing from communism or communist-dominated lands as the category for whom the overwhelming majority of slots would be reserved. In 1968 the United States accepted the United Nations Protocol Relating to the Status of Refugees, which also included the principle of *nonrefoulment* — the prohibition against returning a refugee to a territory where his or her life or freedom would be threatened (Office of Refugee Resettlement 1988). The Refugee Act of 1980 made law the 1968 UN Protocol.[2] Section 101(a)(42) of the Immigration and Nationality Act, as amended by the Refugee Act of 1980, defines a refugee as

A. any person who is outside any country of such person's nationality or, in the case of a person having no nationality, is outside any country in which such person last habitually resided, and who is unable or unwilling to return to, and unable or unwilling to avail himself or herself of the protection of that country because of persecution or a well-founded fear of persecution on account of race, religion, nationality, membership in a particular social group, or political opinion, or

B. in such circumstances that as the President after appropriate consultation (as defined in section 207[e] of this Act) may specify, any person who is within the country of such person's nationality or, in the case of a person having no nationality within the country in which such person is habitually residing, and who is persecuted or has a well-founded fear of persecution on account of race, religion, nationality, membership in a particular social group, or political opinion. The term "refugee" does not include any person who ordered, incited, assisted, or otherwise participated in the persecution of any person on account of race, religion, nationality, membership in a particular social group, or political opinion. (Office of Refugee Resettlement 1988, 2)

The amendments of 1980 assured a more permanent commitment to the admission of refugees, but they did not eliminate the principle of selectivity.[3] The clauses were intended to do away with the ideological bias in U.S. law, which had previously specified that preference should be given to persons fleeing communism and/or the Middle East. But in spite of this law, the president, with the advice and consent of Congress, selected the numbers and the country of origin of the refugees. Furthermore, instead of applying this definition at the individual level, as does the UN Protocol, the U.S. government applied it to entire nationality groups that served a political purpose, thus entangling distinctions of who really "fit." The United States continued to admit only those groups it regarded as most deserving, that is, best able to promote U.S. national interests. Overall figures give a highly skewed distribution of refugee admittances in favor of people coming from communist countries. For instance, while less than 5 percent of those coming from "friendly" governments were granted asylum, the acceptance rate for people originating in "unfriendly" (or Soviet-allied) countries ranged between 60 and 90 percent (American Friends Service Committee 1988, 38; National Asylum Study Project 1992). Refugee policy, foreign policy, and national security have been consistent, with refugee policy *in practice* being a derivative of foreign policy. For every instance of welcome, of an open door, there has been one of exclusion, of a door shut, regardless of the nature of the plight of those calling for help. These contradictions in refugee admission policies provide the context in which to present the Salvadoran case as an example of the legacy of the cold war years.

Salvadorans and the U.S. Government

Throughout the 1980s, when Salvadoran immigration peaked, Salvadorans were denied refugee status or any other form of protection; they were categorized as economic immigrants, and so they were subject to deportation. Recent changes in immigration law have modified this practice, halting deportations of Salvadorans under the Temporary Protected Status (TPS) settlement, which I discuss below. But first we must examine the practice that was in effect during ten of the twelve years that the Salvadoran conflict lasted.

From the outset of the political upheaval in El Salvador, the U.S. government was deeply involved. Fearing a communist takeover such as had occurred in Vietnam, the United States resorted to military tactics. Thus from the conflict's early days (which roughly coincide with the beginning of the Reagan administration) Washington viewed it as essentially a cold war situation. This assessment implied the need to contain, or even reverse, Soviet/Cuban expansionism, and El Salvador became a battleground where communist forces were to be defeated.[4] The Reagan administration concentrated on fighting the Marxist-Leninist threat in El Salvador with the largest military buildup in Central American history and took a firm stand against negotiations with the rebels, thereby relegating political and social reforms, as well as human rights issues, to second place. By igniting anticommunist sentiments and citing the close geographic proximity of Central America to the United States, President Reagan and other policy makers urged Congress to take note of the region's vital role in national security. Congressional response included the largest aid package the United States has ever given to an ally in the history of U.S. aid, even exceeding that given to South Vietnam at the height of the Vietnam War (American Friends Service Committee 1988).[5] The money Washington sent to El Salvador was "disproportionate to any conventional conception of the national interest" (Long 1992). Although at times the U.S. administration vacillated about whether to continue such a large aid package, U.S. policies toward El Salvador did not change throughout the twelve-year conflict.

Against this background and given the history of U.S. policy toward refugees, it would have been antithetical to conceive of a generous policy of admission for Salvadorans, even if many were de facto refugees from the war. Based on the logic of U.S. policy toward Central America, Salvadorans could not migrate en masse to the United States from a country that was fighting communism and attempting to establish a democracy, with full U.S. economic and military support. However, throughout the twelve-year conflict there were countless reports, including lengthy accounts by the State Department itself, depicting serious and widespread abuses of human rights, disappearances, and deaths due to political violence in El Salvador. For instance, the U.S. Embassy in El Salvador reported 6,116 deaths attributable to political violence in 1981 alone; in some months the number of deaths reached 1,000 (reputable independent organizations and church officials place this figure higher). The State Department noted that "the large number of corpses routinely discovered throughout the country dictate quick interment, and thus, identification of the bodies is nearly impossible" (U.S. Department of State 1982, 424–425). During the same year, the U.S. government did not admit *any* refugees from El Salvador, granted political asylum to only two people (Office of Refugee Resettlement 1985, A11–12),[6] and deported 3,683 Salvadorans (U.S. Immigration and Naturalization Service 1981, 95–96).[7]

For many years the State Department's policy toward El Salvador seemed to be contradicting itself. Even if it acknowledged the troubling human rights situation in El Salvador, the U.S. government refused to admit Salvadorans as refugees, and only a handful were granted asylum during the war years. It must be made clear, however, that the U.S. government *did recognize* that the political upheaval in El Salvador caused major population dislocations, as it acknowledged that there were approximately a quarter of a million refugees in the Central American region (Gibney and Stohl 1988). The United States not only recognized the presence of these refugees but also aided them and encouraged their resettlement there. Patricia Weiss Fagen (cited in Gibney and Stohl 1988) notes that, in addition to its regular contributions to the UNHCR, the United States earmarked aid for Salvadoran refugees in the Central American region. Thus the issue was not that the United States failed to *recognize* that people were fleeing the Salvadoran civil war; it was that it would not admit *any* of these Salvadorans as refugees on its soil.

In line with U.S. foreign policy and national interests, the INS consistently maintained that Salvadorans were no different from thousands of other economically motivated immigrants. But even for INS officials, the distinction between political and economic immigrants in the Salvadoran case was blurry, as Doris Meissner, the INS commissioner, commented: "You take the El Salvadorians in the last decade. It would take Solomon to decide were they economic immigrants or political immigrants? But they were not coming here for health care" (quoted in Sandalow 1993). Even if violence in El Salvador was acknowledged, it was argued that democracy had been restored in the country and that those who genuinely suffered political repression and persecution should seek protection in adjacent countries in Central America or Mexico. If migration flows, including refugee flights, were merely mechanically conditioned by "push-pull" factors in which human agency and historical-structural links did not play a role, this argument might hold up. However, Salvadorans who migrated during the civil war went to the United States because they had already established informal networks with friends and family, forged through a long history of close links between El Salvador and the United States. As has been observed, the emergence of regular migratory flows requires the prior penetration of the strong state's institutions into those of the weaker one (Portes and Böröcz 1989). Notably, in this case such linkages were structured by U.S. foreign policy and military intervention, which shaped the politicoeconomic conditions that Salvadorans (as well as other Central Americans) fled to begin with (Rumbaut 1994a, 598). Hence, at this particular historical juncture, the United States emerged as the destination of choice for the thousands of Salvadorans who fled the conflict.

Meanwhile, U.S. tourist and visitor visa requirements for travel to the United States were becoming overwhelmingly difficult for ordinary citizens to meet. People had to present proof of bank accounts with high minimum balances, titles to property, and similar documents that would assure U.S. officials that they had reasons to return to El Salvador. This practice excluded large groups of people: those whose usual places of residence had been bombed (usually the poor in rural and urban areas); those who lived in areas of intense fighting and had lost their mostly working-class jobs as a result; those of the urban and rural poor whose family members had been involved in the conflict, causing them to be targets for persecution; and those who lacked the resources and contacts to be able to cope with life during the civil war. The situation unleashed a booming transportation business of undocumented persons to the United States, mostly catering to those who lacked the financial means to obtain visas.[8]

Once on U.S. soil, Salvadorans were able to apply for political asylum. However, in practice the asylum process was almost meaningless for this group during the 1980s: approximately 2 percent of Salvadorans were granted asylum (National Asylum Study Project 1992). Applications for asylum were sent to the State Department, which in most cases recommended against it. Applicants then had to go through a hearing, where the burden of proof was enormous and there was little chance for success. A former labor organizer I met at a community association — not a study participant but someone whose documents I helped translate — could not effectively prove to the forum that his life would be in danger if he returned to El Salvador. This was true even though he showed the judge many tiny scars on his back from cigarette burns inflicted during torture sessions. Seemingly unmoved, the judge explained that he had heard similar stories from alcoholic men who were too drunk to realize that they had burned themselves with their own cigarettes.[9]

Furthermore, many Salvadorans were not eligible for amnesty under the Immigration Reform and Control Act of 1986, since its provisions stated that only undocumented immigrants who entered the United States before January 1, 1982, and a special category of agricultural workers (the SAW, or Special Agricultural Worker) were eligible for amnesty. More than half of Salvadorans now in the United States arrived after 1982. Because most Salvadorans were ineligible for refugee status and many did not qualify for amnesty under IRCA — to say nothing of the fact that most asylum applications were denied — a high percentage of Salvadorans in the United States have been, and remain, undocumented. In 1994 the INS estimated the number of undocumented Salvadorans at slightly over 60 percent (Warren 1994),[10] very close to the more recent estimate of 335,000, or a little under 60 percent of the entire Salvadoran population in the United States (U.S. Immigration and Naturalization Service 1997a).

Because IRCA entailed sanctions against employers who hired undocumented workers and because recent ballot measures in California
have sought to cut undocumented immigrants' access to social services, Salvadorans have found themselves in an extremely precarious
situation. Salvadorans (along with Guatemalans) have been depicted
as constituting "perhaps the most vulnerable national-origin group in
the United States because they are among the most undocumented.
. . . Their claim to refugee status has never been recognized; and they
are about to lose what temporary protection against deportation they
had" (Lopez, Popkin, and Telles 1996, 287).

Legality is crucial for Salvadorans — no other issue among the people with whom I spoke was more important than having proper documentation.[11] Evelyn S. told me that even though she spoke a bit of
English, she felt as if her hands were tied because she lacked documents. She said that opportunities in the United States and in El
Salvador are about the same: "Over there you need education to get
ahead, but here you need documents. In the end, one loses out anyway because both are equally hard to get." This need is so pressing
that people do whatever they can to acquire legal residence status, and
one of the easiest ways is to marry a U.S. citizen. Chentía A., a friendly
woman from a village in eastern El Salvador who is in her late forties
and has a first-grade education, had married twice in efforts to obtain
her documents but was still undocumented because each marriage
had failed. Laughing at her own story, she said next time she would try
a different method: "I have no luck in marriage. Back there [in El
Salvador] I was married twice too. But whether they are 'true marriages' or for business, it [marriage] is probably not for me [laughs]."
Purchasing fake social security or green cards, although popular, only
provides a means to obtain employment, not to become legal. Those
who have come to the United States with proper documentation are
always quick to recognize this advantage. Without having been asked,
Ileana A., a twenty-year-old from San Salvador who left her country
right after completing high school, commented on her legality: "I am
here legally, you know. What else can I ask for? I think I'm very
lucky." Contextualizing the importance of legality for Salvadorans,
Chentía said, "We need our papers. If we came from a country that is
near, like Mexico, it wouldn't matter so much. Look, I'm not saying
that the poor Mexicans don't need papers. But for them it's no big

deal to be deported; they can come back in no time. But we [Salvadorans] come from farther away. For us, it can cost us our lives. If we get deported, oh, it's — God forbid. Our whole life depends on that tiny card that we call green but now it's pink. Tell me, am I not right?"

Treating Salvadorans as economic immigrants has meant that they are not protected by the 1980 Refugee Act or article 45 of the Geneva Convention IV, which prohibits the transfer of a protected party to any country in which the Geneva Convention is not being honored (American Friends Service Committee 1988, 37). Although El Salvador did not honor the Geneva Convention, the United States continued to deport Salvadorans until fall 1990. But under mounting pressure from immigrants' rights groups in late 1990, the Justice Department agreed to provide Temporary Protected Status to Salvadorans and immediately halted the deportation of those who had entered the United States on or before September 19, 1990. This discretionary procedure included the option to apply for work authorization, and, according to an immigration officer, more than 95 percent of the TPS applicants obtained such documentation. TPS was not a blanket amnesty to all Salvadorans; it was a temporary stay of deportation and, technically, did not confer refugee status. Concomitant access to social services was still denied because the status protected de facto refugees, that is, people who fled potentially dangerous situations but who were still not de jure refugees.[12]

The TPS program was supposed to last eighteen months (although Salvadorans had to reapply every six months), ending June 30, 1992. But the original decree was replaced by the Deferred Enforced Departure (DED), which exempted registrants from deportation until June 1993 — a period that was extended twice until it expired for good in December 1994. The Clinton administration announced that there were not going to be any more extensions; however, it granted work authorization permits for an extra nine months to ensure a smooth transition. According to the INS, close to 200,000 Salvadorans applied for TPS during the first ten months of 1991 (it was estimated that up to 500,000 were actually eligible, a figure not based on census data but on INS estimates). But this figure does not correspond to the number of people who were protected by the statute at the time of its final expiration in 1994. Many of the initial applicants failed to meet subsequent deadlines to renew their permits, mainly because of confusing last-minute announcements for extensions, while others went back to El Salvador for permanent visa appointments. By the end of this temporary safe haven, there were approximately 90,000 DED holders out of an estimated 327,000 undocumented Salvadorans. Therefore, the fact remains that more than one-half of the Salvadoran population in the United States is still either undocumented or in a legal limbo, in both instances vulnerable to policy decisions that may continue to take place during the high tide of anti-immigrant sentiment. Salvadorans who lack documents have tended to remain in the United States without visiting their country as frequently as legal compatriots do. Though back-and-forth travel has not been as common among Salvadorans as among Mexicans (for reasons explained in chapter 3), the increased militarization of the border has made it even costlier and riskier for undocumented Salvadorans to travel to their homeland. In fact, in roundups by the INS it has been noticed that, when apprehended, it is more likely for Mexicans to accept deportation and for Salvadorans to request a hearing.

Also, roughly at the same time that TPS became law, the INS agreed to settle a class action suit on behalf of Salvadoran and Guatemalan asylum seekers that charged bias in asylum adjudication procedures (Frelick and Kohnen 1994, 14). The suit, *American Baptist Churches* [*ABC*] *v. Thornburgh*, was filed in May 1985 in federal district court by more than eighty religious organizations. It resulted in a provisional settlement that allowed Guatemalans and Salvadorans whose cases were denied, or still pending, new asylum hearings by the new corps of asylum officers established under the 1990 immigration reform. Applicants for TPS were automatically included as part of the class action settlement, which required the INS to inform them of their right to apply for asylum on expiration of DED. The procedure for obtaining *ABC* benefits required the assistance of trained or qualified legal professionals, because applicants needed to substantiate their claims with additional documentation, something that was not always clear. But the settlement agreement permits claimants to receive work authorization while their asylum applications are pending. Also, Salvadoran DED recipients who apply for asylum under *ABC* are added to the backlog rather than treated as new applicants (Frelick and Kohnen 1994). In all, the prospects improved, and the case represented a major victory for the immigrants as well as for refugees' rights groups. According to the National Asylum Study Project (1992, 17), there was an overall improvement in the rate of success of Salvadoran asylum applicants, from 2.8 percent between 1983 and 1991 to a high of 28 percent in fiscal year 1992. But this rate has since leveled off and declined. According to the INS's latest estimates, the success rate for applications stands at about 3 percent, very close to what it was throughout the 1980s (U.S. Immigration and Naturalization Service 1995). At the end of fiscal year 1996, 191,309 Salvadoran asylum applications were pending (U.S. Immigration and Naturalization Service 1997b), most of them filed under the *ABC* program.

Certain Salvadorans were included as beneficiaries of the 1997 Nicaraguan Adjustment and Central American Relief Act (NACARA). Designed for Nicaraguans, this act also included Cubans and nationals of former Soviet bloc countries. Salvadorans who entered the United States before September 19, 1990 (the same cutoff date established for TPS), and registered under the *ABC* settlement, or who had filed an asylum application before April 1, 1990, could be granted a "cancellation of removal." Though NACARA provides an opportunity for Salvadorans to regularize their status, it does not confer permanent residence automatically. To be eligible for NACARA, Salvadorans also have to demonstrate seven years of continuous residence in the United States, good moral character, proof of income tax returns, and extreme hardship if deported. This is a special discretionary relief that, if conferred, permits an individual who is subject to deportation to remain in the United States. Salvadorans already placed in deportation procedures, and therefore required to appear before an immigration judge, can request a cancellation of removal. If the request is granted, the individual's immigration status will then be readjusted to that of a permanent resident (U.S. Immigration and Naturalization Service 1998).[13]

Other recently passed immigration legislation may have important repercussions in Salvadorans' lives. The Illegal Immigration Reform and Immigration Responsibility Act of 1996 includes some of the toughest measures ever taken against undocumented immigration. Among its provisions, it requires that the number of border patrol agents be doubled to ten thousand over the next five years; it establishes new penalties against alien smuggling and document fraud; it revamps existing deportation and exclusion proceedings, allowing for summary exclusion and sweeping power of immigration officers to order the removal of immigrants who arrive with false documents or with no documents, without the right to a hearing before an immigration judge; and it provides new grounds for exclusion and deportation. One of the most significant provisions is that lawfully admitted aliens who overstay their visas for an aggregate of 180 days to 365 days will be penalized by a three-year period of exclusion, during which they would be ineligible to receive immigrant or nonimmigrant visas. If they overstay their visas for more than 365 days, they will be subject to a ten-year period of exclusion. Under this act, most future immigrants will be barred from applying for benefits under federal means-tested programs for their first five years in the United States. One of the most controversial measures is that a permanent resident can be deported under many new terms, one of which is a crime of violence, which now constitutes an aggravated felony if the term of imprisonment imposed is at least one year. This law applies retroactively.

The effect of this new law on Salvadorans remains to be seen, but it could make it more cumbersome to obtain political asylum and to regularize a person's legal status under family reunification, and it places permanent residents in a vulnerable situation. A community agency that in the past assisted Central Americans in the United States has now opened an office in San Salvador to help the deportees resettle in their country, as many find it difficult to do so because they have been labeled criminals, even though for some their infractions have consisted only of driving under the influence, traffic violations, or civil disobedience and the like.

Since changes in the law that provided TPS to Salvadorans occurred during the time when I was conducting fieldwork, I had the opportunity to ask my informants about these procedures. For many, TPS had increased the fear of eventual deportation, and these Salvadorans were reluctant to apply. Having been afraid of and harassed by the INS for so long, they had learned not to trust the institution. Amparo A. told me that she had heard that once the INS obtained your name and address, you were practically signing your own deportation orders because TPS was a new INS tactic to obtain as much information as possible from undocumented immigrants. Others mentioned that they did not apply because they could not take time off from their jobs; still others said that they did not have the financial resources to file the application. I inquired into this matter and discovered that indeed the application procedure was beyond the economic reach of many potential applicants. A lawsuit filed in San Francisco forced the INS to waive the $75 application fee per person, set a family cap of $225, and eliminated re-registration fees, but the fee for work authorization permits remained at $60 for each six-month TPS period.[14]

Therefore, despite the political violence in their country, Salvadorans were continually denied the "structure of refuge," as Rubén G. Rumbaut (1989) termed the aid package that the U.S. government makes available to officially recognized refugees. The resulting instability, as we shall see in the following chapters, has profoundly affected these immigrants' long-term plans and their ability to establish enduring informal networks. But whereas government decisions regarding immigration policies affect everyone who enters the United States, the dynamics of the economy vary from one geographic region to another. The inextricable linkages between the state and the economy bear on the local labor market and the opportunities (or lack thereof) for Salvadoran immigrants.

The Local Economy: San Francisco's Labor Market

Immigrants enter an ambit shaped by the economy and the polity, the confluence of which is place-specific. In some respects San Francisco's economy differs sharply from that of other cities to which Latin Americans migrate in that it offers fewer opportunities for factory work. But in many ways San Francisco offers the same sights that can be found in other cities that have a large influx of Latin American migrants: men huddled on street corners (hoping to be picked up for day jobs mainly in construction and landscaping) while potential employers cruise by and hire a crew for the day, no questions asked.

Following trends in other major U.S. cities, San Francisco's economy has undergone structural transformations, some of which have been ongoing since the early 1970s; others have developed more recently, in the late 1980s and early 1990s. Global processes of industrial restructuring have reduced the number of jobs in traditional man-

TABLE 7   Employment by Main Industry Concentration (Percentages)

	General Population	Salvadorans		Central Americans
	San Francisco	San Francisco	Los Angeles	San Francisco
Construction	4.3	6.2	8.3	8.0
Manufacturing[a]	9.2	10.8	26.7	10.1
Retail trade	17.4	23.2	17.8	21.7
Services[b]	41.9	40.3	34.2	40.8
Finance and real estate	10.8	6.9	2.8	7.5
Transportation and communication	8.3	6.8	3.3	6.6

SOURCE: Census of Population and Housing, 1990 (Summary Tape File 4).
NOTE: These are general figures for these populations and do not take into account time of arrival.
[a]This category includes all manufacturing, nondurable and durable goods (the majority of workers in all groups are concentrated in nondurable goods).
[b]This category includes all services, such as professional, educational, health, entertainment, and personal.

ufacturing and have led to a downgrading in this sector due to a reduction in the share of unionized labor, a deterioration of wages, and a proliferation of sweatshops and homework (Sassen 1988, 1991). Meanwhile, the service sector — both the highly paid and the low-wage ends — experienced an increase in jobs related to the requirements of residential and commercial gentrification (Sassen 1991). This pattern was deeply felt in the San Francisco Bay Area, where jobs in traditional manufacturing declined 9.6 percent during the 1980s. At the same time the upper end of the service sector grew by 50 percent (McLeod 1992a). (See tables 7 and 8 for a comparative distribution of employment by sector and occupation for San Francisco, and for Salvadorans and Central Americans in this city, showing variations between groups in the same location. Tables 7 through 10 also include information on Salvadorans in Los Angeles, for a comparison across locales.)

The steady decline in San Francisco's manufacturing sector during the 1970s and 1980s was countered by an even greater employment increase in the upper echelons of the service sector. For instance, at the upper end of the service sector, executive and administrative jobs

TABLE 8   Main Occupations (Percentages)

	General Population	*Salvadorans*		*Central Americans*
	San Francisco	San Francisco	Los Angeles	San Francisco
Managerial and professional	34.7	9.1	5.3	11.1
Technical, sales, and administration	33.9	22.6	17.4	24.9
Service occupations[a]	15.7	38.7	30.1	38.2
Precision craft, repair[b]	6.3	9.2	14.8	10.1
Operators, fabrication laborers	8.9	14.6	30.6	14.6
Agricultural, farm-related[c]	0.5	1.3	1.8	1.1

SOURCE: Census of Population and Housing, 1990 (Summary Tape File 4).
NOTE: These are general figures for these populations and do not take into account time of arrival.
[a]This category includes workers in personal service, in private household service, in food preparation, in restaurants, in cleaning and building service, in protective services, and in child care.
[b]This category includes mechanics and repairers and workers in construction trades, such as carpenters, electricians, and painters.
[c]This category includes workers in farming and in forestry, including groundskeepers and gardeners.

grew by 52 percent, and engineering expanded by 44 percent, whereas the number of machine-operator jobs shrank by 10 percent from 1980 to 1990 (McLeod 1992a). In fact, San Francisco was believed to have made the transition from manufacturing to services with relative ease, in part because its prosperity had long been based on those industries that were expanding, namely, finance, retailing, government, law, and tourism. The growth of San Francisco's white-collar economy generated new jobs in the skyscrapers of a burgeoning downtown and fueled the process of urban revitalization. The "Manhattanization" of San Francisco was evidenced in a doubling of office space in the city between 1965 and 1983 (Godfrey 1988, 9–10). But the decline in manufacturing in San Francisco was not accompanied by a surge in the low-wage, downgraded manufacturing sector, as had occurred in other cities that underwent economic restructuring, such as Los Angeles and New York. San Francisco lost unionized jobs in the skilled and semiskilled industrial sector that were never replaced by the boom in the garment industry that occurred in Los Angeles.

As San Francisco became an important financial center, it also became a mecca for immigrants. The yuppie lifestyle of the new professionals required specialized services that immigrant labor fulfilled. The consumption patterns of the newly affluent managers and professionals were noticeable in the proliferation of boutiques, restaurants, laundries, and gourmet shops. Immigrants worked as busboys, washed dishes, or prepared food in restaurants and also took jobs in housecleaning, construction, and landscaping in the increasingly prosperous residential areas. Growth in tourism and business conventions opened up opportunities for immigrant workers in hotels and restaurants. The expansion in finance and real estate also created jobs for immigrants, mainly as janitors in high-rise buildings. According to the 1990 U.S. Census, of the 38.7 percent of Salvadorans who were in service occupations in San Francisco (in contrast to 15.7 percent among the general population of San Francisco), close to one-third were engaged in food preparation and approximately two-thirds in building cleaning (see table 8). Among the new beneficiaries of the economic boom were the growing number of two-income families, whose relatively high incomes, accompanied by long working hours, facilitated and made highly desirable the hiring of domestic servants (Chinchilla and Hamilton 1992; Salzinger 1991). These new jobs tended to be unstable, poorly paid, and unprotected and to require almost no skills, and they were therefore unattractive to native workers. But a growing number of immigrants in need, particularly the undocumented, were willing to take such jobs. Thus throughout the 1980s immigrants entered an economy in which the only real gains were concentrated in the service sector and the easiest jobs to obtain were the low-paid ones that required few, if any, skills.

However, opportunities for steady work in the lower end of the service sector, albeit poorly paid and unprotected, shrank considerably in the early 1990s. The prolonged national recession, the Gulf War, and the 1989 Loma Prieta earthquake, aggravated by the decline in defense contracting as the cold war ended, deeply affected labor market opportunities for everyone in San Francisco. For example, the estimated number of wage and salary workers in the service industry dipped from 196,400 in 1990 to 189,400 in 1992 (Employment Development Department 1993). Fearing a recession, the corporations that once fueled the economic growth of San Francisco focused on cutting costs, consolidating and merging, and reducing their permanent workforce. The number of jobs in the engineering, accounting, and management industries declined from 29,300 in 1990 to 25,900 in 1992, and those in finance went from 44,300 to 41,800 during the same period (Employment Development Department 1993). Defaults on real estate loans more than doubled, as rising unemployment and personal debt put home owners in danger of losing their property (Evenson 1991). Also, as the recession hit Europe and Japan, the tourist industry in San Francisco, a major source of employment, suffered serious losses (Chen 1991). Layoff threats spread beyond the upper end of the service sector; as the city faced a fiscal crisis, there were layoffs in the local government. Authorities slashed academic programs, threatened to close entire schools, and cut teachers' salaries (Asimov 1992). This was accompanied by major layoffs of accountants, advertisement executives, lawyers, and security dealers and a tripling in the rate of business failures (Trager 1991). The end result was a huge increase in the unemployment rate in San Francisco, from 4.3 percent in June 1989 to 7.8 percent in June 1992 (Employment Development Department 1993). (See table 9 for a comparison of unemployment rates with other groups and with Salvadorans in Los Angeles.)

Not only did the highly paid professionals in the upper echelon of the service sector who once held secure jobs now face increased employment uncertainty, but many other workers did as well. A poll taken in the Bay Area in 1991 indicated that half of the respondents feared unemployment (Marshall 1991), and many professionals began to cut down on their consumption patterns.[15] For instance, the estimated number of workers in the restaurant and bar industry in San Francisco decreased from 32,300 in 1988 to 30,500 in 1992, and in other retail trade from 21,300 to 17,900 during the same period (Employment Development Department 1993). An Anglo professional woman who regularly employed Central Americans as house cleaners and helpers in her catering business told me that she could no longer afford to pay for these services. Recently she had resorted to doing the work herself because she did not have as many orders as in

TABLE 9   Labor Force Participation and Income

	General Population	Salvadorans		Central Americans
	San Francisco	San Francisco	Los Angeles	San Francisco
Labor Force Participation (percentage)				
Employed males	73.7	80.3	85.7	80.0
Employed females	60.7	62.6	64.4	60.8
Unemployed males[a]	6.7	8.0	10.8	9.4
Unemployed females[a]	5.8	9.3	13.2	10.3
Income (in dollars)				
Per capita income[b]	19,695	9,061	6,284	9,315
Median household income[c]	38,669	27,366	21,690	27,927

SOURCE: Census of Population and Housing, 1990 (Summary Tape File 4).
NOTE: These are general figures for these populations and do not take into account time of arrival.
[a]These unemployment figures are annual estimates by the U.S. Bureau of the Census. The figures on page 93 are monthly estimates by the Employment Development Department.
[b]The per capita income for whites in San Francisco was $26,222 and $11,400 for the Hispanic-origin population. The average household size in San Francisco is 2.4, for Salvadorans 4.6; thus it is useful to present per capita incomes.
[c]For households with incomes of less than $15,000.

the past. She also mentioned friends in the same situation. And whereas she had hired an immigrant to clean her house at least once a week before, lately she could only do so once a month. Two-earner working- and lower-middle-class families that used immigrant labor mainly for child care were also affected by the recession and cut down on hiring. This situation resulted in a serious employment shortage for immigrant workers.

Practically all of my fifty informants stressed the difficulties they had experienced in securing jobs in San Francisco, especially in contrast to friends and relatives who had arrived in the city much earlier (although the earlier arrivals had had a relatively easy time finding jobs, they were generally low paid and often without benefits). Mireya C., a community worker who had been active with the immigrants' rights groups that helped to obtain TPS for Salvadorans, shared her frustration with me: "If it wasn't so tragic, it'd be funny. We have such bad luck — it had to happen to us. Remember how hard it was before? We thought, oh yes, with a work permit they [Salvadorans] will make it, so we concentrated on trying to get them their papers. But now that doesn't help. Look, they walk around with their work permits but there's no work. It's sad, but what can we do?"

All my informants were either working or, it seemed, perpetually looking for jobs when I first met them; much of their casual conversations revolved around work-related issues. Thirty of the forty-three who were working when we first met had temporary or part-time jobs (often both), devoid of fringe benefits, and thirty-eight of them were working without documents. (One exception is Chentía A., who worked the night shift cleaning offices in a high-rise building downtown for $11 per hour plus benefits.) Most had to work several part-time jobs to put together what might resemble one full-time job. It was not unusual for a woman to clean houses, baby-sit at home, sell Avon products or similar merchandise, and make food for sale on the weekend, or for a man to do gardening, wash dishes, and work as a parking lot attendant at night, all in the same week. All of them pointed out the financial stress the tightening in employment opportunities created not only for them — given that they had expected to find work rather quickly — but also for the relatives who received them, who had not anticipated the additional burden of supporting the newcomers for so long. In a survey conducted in 1991–1992 among 1,700 Salvadoran newcomers in the Bay Area, only 37 percent of the respondents were working full-time; 46 percent were either working temporarily or not working at all; 55 percent had not held permanent jobs since their arrival; and 73 percent had lost their jobs more than once (Calderón 1992, 14).

Amparo A. shared with me her tale of penury as she tried to hold on to her job in the increasingly tight labor market. She has two children in El Salvador and a toddler with her in San Francisco. She works as a chambermaid in a hotel near the airport. Her job is not permanent: she is "on call." Sometimes she is called to work four days a week, but sometimes a week or two go by with no work at all. She has tried hard to find a more secure job. She was once a housekeeper for an Indian family, but her salary was $400 a month for working six and a half days a week. In addition, because she did not like the

Indian food that she prepared for the family, she had to buy her own food. She told me:

I prefer the hotel because when I work, I earn a bit more. I am on the list of people that they can call to work, but many times they don't call me in several days — sometimes two weeks. What kind of a job is this? But *me conformo* [I resign myself] because at least I am on their list. I feel that I have to sort of grab whatever comes to me, squeezing my way in because there are so many of us waiting for those hours that the hotel wants us to work. Sometimes I feel we are like children trying to get candy from a piñata, but it's not funny, it's tough.

Given her unstable economic situation, Amparo needs to share living costs with others. There are nine people living in her two-bedroom, $900-a-month apartment (the same apartment was being rented for $1,500 in 1998), including her own toddler, her two siblings, a cousin with a husband and a child, and an unrelated couple. As a result the entire apartment had been converted into sleeping quarters. Because there was no living room per se, when I visited we sat on the beds or at the small table that doubled as a cupboard in the cramped kitchen.

The Salvadoran population in the United States is composed of relatively recent arrivals, with 45 percent of those in San Francisco having arrived between 1980 and 1990 (see table 1). Their recent arrival, generally low skill levels, and lack of U.S. work experience, as well as their limited English-language proficiency, have contributed to diminishing their odds of obtaining positions with prospects for advancement. But in recessionary times the undocumented status — or even legal limbo — of the majority of my informants further reduced their possibilities for employment, whether low paid or not.[16] Their legal status has to some extent mitigated the effect that individual differences such as educational level might have had. Regardless of differences in their educational level or age, the men were concentrated in restaurants — mostly as busboys and dishwashers — and in construction jobs, whereas the women held jobs as housekeepers, baby-sitters, and caretakers of the elderly. Increasingly, however, men have resorted to day labor (Chinchilla and Hamilton 1992). But my informants unanimously agreed that such work was a last resort in the struggle for employment. Given their gloomy job prospects, even if they possessed skills and/or documents, many of my informants could not risk looking for better positions because the search could turn into a lengthy process with little chance for success. Lilian M., a woman in her early fifties who was a physics and mathematics high school teacher in El Salvador, wanted to work as a teacher's aide to gain experience so that eventually she could obtain her teaching credentials. But she told me that in the face of the current crisis she could not afford to leave her job as a sales clerk in a small Taiwanese-owned convenience store to look for something better. Alejandro M., who had been close to graduating from medical school in El Salvador, told me, "The job situation — no, it doesn't look good. I think I will continue washing dishes and sleeping at the shelter for a long time to come." He agreed with Lilian that it was better to hold on to the jobs they had for as long as they could, for jobs — desirable or not — were hard to find.

Furthermore, only a handful of my informants worked for Salvadoran or other Latino bosses. Although there are Salvadoran or other Central American businesses in San Francisco, they are not numerous enough to create an ethnic economic enclave with viable opportunities for employment for newcomers. My informants worked in Greek-, Japanese-, or Italian-owned restaurants, for Taiwanese or Korean business owners, for German- or Irish-American landlords, or for Indian and Iranian families just as frequently as they worked in Salvadoran and Mexican restaurants or for Salvadoran or other Central American families. The average wage for men was $6 an hour and for women $40 a day, though few were able to stitch together enough hours or days to earn a permanent full-time wage. By comparison, the median household income for Salvadorans in San Francisco was $27,366 in 1989 (including all persons of Salvadoran origin) while that for all San Francisco residents was $38,669. (See table 9 for income comparisons.) The study participants' are relatively low wages, as San Francisco has one of the highest costs of living in the country. The 1991–1992 survey (Calderón 1992) reported that, based on San Francisco standards, 90 percent of recently arrived Salvadorans earned salaries close to poverty levels.[17]

The fierce competition for jobs has placed many undocumented immigrant workers in an even more vulnerable position, a situation that has been noted elsewhere among Central Americans (Chinchilla, Hamilton, and Loucky 1993). As previously noted, job losses and plant closures have left immigrants in a precarious situation and subject to super-exploitation (Chinchilla and Hamilton 1992). José R., an accountant by training, said that he quit his part-time job washing dishes, where he earned $6 per hour, for a full-time job cutting cheese at a pizza place. He did this because he was promised $400 per week, fixed salary — meaning no overtime. He had to work ten hours a day six nights a week, and if he wanted to take a day off, he had to get someone to replace him and pay the person from his own pocket. A second-year university student in El Salvador (who was staying with a family I came to know well) mainly has taken day jobs. He told me that employers who hire him for the day do not always pay him what they had agreed on and sometimes even refuse to pay altogether. Once he accepted a job carrying bricks at a construction site, where he was promised $4 per hour. At the end of the day, the employer said that he was not satisfied with his performance — even though he had done more than he had been assigned in the hope of being hired on a more permanent basis — and decided not to pay him.

The precarious economic situation has profoundly affected the hopes and prospects of Salvadoran immigrants. It has been particularly troublesome for them because they pride themselves on their strong work ethic, which in Central America had led them to be called "the Germans" or "the Japanese" of Central America. The high labor force participation rates of Salvadoran immigrants in the United States (93 percent for males and 70 percent for females) and a low household level of public assistance use (7.1 percent) may provide support for this notion (Lopez, Popkin, and Telles 1996, 303; see also table 9).[18] Invariably, as they recounted their disappointment in the labor market, the Salvadorans I met in San Francisco would invoke their reputation as tireless workers. They commented on the many things they would be capable of doing if they were given the opportunity to prove themselves as *emprendedores* (enterprising people). In the words of Don Julio A., "It pains my soul to see our compatriots in this situation because they are not the type to sit around waiting to be fed. I remember when Salvadorans would go to Honduras, to towns that were practically dead. They would immediately revive them, they would buy and sell everything. They built. Those towns were alive. And look, here they can't do anything. If they were given a chance, they would get ahead quickly and prove that they're not lazy people hoping to be supported by American *taxpayers.*" His view was echoed by Don Mario M., a seventy-year-old with a ninth-grade education from a city in western El Salvador. Don Mario proudly proclaimed that the Salvadoran work ethic is legendary. He assured me, "If a Salvadoran is a lawyer, he'll try to be the best lawyer; if he's a janitor, he'll try to clean even more than asked; a housekeeper, the same. And even if he's a pirate in illicit activities, he'll be the best of the criminals because we're hard workers and want to succeed at what we do, and we'll always push ourselves. All we need is a chance, and leave the rest to us." The mismatch between the lack of economic opportunities that many of my informants mentioned and their relentless desire to work has had serious repercussions in their lives. As one example, they have not been able to repay their debts to their relatives in San Francisco or to contribute to the families they are staying with.

In addition to the need to find a job to support themselves and repay outstanding debts, many Salvadorans have enormous pressures to remit money to their families in El Salvador, which not surprisingly leaves them with few resources. During the 1980s, Salvadorans remitted more than $1.3 billion a year, which along with U.S. aid and earnings from coffee exports constituted the three largest sources of foreign exchange in El Salvador (Montes and García Vasquez 1988, 36).[19] A recent comparative study showed that in spite of their precarious U.S. situations, Salvadorans remit as much as Filipinos, whose socioeconomic situation is substantially better (Menjívar et al. 1998).[20] This does not imply that resource-poor Salvadorans, such as those in this study, send inordinate amounts of money *individually.* Many Salvadorans — with varying degrees of financial capability — send money back home regularly, and thus, in the aggregate, remittances amount to large sums, but many send between $20 and $100 monthly. The importance of these remittances cannot be overstated. A major Salvadoran bank has opened up branches in several U.S. cities to facilitate remitting and to allow Salvadoran immigrants to conduct other banking transactions, including the payment of debts or mortgages back in El Salvador. I accompanied Chentía A. and her daughter, Amparo, to the San Francisco branch, and it felt as if we had stepped into a bank in downtown San Salvador.

The high volume of remittances can be attributed to the lack of opportunities for the Salvadoran immigrants' families in an economy

ravaged by the civil war and to the immigrants' own uncertain future
in the United States. In the present study, two-thirds of the survey
respondents — both men and women — felt financially responsible for
someone in El Salvador. And it was such a commonplace practice to
send money home, though the amounts were small and, in many
cases, irregular, that even children understood its importance. For
instance, Claudia, Marcela Q.'s seven-year-old daughter, saves pen-
nies or dimes that she finds to "send there [El Salvador]." With her
mother's encouragement, Claudia is building a house there. Marcela
proudly explains Claudia's progress in the construction and her plan to
share it with her siblings who live in El Salvador. And Priscilla F., who
was attending English lessons but had to rush after school to her job
as a waitress, told me, "I have to work, there is no way I can just go to
school or have fun. Of course I feel responsible for sending my family
at least $50 a month, that's the least I can do. Without this money I
feel everything would collapse. I cannot stop earning money. I feel
obligated, I have a daughter and a grandmother there [in El Salvador],
and I cannot just sit back. I have to remain strong, forget my pains and
worries, and keep on going."

One particularity of the urban landscape of San Francisco has further affected adversely the economic situation of Salvadorans in this
city. San Francisco has become one of the most expensive housing
markets in the country; rents for all units increased 30 percent more
than income during the 1980s (McLeod 1992b). The median gross
rents for San Francisco were 46 percent higher than in the rest of the
country, but incomes in San Francisco were only 11 percent higher
(U.S. Bureau of the Census 1993).[21] Furthermore, gentrification and
Hong Kong investment have augmented fears that longtime residents
will be pushed out of neighborhoods such as the Mission District,
where already most convenience stores are run by Asians.[22] Being able
to pay a monthly rent was a common concern among my informants;
Marcela Q. said her principal objective every month was to be able to
gather the $250 to pay the rent on the small garage where she lived. In
fact, one of the reasons that the immigrants in this study were so
mobile (and difficult to keep in touch with) was their inability to pay
the high rents.[23] In Ricardo Calderón's (1992) survey of Salvadoran
newcomers in San Francisco, 75 percent of the respondents mentioned that more than half of their income went to pay rent (see table

TABLE 10   Average Household Size and Median Rent

	General Population	*Salvadorans*		*Central Americans*
	San Francisco	San Francisco	Los Angeles	San Francisco
Average household size	2.4	4.6	4.7	4.7
Median rent (dollars)	653	632	546	617

SOURCE: Census of Population and Housing, 1990 (Summary Tape File 4).

10 for median rents for Salvadorans as compared to other groups). Astronomically high housing costs have led to overcrowded living conditions; the average number of people per dwelling in this study is 6.5 (see table 10 for household size comparisons). Overcrowded living conditions carry great potential for tension, particularly when not all residents are able to contribute financially. In addition, as will be seen, physical separation due to high mobility makes it difficult for people to reciprocate or exchange favors regularly.

The Community and the Politics of Reception

Community ("Refugee") Organizations

To fill the vacuum left by official services Salvadoran newcomers joined efforts with Californians — mostly middle class and white — whom my informants and community workers referred to as "North Americans." Church and private groups, in the form of refugee organizations, funded efforts to provide a range of services to Salvadorans (and to other Central Americans) who arrived during the twelve-year Salvadoran conflict. Although these groups were exceptionally successful in providing a safety net for the newcomers, their financial difficulties grew during the recession, and most soon faced serious setbacks that prevented them from continuing to provide help at the same rate as in the past. Nonetheless, the resources they provided, though sometimes very limited, proved vital to the newcomers who otherwise would have had to rely entirely on their families for support.

One of the largest organization's reports show that it served, with varying degrees and kinds of assistance, about ten thousand Central Americans annually in the greater Bay Area; approximately three-fourths of those served had relatives nearby.[24]

These organizations worked in conjunction with another group that provided organized assistance to Salvadorans in U.S. cities, the Sanctuary movement. In 1985 the city of San Francisco passed the City of Refuge ordinance (otherwise known as the Sanctuary law), a resolution to protect from deportation the officially unrecognized refugees from Guatemala and El Salvador. In the Bay Area there were approximately forty churches, fifteen in San Francisco alone, that became sanctuaries for Central American refugees. Assistance to Central Americans in San Francisco — in sanctuaries as well as in other community organizations — consisted essentially of legal defense and services for those arrested by the INS, or those who were applying to regularize their status. Legal assistance was organized in the form of immigrants' rights groups, which actively pursued cases for Central Americans.[25] Aid also included shelters, information about jobs, health services, English classes, and food and clothing distribution programs. Some of these organizations provided temporary housing and "grants" to pay a month's rent. They also assisted Salvadorans with applications for Temporary Protected Status, with resubmissions for its extension, and with political asylum application procedures. There were, in addition, sympathetic individuals in the greater Bay Area who provided shelter, food, clothing, and even jobs to Central Americans, all of it outside the confines of organized community assistance.

Health care was always in high demand, for even if these immigrants worked, their jobs seldom provided any form of health coverage. Thus one of the most important services that these community organizations provided was health care, most often through a free clinic but also through referrals to private physicians — who sometimes donated their services — and to local hospitals. Catholic Relief Services partially funded a program that included a shelter, counseling and job placement services, referrals to clinics and health advocates, and a food distribution program. The organizers in charge of food distribution mentioned that the need for mental health services was also great, but it so often went unfulfilled that they had to act in the capacity of counselors, even though they were not trained as such. This scarcity has posed serious problems because many of the newcomers still bear searing scars from the civil war. A local priest expressed concern over the potential repercussions that untreated mental health–related conditions could have for Salvadorans, conditions that he believed were the result of both the civil conflict in El Salvador and the dire situation that many encounter in the United States.

In addition, these community organizations informed people of developments in immigration policy and of events and programs in the community. For instance, during the campaign for Proposition 187 (a state ballot measure denying undocumented immigrants access to social service benefits), the organizers of the food distribution program always provided a briefing on this issue before distributing food. Also, they would bring up recent events in Central America; almost every Friday, people were informed about the government-opposition negotiations and the peace process in El Salvador. The people who ran the program were all Salvadorans and worked in conjunction with other refugee organizations in the area, one of which is a cooperative for job placement. The Salvadoran in charge of this cooperative mentioned that there were approximately six hundred members in the cooperative but only about fifty jobs available at any one time.

The fiscal crisis of the early 1990s eliminated funds that had been used for community projects to aid immigrant newcomers. For instance, the person in charge of the food distribution program (a Salvadoran working for Catholic Relief Services) was moved to an office downtown to work with Vietnamese and Cuban refugees. Thus, for a few months, it seemed as though the food distribution had ended. But this person returned, and the program continued and even expanded. And whereas a few years before it served mainly Central Americans, lately the program has provided food to Mexicans, Ecuadorans, Peruvians, Middle Easterners, Filipinos, and even a Bangladeshi family. Although the program represents a welcome source of help, its very presence (and growth) is a disturbing indication of the conditions that immigrant newcomers face in the city. One of the largest community organizations has started to charge for the services they used to provide free, such as assistance with legal paperwork and dental care, because it can no longer obtain the necessary grants. Many residents who contributed monetarily to these organizations or helped the newcomers with food and clothing directly have not donated as much as they used to. For instance, while food donations and contributions to two of the largest soup kitchens in the city declined by almost half, the number of those looking for meals increased at least 30 percent (Burdman 1992). In addition, the changing political situation in El Salvador—though by no means yet resolved—led to the perception that the Peace Accords signed on January 16, 1992, at the Castillo de Chapultepec, Mexico, had halted the war and violence there, and the prolonged efforts to help Central American refugees have produced a cooling-off effect.[26] Potential donors redirected the declining resources to groups that were deemed more needy.

Longtime Salvadoran Residents and Disappointments in the Community

Ethnic solidarity within immigrant groups in the United States rarely happens automatically. Assumptions about unity based on a common nationality do not hold up when there is great social distance between longtime residents and newcomers. A common nationality does not translate into ethnic solidarity—with a viable economic enclave to sustain newcomers—if different waves of immigrants from the same country do not share similar socioeconomic backgrounds or political objectives in the United States or some other common ground. An early example is provided by the Irish, among whom there were substantial cleavages between the middle class that arrived early and the mass of mainly unskilled laborers that followed (Roberts 1995, 64). More recently, Steven J. Gold (1992) and Mary P. Erdmans (1995, 1998) observe among Soviet Jews and Polish immigrants, respectively, that common ancestry, culture, and even frequent interaction do not lead automatically to ethnic solidarity between old-timers and newcomers. The case of the Salvadoran immigrants I met in San Francisco does not differ greatly.

Salvadoran residents who arrived in the 1940s, 1950s, and 1960s tend to be of a higher class background than the new arrivals and have dissimilar lifestyles and objectives in the United States and different political ideologies. This group includes financial executives and professionals, owners of large businesses and expensive real estate, and those who have established links with local politicians and power holders. These Salvadorans are not many, but they do have access to goods that could benefit the rest of the community. Among the newcomers are people who opposed the Salvadoran government, exiles, and the poor — who have no particular political agenda but who suffered during the war. The Salvadoran community, of course, is not so rigidly compartmentalized into old-timers and newcomers, for there are many who fall somewhere in between. Nor can we equate time in the United States with wealth or material resources, because there are poor old-timers and relatively financially stable newcomers. However, here it is the division and general lack of contact between the old-timers (who on average have more resources) and the newcomers (who tend to not have many) that is relevant.[27] The Salvadoran situation is further complicated because politics from back home, as is the case in refugee immigrant communities generally, affect these immigrants' lives in the United States in many important ways.[28] Differences in political ideology have created deep cleavages among Salvadorans that are often difficult to overcome because of the absence of other factors that could bring the immigrants together, such as common class backgrounds or ethnic identity.[29]

Salvadorans working in community organizations to aid newcomers were once new immigrants themselves. They, in turn, organized the reception for those that followed, with little or no assistance from longtime Salvadoran residents, who are in better positions to mobilize resources for the rest of the community. Occasionally some of the workers in community organizations — who had been politically active in El Salvador — openly opposed U.S. policies in El Salvador, a stance that the usually more politically conservative longtime residents did not approve of or could not understand. Differences in class background, compounded by cleavages in political ideology, have prevented the development of cohesive ties between longtime residents and newcomers — and perhaps the semblance of a viable enclave — in the U.S. city that has been host to these immigrants for the longest time.

According to Sonia, a community worker, the different lifestyles of longtime residents whose objective is to "assimilate" into U.S. society prevent them from identifying with the situation of the newcomers, who are mostly from disadvantaged social backgrounds and "look humble." In her words, "Of course they don't want anything to do with

us, you know, the poor. They prefer to distance themselves from us
and ignore us completely. Sometimes two or three come to an event
or give us money for a particular project. But that's not consistent and
it's very little in comparison to what they could do for us if they
wanted to." The result is a noticeable lack of participation of established Salvadorans in community organizations, especially in contrast
to the active participation of many North Americans.

I had the opportunity to talk about the newcomers with a successful Salvadoran couple (residents of San Francisco for forty-three
years) in their home in a foggy, upper-middle-class suburb. Afraid of
the "image" of Salvadorans that the newcomers were creating in San
Francisco (and downplaying the conditions of these immigrants' exit
and entry), the woman told me,

I have nothing against the new ones, but it's not right for them to come to this
country to ask for charity. It gives us all a bad name. We Salvadorans have
always worked hard and have never begged. What's all that about being
refugees? To me this word implies that our country has problems. Besides it
sounds, I don't know, like subversive or communist. Here, *vivimos bien* [we
live nicely] because we worked hard, and I hope they do the same. I know
that you like to go around the Mission talking with them. I still don't know
why — it's ugly down there. But when you write, don't just write about them.
Say something about us, the ones who live differently, the ones who are trying to give the Salvadorans a good name, the respectable and decent ones.
Look at the Mission now, it's dangerous, it's embarrassing because it's all
Salvadorans there.

This woman neglected to mention that, in addition to hard work, she
and the other Salvadorans who arrived about the same time have been
able to "live nicely" because they faced a radically different context of
reception — and of exit. Those early arrivals, already better equipped
socioculturally to live in the United States, encountered more relaxed
immigration laws, abundant job opportunities with real chances for
mobility, and a largely homogeneous community composed of far
fewer immigrants.

Longtime resident compatriots, however, are not the only segment
of the receiving Latino community that has let down the newcomers:
other coethnics have gone even further than merely giving them the
cold shoulder. My informants told me that they have been cheated
and lied to by other Latinos, experiences that have left them with mis-

trust. However, it is these Latinos (including, of course, other compatriots) who see in the newcomers an opportunity to make a quick buck because they too are often in precarious situations with little or no opportunities for advancement. Similar to what Sarah Mahler (1995a) found in New Jersey, this has happened with frequency in the "legal" field. More seasoned Latinos, knowing that newcomers are desperate to obtain documents, sometimes take advantage. I heard of several cases of "notaries" who had charged exorbitant sums to fill out applications for political asylum or Temporary Protected Status, or cases in which these "legal workers" have disappeared with money that people have paid in advance for their services. Several community organizations have launched campaigns to help people with this paperwork, but they cannot serve everyone, leaving many people prey to the services of the "notaries." For instance, on the recommendation of friends Marcela Q. went to a Nicaraguan notary for assistance in resubmitting her asylum application; he was charging her $900 for helping to fill out the application form and prepare the necessary documentation. Alicia N. and her family were trying to come up with the $2,500 "family fee" that a Salvadoran notary was going to charge them for filling out their political asylum applications. These operations often provide services on credit because they know their extremely poor clients cannot afford to pay the entire amount at once.[30]

Hometown Associations, Church Groups, and Political Groups

The community organizations that formed to assist Salvadorans during the 1980s were created for the purpose of helping those who were in need, not as mutual assistance associations.[31] However, there were a few groups that were formed as "hometown" associations, through which people, by virtue of their membership, had access to a web of friends — and often help.[32] Membership in hometown associations is Salvadoran, and all members have the potential, at different times, to contribute to the organization and help each other on equal grounds. A member of one such organization explained to me, "We get together socially, to remember our life back home, to get nostalgic, not to help people here but to help those back home." He told me that people from his town have organized in San Francisco; they have social functions and fund-raisers, even a soccer club with the same colors and a slightly different name from the one in their hometown. The money they raise goes to a charity of their choice in their town in El Salvador. Their latest project was to paint the school and restore the bells of the Catholic church. This organization has more than one hundred members. The man I spoke to said, "We always have a good time celebrating our customs, our folklore, but in a clean way, without politics involved — and with the good conscience that we are benefiting our people."[33] He emphasized that they are "not interested in helping refugees here, but doing good for the poor there." If one of their own members has a problem of any kind, however, the group does try to help. Even though people obtain assistance through their contact with others in these associations, the manner in which such help is provided and the nature of their membership and objectives are fundamentally different from those in the community organizations, which are organized for helping refugees in need.

Other important types of organizations that have extended a helping hand to fellow newcomers in need are those based on political ideology and religious affiliation.[34] Their organizational structure is similar to that of the "hometown" association. Reflecting to a large extent the social reality of El Salvador — where both forms of organization have played a central sociopolitical role — Evangelical and Catholic churches and political groups with roots in the Salvadoran conflict have provided an important place in the Salvadoran community through which newcomers establish enduring ties. Catholic and Evangelical churches have also been found to play a key role in establishing institutional links between Salvadorans in the United States and their communities of origin (Menjívar 1999b). Relative to the number of those in need, however, few people have access to these networks; nonetheless, they are vital for those who belong to them. Members of these groups provide information as well as material assistance to members in need, who in turn help others. Marcela Q., concerned that she was "maybe sinning," confessed that she is an active member of two different churches because she has found support in both. As a member of a Southern Baptist church to which a popular Latin television anchorperson belongs, she obtained everything she needed for her baby with help from this local celebrity. Through friends she met at the Catholic church, she has received information about a job for her brother as well as other forms of assistance, including transportation, small loans, and clothing. Joaquín M., a high school graduate from San Salvador in his thirties who is a former guerrilla combatant, and his roommates, Tony, Armando, and Luis, met through political work in the Bay Area and have been actively involved in helping fellow activists who arrive in need. Ties among people with similar religious beliefs or political ideology are noteworthy, for they constitute one of the most important forms of association (and of community-level sources of assistance) in the Salvadoran community.

Mario, a community worker, mentioned that forming organizations with objectives other than helping those in need may be difficult, but it is not impossible. He said, however, that the great majority of the people with whom he deals have what he calls "a refugee mentality." On the one hand, he explained, there are thousands of people in great need, and on the other, there are people who feel morally obligated to assist. He said that this attitude on both sides makes it difficult to concentrate on longer-term projects or to create other forms of local or community organization. He blamed the situation on the extreme immediate needs of his community, which leaves only a few with time and energy for other projects. According to Mireya, another community worker, organizing is more challenging among these Salvadorans because typically they do not see the need for putting their efforts into long-term community projects: "Because of the uncertainty — they're undocumented, you know — even with TPS, they're not here permanently, and, well, the poverty in which they live, Salvadorans prefer to concentrate on fulfilling their own immediate needs because they don't know if they'll be here tomorrow. We Salvadorans have a lot of experience in organizing, but here people think, what for? We're not here on a permanent basis. So, in general, we take a more individualistic approach to solve problems."

The Backlash

Harsh economic times have impaired community efforts to assist Salvadoran newcomers, but with equally devastating consequences, the recent immigrant backlash that has accompanied the economic downturn is seriously crippling the immigrants' chances for survival.

Hostility toward immigrants typically arises in times of economic crisis, but the current anti-immigrant resentment is perhaps unique to the 1990s, with fears of overpopulation, crime and delinquency, terrorism, and the emergence of a multicultural society (Burdman 1994). Whereas blaming immigrants for draining essential funds from the state would have been dismissed as headline-grabbing rhetoric a few years ago, it is now an attitude embraced by the mainstream. People feel they can "do something" about a concrete problem like immigration, whereas "doing something" about the economy is too vague and beyond most individuals' means. Politicians, in their efforts to attract sympathizers and distract people from more fundamental issues, have exacerbated the situation with rhetoric emphasizing the detrimental effects of immigration.[35] Even in a traditionally tolerant and hospitable city such as San Francisco, these fears have taken root.[36]

For instance, the clause in the City of Refuge ordinance that forbade the police from reporting undocumented immigrants to federal authorities was eliminated in 1993 after the State of California threatened to withhold $4 million for the city's antidrug program (Lucas 1993). Ultimately, the ordinance itself was revoked, so that Central Americans are no longer protected from deportation. And in a poll taken in early 1994, two out of three Bay Area residents favored Proposition 187 (Tuller 1994).[37] Known as the Save Our State Initiative, Proposition 187 was designed to remove funding for undocumented immigrants in an attempt to eliminate the magnet that supposedly attracted them to the United States, specifically to California. It proposed to exclude undocumented students from schools and colleges, to deny nonemergency health care to undocumented persons, to verify the immigration status of persons seeking benefits, to require all service providers to report suspected undocumented persons to the INS and require the police to check on the legal status of those arrested, and to make the creation and use of false documents a state felony. Soon after it passed on November 8, 1994, several lawsuits were filed, and, eventually, a federal court deemed all the measures of the proposition, except for the one that covers the creation and use of false documents, unconstitutional. Although San Franciscans initially supported the proposition and by election time 29.4 percent voted for it, this was one of the lowest county percentages favoring the proposition throughout the state.[38] Even though most of the measures were thrown out, it gave constituents the illusion of action.[39] Lamentably, it did not create or give back a single job, nor did it accelerate the end of the stubborn recession even by one day.

While the constitutional basis of Proposition 187 was being debated, the mere fact that it passed sent shock waves through the Salvadoran community.[40] Many were afraid to search for jobs, and if they did, they felt more vulnerable than ever. As critics of Proposition 187 rightly predicted, many immigrants became afraid to send their children to school or to seek medical care. A community worker, who had earlier mentioned that the day after this proposition passed her offices overflowed with calls from frightened people trying to clarify some of these issues, asked me one day to help her convince a couple to send their children back to school. Apparently, the children had too much free time on their hands while they were being kept from going to school and had started to get in trouble with the law.

The Salvadoran immigrants also have experienced hostility in their neighborhoods, particularly from other impoverished and disenfranchised groups.[41] For example, rivalry for day labor jobs created an unsettling situation. Those with documents, it seemed, denounced their undocumented peers to the INS. Community workers suggested that this resulted from a desire to get back at someone for "stealing" a job, from manipulation by immigration officials, or from animosity between various Latino groups. In Alicia N.'s case, she had not been able to get any toys for her children or a basket of food from a charity organization at Christmas because there simply was not enough for everyone. However, a few African Americans who were in line for the goods shouted slurs at her, adding that she should go back to her country because she was taking what belonged to them. Alicia said that even though she felt humiliated, she understood them: "Look, Cecilia, at least we had people, centers that gave us clothes, food, places where we got help. But the poor blacks, no one does anything for them; they must feel bad seeing us getting something, right?" Alejandro M. recounted his experience:

Americans are nice, friendly. I have no problems with them. I am talking about the white, blond Americans, you know, whom we call *gringos* or *gabachos*, not the others — well, you know, the *morenos* [blacks]. Well, yes, they're Americans too. We're all Americans, as you know, but I'm talking about those, the *morenos* I find in shelters, in buses, in the areas where I have to hang around. They are not nice. They say things to me, well, to us — insults. It is them [blacks] who are in the same conditions, with whom we have to compete for things.

Some informants were not as tolerant or understanding of the position of other disadvantaged groups and expressed anger at those with whom they had to compete for ever-scarcer resources. Some had been victims of crime, which made them buy into stereotypes quite easily. "I am afraid of blacks. If I see one, I move to the other side of the street," said Chentía A. She was especially wary after she had her purse snatched twice, although on only one occasion had the perpetrator of the crime been a black person. But my observations among these Salvadorans regarding ethnic antagonism are not an exception; similar cases have been reported in other contexts, particularly in Los Angeles (Chinchilla, Hamilton, and Loucky 1993).[42]

While many of these immigrants continue to live on the margins of society with very little, if any, formal participation in its institutions and the community at large, this does not mean that they are impervious to what surrounds them. They take sides on the different local and national political debates, fervently supporting or opposing politicians — though, as one informant once said, "even if no one cares about what we think, we behave and have opinions as if we counted." Most were well informed about the issues that affected not only their immediate communities and neighborhoods but also the city, state, and country. (The Gulf War sparked heated debates among some of my informants.) And as it sometimes happens with recent immigrants, their expression of patriotism and love for their new home surpasses that of even the proudest native. For instance, when the San Francisco 49ers won the Super Bowl in 1990, the celebration in the Mission District was huge, even though many did not quite understand the relevance of the victory, or the game itself for that matter. As someone explained to me, "The 49ers are our team, and they won — how can one not celebrate?"

The community that has received these immigrants, however, has been shaped in important ways by the short history of large-scale Salvadoran migration to the United States. The anti-immigrant backlash that has contributed to decisions to limit the resources of community organizations and that powerfully affects the lives of those who are perhaps most vulnerable does not show signs of abating, at least for the moment.

Conclusion

During the time that U.S. policy provided for active support of the Salvadoran government, Salvadorans entered the United States in massive numbers but were not officially recognized as refugees because doing so would have been contradictory to U.S. foreign policy. In practice, this meant that even those who fled extreme violence and outright persecution were not provided resettlement assistance. Although official immigration policies affect everyone who enters the United States, the dynamics of the economy and labor market opportunities vary according to the specific locale the immigrants enter; these two are, of course, not independent of each other. Immigration policy is played out in specific ways according to particularities in the context of reception. The local economy of San Francisco, reflecting a nationwide trend, entered a recessionary cycle in the late 1980s and early 1990s that seriously affected labor market opportunities for Salvadoran newcomers, particularly given their uncertain immigrant status and limited human capital. As employers of immigrant labor focused on cutting costs, there was increased competition for fewer jobs. This situation left Salvadoran newcomers, particularly those without documents, in an even more vulnerable position, working jobs that were part-time, temporary, and low paid.

Several community organizations were created during the 1980s to aid Central American refugees who did not have access to government support for resettlement. However, these organizations were privately funded, and their already tight budgets suffered irreparable losses during the recession as donors were not able to contribute as much as before. And the perception that Salvadorans have been here long enough to establish themselves has meant that those who have recently arrived received less support through these crucial channels. Equally important, the anti-immigrant sentiments brought about by the recent recessionary cycle have created a hostile environment in one of the most hospitable cities, with serious repercussions for the immigrants' lives.

The structure of opportunities for Salvadorans — as shaped by the polity, the economy, and the receiving community — has been characterized by instability and a general lack of resources (both tangible and intangible). In the face of such poor prospects, informal social networks based on friendship, kinship, neighborhood, or region of origin would be expected to be salient in providing the newcomers with support. But these social relationships do not exist in isolation from the structures in which the immigrants live; their viability may be compromised for those who may need them the most. This point is the focus of the discussion in the next chapter.

Chapter 5

The Dynamics of Social Networks

People become inhuman when they don't have anything. It gets to a point where they don't care about anything. It makes one go crazy to be in a strange land, in debt and poor, without being able to do anything or say anything because you can't express yourself in the language. People lose their minds, believe what I'm telling you. Look at my mother. She helped us to come here and now we owe her a lot of money. So she became desperate because she borrowed this money from other people. But put yourself in my position, Cecilia, and picture this, your own mother threatening to call the *migra* [immigration authorities] on you and to tell the owner of the apartment building that we lived there illegally. The thing is, she'd be in trouble too, because she's as illegal as we are. You understand? It's not normal, it's not human. What people do here is not what people do. I don't want to have anything to do with her or with my sister now. I feel as if my mother doesn't exist for me anymore.

Gilberto F.

Gilberto's distressful words convey his disappointment at having been let down, for he had expected more support from his mother, the only person he was counting on. As his, and others', experience will demonstrate, asking for and receiving help is a jagged process filled with unanticipated results.

Assistance is obtained and exchanged in various, sometimes ambiguous, ways. An individual may mobilize resources for particular purposes at one point in time, but as objectives change, the source of help may also change. At the same time, the different facets of a person's life may provide access to various networks simultaneously, and thus he or she might muster help from multiple sources at any one point. One belongs to networks at home, at work, and at play, to name a few places; often these overlap and change as one moves through his or her life cycle. Sometimes people mobilize networks to attain a particular objective, but these can assume an ephemeral existence; after having fulfilled their objective, they may disband, and a new network may not have the same composition.[1] Social distance also matters, for people have different expectations of relatives and friends. It is expected that close relatives will help more than distant ones and that family ties will provide more support than friendship. But expectations are often determined by interfamilial relations and can be situational; distant relatives and friends may sometimes provide more assistance than close relatives.[2] Obtaining and exchanging help entails a *negotiated process* of mobilization of resources, in which decisions to ask for and to provide help are contingent and fluid, not predetermined or fixed.

The process of receiving and giving help among immigrants' friends and family is in large measure conditioned by the structure of opportunities that immigrants encounter in the receiving context. Key institutions such as the state — through policies that grant or deny immigrants security of residence and rights to the labor market and social programs — and the local economy — through the absence or presence of stable employment opportunities — directly influence the viability of immigrant social networks. A favorable reception context will positively affect the dynamics of social networks because members will have more (and perhaps better) resources with which to help one another; an adverse reception will have the opposite effect because immigrant social networks are grounded in specific contexts.

As each immigrant group (and the same group at different times and places) faces a historically specific confluence of factors in the receiving context (Menjívar 1997a), the content and form of and potential for assistance from their informal ties will differ. This conceptualization buttresses the notion of exchanges within immigrant social networks as dynamic processes with great potential for change and eschews the presumption that these ties work independently of, or even counteract, the effects of broader structural forces. As a result, I downplay assumptions of altruism and universal consensus within these immigrant institutions in favor of an approach that emphasizes their contingent, shifting nature.

In this and subsequent chapters, I shift gears to discuss how, within the structure of opportunities in the receiving context, Salvadoran newcomers go about mobilizing resources to procure and

into their own studio when news came that her partner's father had fallen ill in El Salvador and relatives there needed money for his medical treatment. To Carmen's disappointment, their plans for better living conditions were indefinitely delayed. Marcela Q. said that she often feels suffocated because there are too many people making claims on what little she has, and when she cannot stretch her resources enough, people resent her. She even had the telephone disconnected twice because she could not pay the large bills, mostly from collect calls from her relatives in El Salvador (asking for money). Now she is paying the telephone bill in installments and tries to restrict the times she accepts collect calls. In her words:

I feel like running out and never looking back again. Look, I have my two children back there [in El Salvador], then I have my girl here, and I can barely provide for them. Sometimes I send [money], but other times I can't. I really can't. Then I have my debts. When one is poor, one always has debts. And then I have my youngest brother here who never gets a good job. Sometimes I even have to buy clothes for him. And on top of that, this lady, Doña Berta, wants me to lend her money for the rent. No, I can't do it. I think I'll go crazy one of these days. Just because sometimes I work doesn't mean that I have to support the entire world. I don't care if people get upset at me because they think I'm stingy. I know what I can and what I can't do.

This situation, as Marcela and Estela Z. make clear, also has serious repercussions for broader networks. Many of these immigrants are left with few or no material resources to enable them to establish enduring reciprocal ties outside of relatives in the United States. Marcela, for instance, could not lend her neighbor Doña Berta money for rent; she said she was well aware that this would affect the way Doña Berta would later respond if she were to ask her for a favor. Doña Berta used to baby-sit Marcela's child, and in exchange, Marcela would bring her sweet bread, lend her a bus pass, or sometimes even lend her small sums of money. On one occasion, when I stopped by Marcela's place and she was not there, Doña Berta, with whom I had already spoken a few times, invited me to her apartment. Over a cup of coffee and a few-days-old sweet bread, she vented her frustrations and resentment. She said that she had always tried to help Marcela but she felt Marcela had increasingly been taking advantage of her kindness. "You know how I've been with Marcela," she said, "always giving her advice, trying to help her out with a little thing here and there. But she's *malagradecida* [ungrateful], and from now on, when she asks me if the girl can stay with me, I'll start to charge her, like other people would do. We are all poor, and we can't behave like this. If she chooses to behave this way, I'll also behave in the way I choose. She doesn't know, but I will change the way I am with her. She can't behave like I'm a stranger."

As the case above indicates, members of this immigrant group have come to pay for services that normally would have been part of reciprocal exchanges among them, something that Sarah J. Mahler (1995a) also observed among the immigrants she came to know on Long Island. In addition to this commodification of social ties (in Mahler's conceptualization) among coethnics, I noticed that it also took place among people united by closer ties, such as *compadres* (co-parents; a child's parents and godparents), in-laws, and partners living under the same roof. The cases I observed, however, were clearly linked to the material conditions in which my informants lived, which undermined obligations of assistance to close ones that are usually taken for granted. For instance, Amparo A. dropped off her daughter at her cousin's for baby-sitting every morning at 6:00 A.M. She paid $5 to the godfather of her daughter each time he gave them a ride to or from the cousin's house, plus $12 a day to her cousin for baby-sitting. And Mayra B. and Ricardo R.'s neighbor and his three cousins, who shared a small one-bedroom apartment, would each buy his own food. If someone ran out of bread or coffee, he could borrow from the others but later had to either replace it or pay for it, to avoid "problems." When I inquired about these arrangements, Amparo and the neighbor gave very similar answers and did not question or seem to be upset by them. They quickly related it to their lack of material resources. As Amparo put it, with a shrug of a shoulder, "If one wants to do a favor, one has to charge, otherwise one is left with nothing. Sounds funny to charge for favors, sounds less like a favor and more like business, but at least it is help, right?"

Expectations and Disappointments

The expectations immigrants have and the reality that awaits them in the United States play an important part in how their informal ties are eventually reconstituted. Many of the immigrants I met expressed disappointment. Some talked about the physical environment, that they had "imagined" the United States quite differently. They had constructed images about life here from tales they had heard back home, and many impressions were based on the gifts and pictures that U.S. relatives and friends sent, especially the remittances that they had either directly benefited from or seen others get. Unfortunately, most of these images had very little to do with the reality that these immigrants confronted on arrival in the United States. One day Amparo A. and I were looking for a parking space near her apartment, and seeing the potholed pavement, untidy streets, and dilapidated walls covered with graffiti, she mused, "When I came here, I thought everything would be very different." "In what sense?" I asked. "Like Manhattan, that it would be there, close to the water, like one imagines it. But when I came here, I asked my mother, 'Is this the United States?' This is dirty, ugly, almost like over there [in El Salvador]. I thought everywhere here would be like downtown San Francisco, with tall buildings and all that — not like where I live. I don't even need to speak a different language because everyone around me speaks Spanish. Yes, I wondered, is this the famous United States? I couldn't believe it."

As we have seen, many others were disappointed at not finding jobs, which they thought would be plentiful, and by their miscalculations about the importance of legal documents. Some admitted that they had not wanted to pay heed to admonitions from those who had repeatedly told them about the difficulties of life in the United States. Lety R., for example, who left five children in the care of her mother in El Salvador, kept on repeating, with her eyes watery, what life in the United States has been for her: "My brother-in-law told me, I knew it would be hard. He said, 'I won't lie to you, Lety, but life is really awful and you have to be very strong. People without documents live in torment.' He said it clearly. But I also had to think about the five mouths that I have to feed there [in El Salvador]. If I don't send them the $100 a month, they don't eat. What do I do? Face the situation and keep on going." Mayra B. talked about what she thought was the "stubbornness of the immigrants." She quipped, "We immigrants, we're always going to insist, no matter if we are welcome or not, or if the laws are enforced, even if reality tells us differently and we're deep in a hole, we're always going to insist that this is a great country."

As Mayra commented, no matter how precarious their situations, most of my informants thought that the United States had much to offer, that it presented many opportunities, that if they only applied themselves harder, they would get somewhere. When complaining about the lack of jobs, they sometimes simply attributed it to bad luck, but at other times they blamed friends and relatives for not informing them about or recommending them for jobs. And even though many thought that it was a common, broader problem, no one expressed disillusionment with the system that had triggered the recessionary cycle that resulted in the lack of jobs in the first place. Perhaps it was a way to reach a psychological balance between reality and expectations to help them to carry on. Because many were pressured to stay (and generate incomes), they insisted that opportunities were still within reach. To think otherwise would mean to give up a great deal, perhaps too much. As Don Armando Q. put it, "It's optimism mixed with fear that keeps us here." Carlos G., a high school graduate in his fifties from a city in western El Salvador, had been in and out of a shelter almost since he arrived in San Francisco. He said,

Even if I live in a shelter and I am depressed because I don't have a job and I don't know what I'll do to eat tomorrow, this is still the promised land, the land of opportunity. And I know everything will get better. Even now, if I don't find a job, I go out collecting bottles to take to the recycling place. I even go around looking in the garbage of restaurants because they throw away so much. The thing is that in this country, if you don't sit idle, you don't go hungry. And that's a blessing. Sometimes, from the street where I practically live, I can see the [Golden Gate] bridge, and I say to God, thank you for bringing me here. That's why the day of the turkey [Thanksgiving] is the greatest day for me. I didn't know what it meant until I came here, but now that I know its significance, I celebrate it in my own way by giving thanks again, and even by eating what the restaurants throw away on that day.

The clash between expectations and reality has shaken many who expressed disappointment at the reception they received from their families. The assistance from relatives in the United States, mostly in the form of a loan to make the trip, had led many to believe that these relatives were doing much better financially than they really were. They believed that their families would continue to help them, at least until they got a start. But the reality was very different. These disappointments often had serious repercussions for networks of assistance.

The case of Rosario E. exemplifies this point. Rosario eventually moved out of her cousins' house and into a one-bedroom apartment that she shared with four friends, where with help from a community organization and a new job cleaning houses three times a week she managed to pay for all her needs herself. Living with friends, Rosario explained, was easier, because she never expected them to help her financially or materially, which in her eyes eliminated the potential for conflict and disappointment. Rosario seldom contacts her cousins because she fears that they may think she needs a favor.

Many Salvadorans and their families were separated for long periods as one member of the family migrated and the others stayed behind. Eventual reunification proved much more difficult than anyone had ever imagined. Very often they found they had little in common to share as a "family," and thus the obligations implied and expected by this relationship were difficult to sustain. Sometimes, especially when children had been left behind, those in the United States and those in El Salvador had been exposed to such different conditions that they could hardly recognize each other as family. Priscilla F. said that she had to struggle to become reacquainted with her mother, whom she had not seen in twelve years. Not only did she find that she and her mother had very different tastes and could not agree on even the smallest things, but her mother had remarried and had other children, which made it impossible for Priscilla to live with her again. In her words: "I don't even call her *mamá*, I call her by her first name. Just because we see each other again doesn't mean, oh yes, let's hug each other and act like nothing happened all these years. She's like an aunt or something like that to me — someone a little strange. I don't have the *confianza* [trust] to ask her for something or to confide in her. I feel better with my aunt, who used to live with me in El Salvador."

One of Joaquín M.'s roommates, Luis, had a similar experience. Luis explained that after he arrived in the United States he quickly moved out of his relatives' house because he realized they did not have enough even for themselves, but also because they had very different views about the world. Luis found others who share his views and who work to promote the ideals he so cherishes. Now Joaquín, Armando, Tony, and he are close friends who share not only living expenses but also, and more important, political ideology. This living arrangement is more suitable for them; it facilitates their exchange of ideas, and it allows for enduring ties to develop among them. For instance, Luis, Armando, and Tony always make sure that Joaquín — who is confined to a wheelchair — has a ride whenever he needs to go somewhere that might have difficult access. They are also careful that Joaquín does not undertake physically demanding tasks at home. In return, Joaquín cooks, lends them money when they need it, and helps them out with simple translations. Luis and Armando visit their relatives regularly but are aware that in times of need it is their friends to whom they will turn.

It was not only the new arrivals who felt let down but also those who were waiting in the United States. The disappointment of the receiving families derived from the seeming inability of the newcomers to procure stable jobs that would help to repay debts, money the receiving relatives desperately needed. Also, by not being able to start earning an income quickly, the newcomers became a burden for much longer than the U.S. relatives had anticipated. Paula A., a friendly woman in her mid-twenties from a small town in central El Salvador and with a fourth-grade education, is a case in point. Her siblings had paid for her trip and were not expecting any money in return, but they wished that she would get a job soon, so that she could start supporting herself and her toddler and contribute to the household. The siblings became increasingly upset at Paula's unsuccessful attempts to get a steady job and one by one decided to stop supporting her. Paula ended up living in a shelter for Central Americans. She reestablished contact with one of her siblings but was reluctant to visit the others.

Then there was the case of Conchita F., a barely literate woman in her mid-sixties, and her family. When I first met Conchita, she seemed sincerely concerned about the grave situation that her son, Gilberto F., and his wife, Alicia N., were going through. After spending four months in Guatemala — where members of her church had arranged for her to live and work embroidering tablecloths — at the insistence of Conchita, Alicia and her three children moved to San Francisco. Conchita had managed to gather the money for Alicia and the children's trip. Gilberto, a radio technician by training, had been living in Los Angeles but soon joined Alicia and the children in San Francisco. They stayed with Conchita along with six other friends and relatives, all of whom had arrived in the United States within the previous three years. This living arrangement was highly unstable because the apartment was limited to three occupants. Only two adults held full-time jobs, and Conchita worked cleaning houses on an irregular basis; all worked without documents. Conchita was particularly upset because her son's family became a burden on the already fragile financial stability of the family.

The situation in this household became unbearable and erupted in a serious confrontation when Gilberto discovered that Conchita had collected clothes and money donated to her by her employers to send to his children while they were back in El Salvador but had never sent them. Conchita said that the clothes were worn out and were not worth sending all the way there. Besides, she had other needy family members already in San Francisco who could better use those items, particularly the winter jackets and wool sweaters she had received. When Gilberto confronted Conchita, she asked him and his family to leave her house at 10:00 P.M. They had nowhere to go, but a friend of Alicia's from church offered them a place to stay for a few days. When they located an apartment, Alicia's congregation came to their rescue by collecting the $750 they needed for the first month's rent. Only Alicia, a deeply religious person who could not live with rancor in her heart, keeps in touch with Conchita. Gilberto, however, was crushed. A recovering alcoholic, he had another drinking bout as a result of the confrontation with his mother, which cost him his job as a handyman with a German landlord who had helped him on many occasions, including giving him a used car as a gift. Conchita's version of this incident was different. To her, Gilberto and Alicia, who had not been able to find stable jobs, were burdens that she and the rest of the family could no longer tolerate. In addition, Conchita was very tense because Gilberto and his family had not been able to repay even a penny of the close to $5,000 she had borrowed from her employers. She was afraid that her employers would send her to jail or have her deported as a result.

It is important to note that the disappointment on the part of both the newcomers and the receiving persons came from specific expectations that neither party had been able to fulfill; it was not based on normative expectations that relatives or friends should help one another. Although the war may have disrupted social relations of trust and support in El Salvador, the newcomers did expect assistance from family members (especially if the relationship was a close one, such as parent-child) on whom they had previously relied, particularly for the trip and often for remittances, but who could no longer fulfill this important social obligation. For instance, given the early involvement of U.S. relatives or friends, the newcomers expected that this help would continue. In fact, of those survey respondents who received such help, more than three-fourths were confident that the *same* person who helped them migrate would continue to lend them a hand in the United States (see table 5, p. 59). However, these study participants did not have any expectations of help from people who had not been involved in providing them aid in the past, whether these were family, friends, or coethnics in general. When I asked my informants to compare assistance from informal networks in El Salvador with those in the United States, some of them recognized that distance sometimes blurs memories. As Victoria O., a reserved woman in her thirties from a town in central El Salvador and with a sixth-grade education, explained, "Oh yes, I can tell you that I *añoro* [long for] the warmth of people there [in El Salvador]. But what happens is that when you're far away you think everything is better there. But reality is probably different." Others made no attempt to romanticize informal networks back home. Never short for words, Marcela Q. simply responded, "There or here, it's the same. If someone sees you standing by a precipice, instead of giving you a hand to move away, they push you."

Some informants, particularly those from small cities or rural areas, however, assured me that "people are better there" and seemed to miss the close-knit and more personalized connections that were often the basis for enduring ties of assistance in the small-town atmosphere they were accustomed to. Chentía A. said that she has been disappointed at what she calls the "lack of charity" in the area where she now lives. For instance, when she did not have enough money to pay at the corner store back home, there was no question that the owner would give her what she needed *fiado* (on credit) simply because they knew each other. It is a different story here. Chentía explains:

Here it is different, one cannot compare. If I don't have the exact money when I go to the Chinese's store at the corner — and by the way, he charges more than Safeway — even if I go there every day and one day I'm short two cents, he doesn't let go of one sad tomato. Or much less at K-Mart. Can you imagine telling the cashier, "I'll be back with the rest of the money tomorrow?" She'll call the police or, better yet, the psychiatric hospital because people don't do that here. But those things, for us the poor, one misses them here. Here money talks more than feelings.

Others offered similar, but somewhat qualified, views. For instance, Chentía's daughter, Amparo, put it in perspective as follows:

The problem here is that everything is more expensive, so if you want to help you have to spend [money]. Over there, no, one could help one another with little. Look, when I needed someone to care for my boys, I could leave them with the neighbor and then I would bring back from the market some plantains, a papaya, or something for her. If a neighbor wanted me to make tortillas, she would give me a chicken — like that. But here? I can't just give the baby-sitter a bunch of bananas for caring for my baby [laughs hard]; she'll think that I'm crazy!

Although some of the newcomers' informal ties might have been weakened *before* migration, in the absence of any formal infrastructure for resettlement, informal ties with friends, family, neighbors, or even coethnics represented their *only* hope in the United States. They were the sole potential source of social support in a foreign and often hostile land. Expectations of support from the people who looked familiar, attended the same churches, lived in the same neighborhood, and spoke the same language grew as the newcomers confronted the harshness of life in the United States. Thus my informants expressed disappointment with acquaintances they knew from back home, compatriots they met in San Francisco, other Latinos, or in general the community in which they lived. Carlos R., a man in his early fifties from a city in central El Salvador who dropped out of school one year before completing high school to help his widowed mother, felt terribly disappointed by his Mexican landlord. Carlos and his wife were renting a basement for $600 a month, including utilities. The landlord kept on complaining that they were using too much water and electricity, and he wanted to raise their rent. Carlos went to a community organization, where he was told that what the landlord was trying to do was against the law and that in fact the entire operation was illegal because the landlord did not have a permit to rent the basement as a separate unit. The landlord backed off when Carlos confronted him with the information he had collected. Carlos felt better but was still quite saddened by the experience. He told me, "I can't believe another Latino did this to me. I would have expected this from an Anglo, but Anglos are much nicer than my own people. I don't know what to expect anymore. We're eating each other alive here."

Other informants extended their feelings of disappointment to all Latinos. Marvin C., a high school graduate from San Salvador in his mid-twenties, explained that he does not trust Latinos because they often take advantage of newcomers whose weaknesses they recognize. A cousin of one of my informants told me that he prefers to work with non-Latinos to avoid envy and gossip, which, according to him, "Latinos are good for, especially when they think they are in competition with one another." Other informants, longing for better relations and more support among Latinos, wondered about the situation in other groups. Lety R. said, "You should see the Chinese, or the Jews, they are so united, *da gusto* [it pleases one] to see them. If one of them needs something, even if the others don't know him, they hurry to help him. Oh God, with us Latinos it's the opposite; they run the other way if they sniff that you may ask for help. I think we would be in a different situation if we were like the Chinese, or the Jews. More united. No, we Latinos don't learn that. We only know how to cheat one another."

Very often people would simply respond with a vague "people change" when asked about these situations. On other occasions they were more specific. For instance, Armando L., one of Joaquín M.'s roommates, thought that Salvadorans change in the United States because they "become consumed by capitalist greed and forget about human relations." Others were less articulate but in essence conveyed the same opinion. José R. said that because Salvadorans are such hard workers and because the United States is a "society that lives to work," they find a perfect niche for this aspect of their "culture."

Despite the fact that some had unexpected negative experiences with compatriots, others had been able to find solace among them. In the words of Luis, another of Joaquín's roommates, "Here I see people from other countries, and I think, our people are good. If a Salvadoran has only beans and rice, he shares them; even if he has only one egg, he cooks it and shares it with you. I didn't know it would be like this in a foreign land, but it feels good because many times, what my own family has not done for me, a compatriot has." This view may be influenced in part by his own experience of living in the "community" of political "comrades" (as he would sometimes refer to his friends). It seems that those newcomers who had been involved in political activities back home were able to rely on these ties of solidarity to forge important networks in the United States that were of much benefit to them. This, in turn, placed them in a better position — materially and socially — to reciprocate favors.

One of the most disappointing situations the Salvadorans in this study have experienced is with the more established Salvadorans, those who have lived in San Francisco for three decades or longer. On several occasions my informants mentioned that these Salvadorans behaved as if they were complete strangers; they even felt unwanted by these compatriots, and no one expressed a "community" feeling toward this group. Sometimes the more established Salvadorans would hire newcomers to work in their businesses, but it was neither commonplace nor a practice from which the newcomers could benefit. In fact, in a few instances the newcomers had felt cheated by more established compatriots. The established Salvadorans, for their part, as we have seen, did not particularly identify with the newcomers and therefore could not see why they should become involved in assisting them.[6]

My informants' disappointment — with the situation in the United States, with their families, or with their community — prompted many to be uncertain about whether to remain, relocate, or return. The overwhelming majority of the respondents to my survey, for instance, were not sure where they were going to be in two years. Some mentioned that they would go to other states, where they had heard the situation for undocumented immigrants was better than in California. Others said that an altogether different country would be a better option, particularly Canada or Australia.[7] Still others toyed with the idea of returning. Though it was not a concrete option, several informants not only remitted regularly but also purchased land and houses in El Salvador and even sent home appliances and the like. According to one of them, "Everything is more secure there. One doesn't know what will happen here, so why accumulate a lot of things here if tomorrow I may be kicked out, and I would have to leave in a hurry and leave all my belongings behind?"

I was given various reasons for why my informants thought friends, compatriots, and other Latinos in the United States had failed to assist them. My own observations and my conversations with many people who were expected to give and obtain assistance lead me to agree with José R., who felt that their own straitened circumstances (in his case, his brother's) prevented people from helping others. Several people were evidently anguished about their inability to fulfill relatives' and sometimes friends' expectations. Milagro V., a woman in her early fifties from a city in eastern El Salvador and with a sixth-grade education, has worked very hard but has not been able to gather enough money to help her nieces. She explained:

I feel very bad because the poor girls, they counted on me. I feel responsible for them. They only have me here and *les he quedado mal* [I have not delivered]. They break my heart. But as you've seen me, my situation here does not allow for more. If I don't support them it's not because I don't want to, it's because I just can't do it. I kill myself working, but it's not enough. I love them dearly, but unfortunately they can't eat from that. What they need now is money, food, clothes, and love comes second because you can't survive on love alone.

Helping Each Other Out:
The Process of Seeking Assistance

Even in the face of disappointment and disillusionment, some of my informants managed to establish reciprocal ties with relatives, neighbors, compatriots, other Latinos, and members of their immediate community. In the absence of a formal infrastructure of resettlement and with resource-poor community organizations, informal ties of support proved to be the only social shelter available to the immigrants in this study. However, very seldom did assistance come automatically from the first person asked or, for that matter, from the person of whom it was expected. Also, different kinds of help came from different people, and there was a tacit understanding about who could ask whom for what. Often "networks" would change in composition with time, and as other needs arose, other informal ties would replace them. Importantly, however, these ways of cooperating with one another cannot be conceived simply as "pooling" resources, a term that conveys an idea of unity and uniformity of objectives. The concept of patchworking suggested by Kibria (1993) is more relevant here. Patchworking, Kibria explains, "conveys the uneven and unplanned quality of members' contributions to the household, both in substance and in tempo" (1993, 77). Also, patchworking connotes the merging of different resources, such as information, services, and education. Whereas Kibria uses this concept mainly to examine the dynamics of economic cooperation among families, I believe its heuristic value can be extended to examine cooperation beyond families, such as among friends, neighbors, and compatriots. The notion of cooperation being uneven and sometimes haphazard that is embedded in patchworking is particularly pertinent here, as it conveys more powerfully the process of obtaining help among immigrants with very few resources to share.

The cases of Mauricio A. and Paula A. exemplify the process of obtaining help. Mauricio, a San Salvador native who is in his mid-twenties and has a high school diploma, arrived in San Francisco with the help of his aunt and uncle, who had been living in the United States for more than two decades. He was able to get a job installing car stereos within three months of arrival, thanks to a friend of the family who recommended him to the Peruvian owner. When Mauricio needed money to purchase a car, however, he turned to different people.

I needed exactly $750. Naturally, I asked my aunt first, but they are kind of old, you know, and they don't have much money. My uncle doesn't work anymore, so it was too much for them. So I asked my cousin, their daughter, but she couldn't lend me the money because she's going to get married, and so that stopped right there. I said, God, what bad luck I have, but I didn't give up. Meanwhile, the guy who was selling the car kept on asking me if I was interested, and I kept on saying, yes, yes, wait a bit longer. I only have a few friends *de confianza* [whom I can trust] here, but they are all *fregados de dinero* [in a bad financial situation]. So finally it occurred to me to ask this uncle in Los Angeles, and he said yes, that if I'd use the car for work and to go to school, he'd lend me part of the money, and the rest he'd give to me as a gift. So, of course, I said, yes, yes, it'd be used only for good purposes [laughs], I'll even go to mass now. But this took about one month. I almost didn't get to buy the car.

Paula came to San Francisco with her youngest son at the urging of her sisters and brothers, all newcomers themselves, who had pooled money to pay for her journey. Initially Paula lived with her brother, until he could not support her. She searched everywhere for a regular job but was only able to find a house or two to clean every couple of weeks, generating a meager income insufficient even to buy diapers and milk for her son. Her brother had lost one of his two jobs and was having a difficult time finding another, and his wife was cleaning fewer and fewer houses. Paula went to live with her sister, for whom she briefly baby-sat. The sister had a regular job, but she was solely responsible for the support of the four children she had left back in El Salvador with her mother-in-law. Paula was forced to move in with her third brother, who, in addition to reprimanding her for not being able to find a job, ended up accusing her of being lazy and of stealing money from him to buy clothes for her son. Paula said she had obtained the items at a Christmas function at which clothes were distributed. Paula was deeply offended and decided to move out, even without having a place to go.

Paula and her toddler son spent two nights sleeping in the stairwell of the apartment building where her brother lived, but the brother seemed oblivious to her situation. A tenant informed Paula about a refugee organization that ran a small shelter, which is where I met her. While she lived at the shelter, Paula maintained contact with only the first brother, with whom she had reestablished amicable relations, albeit on different terms. However, the shelter had to close down because the organization that ran it had suffered severe budget cuts. They could help Paula with food only once a week. When Paula thought about her situation, tears rolled down her cheeks. One day, as we sat in the living room of the shelter, Paula offered me a cup of coffee but added that it had to be black because there was no milk in the house that day. She recounted the perils of her trip and added, sobbing, "My own blood, my own brothers and sister have treated me like garbage because I don't have anything. Aren't we supposed to help those in need? No, they want nothing to do with me because *estoy en la calle* [I am in the street — I have nothing]." Eventually Paula moved to Canada with her partner. Paula's case is different from Mauricio's in that she ended up not obtaining the help she expected from her siblings. However, both convey the processual nature of obtaining help, even if only temporarily and not without negative consequences.[8]

Often a person could appeal to several sources of help simultaneously for the purpose of achieving one objective. One incident in

Marcela Q.'s life illustrates this point. When I met Marcela, she was living with a Peruvian woman who had allowed her to stay at her house temporarily. Marcela did not feel secure there because many strangers frequented the house every day, which made her suspect that the woman's relatives were dealing drugs. A Nicaraguan neighbor, who needed to rent out her garage, learned of Marcela's situation and offered the rental to her, which Marcela gladly accepted. However, when Marcela moved in, she realized that the garage was not equipped as a residence; only the landlord's dogs had lived there before. It lacked everything, including heating and appropriate ventilation, even a bathroom. Marcela told me that she could not pass up the opportunity to live there because it was only going to cost her $250 a month, so she decided to fix it up. To do this, she enlisted the help of several people and also received some assistance from a local organization that served Central American refugees.

To purchase the necessary materials, she borrowed money from another Nicaraguan neighbor who was related to her new landlord and from the community organization. To help her install the bathtub, toilet, and sink, she asked people she had met through community organizations, mostly Salvadoran men. To purchase a used portable heater, she asked Doña Berta's niece for a small loan. To help her transport some equipment, she asked a Salvadoran man who had been courting her. She even recruited me to drive her around to find a good deal on the materials. She explained how she had decided to ask each of us for help.

For money, I ask people that would not think that I could pay in other ways. You know, I wasn't going to ask Ricardo [her suitor] or other men because they could think that I wanted something more with them — you know how men are. I couldn't ask my cousins because with them one is never sure. One day they're on good terms with me and the next day they aren't. And she [the Nicaraguan woman] is nice, and knows that I'm responsible. Plus, *le tengo confianza* [I trust her]. The men who installed the stuff are good. Mireya knows them, *son de confianza* [they can be trusted]. So that's that. Oh, and then, I asked you because you have a car and you have done favors for me before and haven't charged me [laughs].

Marcela's contact with Mireya illustrates another aspect of how people obtain help. Often my informants personalized their relations with those running community organizations, allowing them to transform these relatively more formal ties into informal contacts on whom claims for assistance outside the structure of the organization could be made. Marcela explained that she felt confident about asking people for help because she had done small favors for them in the past. Also, to the best of her ability, she expected to assist them in the future.

When the objectives change, the people an individual calls on for help may also change. And at different times a person may have access to different people for assistance. A little over one year after fixing up her garage apartment, Marcela Q. had another project. Marcela's younger brother had repeatedly attempted to migrate to the United States but had failed each time. Apparently he had run into difficulties in Mexico and had never been able to make it even close to the Mexico-U.S.border. Marcela believed that her brother was not good at faking a southern Mexican accent (which is what helped her to make it through). So she decided that he needed Mexican *papeles chuecos* (fake documents). This would help him get across Mexico and enable him to "demonstrate a Mexican nationality" either to Mexican or to U.S. immigration authorities, in case he was caught.

At the food distribution program, a Salvadoran acquaintance of Marcela's had been talking about the fake U.S. and Mexican documents she had obtained from a person who traveled to Los Angeles regularly, where these are manufactured apparently almost to perfection. With the necessary information in hand, Marcela proceeded to obtain documents for her brother. For this purpose she sought a different group of people than those she had contacted for her bathroom project. The fake Mexican documents, though not as expensive as fake U.S. documents, were going to cost anywhere from $50 to $150, depending on the particular document (or set of documents, for there were package deals) and the quality. This time Marcela mostly needed money. When I inquired about whom she had asked, she explained:

You know, my cousins *están de buenas* [are on good terms] with me again, so I asked Sonia for $50. She gave it to me, but because I'm baby-sitting for her, she said she'd discount it from what she pays me. Then I asked Carmen — remember her, the pregnant woman that we took to get WIC [Women, Infants, and Children Nutritional Program]? She lent me $25. I went to ask Doña Berta, you know, that old lady I introduced to you the other day, but she didn't have anything. So I could only get him [the brother] a *credencial* [a Mexican identification card], the birth certificate was more expensive. I have met good people. Without them, I couldn't help my brother.

As Marcela's case demonstrates, there can be much specialization in a person's network; some people are called on to provide certain kinds of assistance, and others are called on for different needs. This is not an uncommon pattern. Several researchers have observed it (Gulliver 1971, among the Ndendeuli in Tanzania; Wellman and Wortley 1989, among East Yorkers in Canada; Lamphere et al. 1993, among working mothers in Albuquerque, New Mexico; Espinosa 1995, among Mexican immigrants in the United States). Rosa María B. is a woman from a small town in western El Salvador in her early thirties and with a sixth-grade education. She told me that even though her Salvadoran neighbors had been friendly, had helped her carry heavy things to her upstairs apartment, and on occasion had asked to borrow her telephone, she could not conceive of borrowing money from them. For that kind of help, she explained, "You go first of all to relatives, and if they can't lend you money, you go to people that you know very well, *gente de confianza* [people of trust]." Marvin C. echoed Rosa María. He also made a distinction between material help (essentially food and shelter) and financial help. Relatives or close friends could provide the former, as it was easier to let someone sleep on a couch or to let them at least eat tortillas, but financial help involved a closer, more enduring relationship, and for this he thought relatives should be asked first. However, although they both emphasized the importance of relatives, they quickly added that very often relatives could not provide help. In such cases, close friends are called in.[9]

Almost invariably a person would assess the potential provider's means before deciding whether to ask for help. Several informants told me that even if they had *confianza* [had trusted] a relative or a friend enough to ask for a favor, they sometimes could not do so because they knew the person's situation would not allow it. The case of Marvin C. is an example. When Marvin came to join his siblings in the United States, he decided to live with his sister in San Francisco because she "was more stable" than his brother, who had been having serious financial problems. It would probably have been easier to live with his brother: "We're both men and it's easier to share more things, like a room, even clothes." When it came time to borrow money to enroll in a vocational program, he again asked his sister and not his brother, for the same reason. In both cases his sister had come through with help. Although Marvin now lives with roommates, he still counts his sister among his main sources of support.

When newcomers discovered the conditions under which their U.S. relatives were living, most realized that asking them for help would impose an unbearable burden on them. Barely surviving, my informants' families simply could not afford to help as much as was expected. José R., for instance, spoke of his surprise at seeing that his brother in San Francisco was not doing nearly as well as their family in El Salvador had thought: "How in my five senses could I ask my brother for help?! No, I couldn't, reality is different here." This kind of situation, however, often contributed to a weakening of ties between relatives. José moved out of his brother's house and only visits occasionally so as not to appear as if he is asking for a favor.

A valuable form of assistance among the immigrants in this study is the provision of information about jobs, health care issues, daily life, housing, and community programs. My informants agreed this is as useful as material or financial help. Alicia N. said, "No, help like economic, no, I don't expect that because we're all so poor here, but moral support or advice, yes, this information is very helpful. That someone can tell me, go here or there, they can help you here or there. That's important help." Information about jobs (a precious commodity) was often shared among friends or even acquaintances. Vehicles for sharing this information were varied. I often overheard people in the food distribution program talk about jobs and housing, informing each other about vacancies that they had heard about. Carlos G. learned about a new way to make money at the corner he frequented in his search for a job. There, a Nicaraguan acquaintance tipped him about collecting cardboard and glass that he could take to a recycling center when no jobs turned up for him at the corner. Estela Z. learned from a Salvadoran acquaintance that she met at a bus stop about an apartment vacancy. On buses too, people often exchanged myriad kinds of information, from job-related matters to health tips to housing availability.[10]

Although most of my informants (and more than three-fourths of the respondents to my survey) had learned about their jobs through friends, or even friends of friends, a job recommendation was an altogether different issue. This required a closer relationship, such as a close friend or relative. Chentía A.'s husband, Don David M., an apartment manager, said that he often told people of job vacancies he knew about, but that he would never recommend anyone for a job, fearing that they would misbehave. Chentía told me, "It's too much responsibility to recommend someone you hardly know, especially how people behave here; if they do something bad, you're responsible. I never do that." Similarly, Victoria O. said that when she was out of work for four months, people would tell her about openings here and there, but it took a neighbor whom she had befriended and who knew of her situation to actually take her to an employer and recommend her. Otherwise, she admitted, no matter how many jobs she heard about, she would not have obtained one. This point illustrates a distinction that Mark S. Granovetter (1995) makes between two kinds of resources — information and influence. Weak ties are useful in spreading information; strong ties may be more advantageous in accessing influence, which is more costly and difficult to obtain.

Although information channels were quite effective in disseminating useful information, sometimes they were conduits for *misinformation*, as the exchange of information was done in very unstructured ways. This was particularly the case when people passed on news that was deemed important, sometimes vital and anxiety-provoking, but based mostly on rumors. When new guidelines for applying for the various immigration statuses came out — and there have been several for Salvadorans — all sorts of misinformation circulated, from people talking about massive deportations to blanket amnesties to special permits for certain community members. Smiling, Marcela Q. explained that she is often skeptical about things she hears through the grapevine.

You know, people talk a lot when they get nervous. They get confused and can't tell the difference between things that are useful and common gossip. When I hear something good, I wait and think, oh God, could this be true? Then I run to Mireya or someone there [at the community organization] and ask. When I hear something bad, I do the same, but most of the time bad news is always true. But you need to ask informed people anyway. Otherwise you may commit suicide if you only listen to all the people in the street [laughs].

As I got to know my informants, I discovered the importance of emotional and moral support in their lives.[11] Several of them expressed feelings of nostalgia, deep sadness, and depression, linked perhaps to war trauma in their home country and exacerbated by the conditions of their existence in the United States.[12] A psychologist who volunteers in a community organization told me that these were obvious signs of post-traumatic stress disorder that he has seen among many Salvadorans. In fact, research has found that a large number of Salvadorans suffer from this disorder, due to conditions in their country but also to migration itself (Cervantes, Salgado de Snyder, and Padilla 1989). They experience greater stress in the resettlement process than Mexicans do (Salgado de Snyder, Cervantes, and Padilla 1990). Though, to the best of my knowledge, these feelings did not directly interfere with their daily lives and their zeal to "make it," they were nonetheless an important part of many of my informants' lives. They often suppressed this part because there was little they could do to ameliorate it. As Lety R. explained,

It's a sorrow, an affliction we all carry inside. We worry about our situation here, about El Salvador; one lives *con el corazón en la mano* [literally, with one's heart in one's hand, meaning extremely worried] here. It's difficult to explain to others. Sometimes I get very sad and I don't want to go out or see anyone — and, excuse me, but I feel like I have no love for anyone. Some days, it's repugnant for me to see people. Yes, it's, I don't know, like a profound anguish, but I can't cry even one tear. It lasts like three or four days at a time, and then it goes away. But we can't lament constantly. We can't dwell on it, or else we'd go crazy. Yes, we'd lose our minds just thinking, because there's nothing one can do about it.

Under these circumstances emotional and moral support proved a vital form of assistance. Very often, however, my informants said that they had no one to talk to; others were too busy working, or they did not want to let everyone know about their problems. My informants called on both friends and relatives for this kind of assistance, and in some cases even on casual acquaintances. Those who could count on someone for this kind of support were quick to acknowledge its importance. Amparo A., for instance, who still had nightmares about the days when her small town in El Salvador was severely bombed, said that she has suffered her fair share and that without her mother's emotional support she could not survive. "I feel as if I live in a valley of tears, everything is a problem, I get very anxious and nervous, and sometimes I feel like I need to *desahogarme* [let it all out]. When I feel like that, I sit with my mother; sometimes we have coffee and sweet bread, or sometimes we just sit and she listens to me. I go to her for everything." Others, however, are not so quick to turn to their families or friends for this kind of support. Edwin M., in spite of having a close family, prefers to confide in friends because he feels that if his family found out his thoughts, problems, and true aspirations, they would behave differently with him. And Evelyn S. and Priscilla F. talk with their babies instead of their families or friends, because they feel that children will not betray them or spread rumors about them. José R. has become ardently religious since he arrived in the United States and finds consolation in reading the Bible instead of visiting or talking with anyone. Victoria O. prefers to be alone, and in the solitude of her small room she cries for hours until she falls asleep. "Only like that [crying] *se me pasa* [it goes away]," she told me. And Milagro V., who confessed that there have been times when she has contemplated taking her life, works even harder and more hours, so as to keep her mind occupied with other things. Even the solitary ones recognized the importance of having someone in whom they could confide. At times, however, fears of betrayal or gossip prevented them from seeking this kind of support from others.

When discussing matters of support from the point of view of those providing assistance, my informants' explanations were similar. The most salient distinctions were in providing financial help, material assistance, and information. People were more likely to lend money to those whom they could trust, with whom they had established an enduring relationship, and who would not disappear from sight — whether they were friends or relatives. The high mobility of this group, as Estela Z. mentioned, posed difficulties here. Some informants were reluctant to lend money to friends because it was too easy to lose track of them. Others, however, were unwilling to lend to relatives; they explained that relatives assumed that because they were related, they did not have to repay the debt, at least not as promptly as the lender expected. Providing material assistance seemed to be a tricky business. On the one hand, as Marvin C. mentioned, it was easier to let someone stay in one's apartment, or to share some food with a needy person. On the other hand, a person who had been invited to stay for a week could end up staying for months, at which point it became difficult to ask the person to leave. Similarly, allowing a person to share one's meals for a few days could turn into a habit that, as time went by, could become too difficult to stop without creating hostility.

Sharing information with relatives, friends, or even acquaintances did not require a commitment and thus was a resource more freely exchanged. Most informants indicated that they did not have much hesitation about providing information. In the words of Estela Z., "If she [an acquaintance] is not taking anything from me, why can't I tell her where to get food?" People mentioned (and many times I witnessed) that they informed others about the food distribution program, a free clinic, the requirements for TPS, free bread that a Presbyterian church was handing out, how to take the bus, how to enroll children in school, and the like. Providing moral or emotional support was not done as easily as sharing information, for it required a certain degree of closeness and responsibility. But people almost always seemed ready to provide this important form of support to relatives, friends, or even acquaintances. Marcela Q. said that because she has gone through so much, she understands the importance of a kind word or a piece of advice in a desperate situation, and so she is always willing to help in this way: "If I can help someone with a word of comfort or advice, I do it. In my position, it's about the only thing I can help with." Others thought that they needed to be more careful about offering advice, because people are sometimes so distraught that they take advice word for word and get into worse trouble and blame the person who volunteered the advice. Or worse, it leads to uninvited gossip, with which everyone seemed to be especially concerned.

From my observations it seemed that material and financial assistance usually came from relatives, information mostly from friends or acquaintances, and emotional help and moral support from both. This is not by any means a clear-cut distinction or categorization, for relatives also provided information and friends sometimes provided financial help. But, for instance, channels of information did not require established ties where reciprocity norms were expected to be upheld. People also obtained information through broader contacts, from friends, friends of friends, or casual acquaintances, often in haphazard ways. These contacts did not need to be personalized or based on expectations of reciprocity as in the cases of financial or material help. In Granovetter's (1995) conceptualization, these "weak" ties facilitated access to resources. Emotional support was a bit trickier. As in the case of other forms of support, it did not come automatically from people who might have been expected to provide it, and it did not depend solely on the level of trust a person felt toward another. It depended more on how the relative or friend *handled* the information received. A person could not trust someone who might gossip, or who might act on the information provided. In this sense, it was not only the type of relationship between two people that mattered but also an assurance that the confidant would not divulge or misuse important personal information.

Alicia N. and her family and Alejandro M. illustrate another aspect of the evolving, changing nature of networks. When I first met Alicia, she was living with Conchita F., her mother-in-law, but after Conchita's altercation with her son, Gilberto, they had to move out. This move affected informal exchanges between Alicia and Conchita and the rest of Conchita's relatives, since they remained physically and emotionally distant. A year after the incident Alicia had reestablished amicable relations with Conchita, who would occasionally drop by with a chicken, sweet bread, or tortillas for Alicia and the family. Gilberto, however, was still upset and not on speaking terms with his mother, or sister, who had taken the mother's side. More than two years later Gilberto still was not speaking to his mother or sister but had reestablished relations with his sister's husband. He said that he could not forgive his "own blood" for what they had done but did not feel as strongly about his brother-in-law.

Alejandro M. arrived in Los Angeles first but moved to San Francisco to join his cousins because, as he said, "I wanted to be with family." Initially, while he looked for a job, the cousins let him stay with them. After several unsuccessful attempts, Alejandro finally landed a job as a dishwasher and started to pay back loans he had incurred from his cousins. Without documents, however, he was apprehended by the INS and deported. He told INS officials that he was a Mexican national so the trip back would be much shorter and cheaper (and safer) than if he had been sent all the way back to El Salvador. Of his three cousins, only one helped him to return; the others refused on the basis that he might get deported again and never repay his loans. Alejandro was deeply hurt and assured me that he would not have anything to do with his cousins ever again. A couple of months later, when I saw him at a shelter into which he had moved after the rift with his cousins, he was thinking of moving to New Jersey, where he had friends from back home. A little less than two years later I saw him at a community organization inquiring about resubmitting his political application form. He told me that, indeed, he had left for New Jersey but then returned to San Francisco because his mother, now a widow, had moved there. The presence of his mother apparently had softened the friction between Alejandro and his cousins, although he insisted that he would never forgive them. He said, "For my mother I talk with them again. If it was up to me, forget it. They're good for nothing. Sometimes I even have to swallow my pride and do favors for them, but that's only for my mother, because she insists. I behave decently with them so I don't have any problems with her."

Al Que a Buen Árbol Se Arrima:
Social Capital Formation and Access to Resources

The aspects of informal networks presented in the previous sections are all interrelated. Here I discuss their significance as a whole, as they relate to the generation of social capital, a term derived mostly from Pierre Bourdieu's (1986) theory of social reproduction and James Coleman's (1988) work on rational action.

Social capital, Bourdieu (1986, 248–249) observes, "is the aggregate of the actual or potential resources which are linked to possession of a durable network of more or less institutionalized relationships of mutual acquaintance and recognition . . . which provides each of its members with the backing of the collectivity-owned capital, a 'credential' which entitles them to credit, in the various senses of the word." For Bourdieu, the same laws governing the exchange of economic capital are also applicable to different forms of human social relations. Coleman (1988) explains that social capital resides in the benefits derived from relations of trust and collaboration; it inheres in the relations between individuals in a group, not in the individuals themselves.[13] According to Coleman, social debts (obligations) make it possible for resources to be available either on request or on perceived need. In this conceptualization, to possess social capital (not to be confused simply with having friends or family) does not mean to use it but to have the *potential* for use. Unlike physical or human capital, social capital *increases* with use, and it is *depleted* if not used. An important point is that social capital is not generated automatically as members of a group simply interact. It depends, among other things, on the resources available to the individuals in a group. In this regard, Fernández-Kelly (1994, 89) observes that social (and cultural) capital is *toponomical;* that is, it is conditioned by physical and social location. Bob Edwards and Michael W. Foley (1997) observe that social capital depends on the social location of the individuals, just as other forms of capital are differentially available on the same grounds. And Portes (1995, 252) notes that, in the case of immigrants, among the structures through which social capital is generated are their mode of incorporation and the networks that emerge among the members. Thus the social context in which immigrants live and their social position dictate the quality and quantity of resources they have available; and so it circumscribes the immigrants' ability to uphold obligations of reciprocity. As shown earlier, when people, by virtue of their circumstances, lack enough resources to exchange with others, informal exchanges will be limited and ties will be weakened, leading to a decrease in the potential of these ties to generate social capital. In impoverished conditions, when resources to share are unavailable, social capital may not be generated, in spite of strong ties.

The Salvadorans depicted in this study often find themselves unable to reciprocate favors or cut off from access to resources, effectively diminishing their opportunities to help one another. In this case the potential benefits commonly associated with social capital may not be available. It is not that these immigrants live in isolation from one another. What is important are the *kinds* of resources (and, consequently, of social capital) that are available to them, given the conditions in which they live. If these immigrants do not have access to desirable goods and information (or to people who control them), their ties, no matter how strong, may not yield any benefits. A few examples illustrate this point.

Some informants wondered where to obtain information about resources that were beyond their friends' or compatriots' immediate reach, for instance, about access to vocational programs or better-paying jobs. This kind of information was indeed very scarce because people in their surroundings did not have any experience with it. One person had an urban middle-class background, another came from a rural, small landholding family, and a third grew up in an urban working-class family. None of these three informants had legal documents.

However, all three had a minimum of a few years of college education (if not completed professional degrees), had white-collar work experience, spoke at least some English before migrating, and had experience traveling abroad before migrating to the United States. Thus all three had a degree of human capital that would have allowed them to enter life in the United States differently, provided they had had access to goods and services that would have helped them translate their human capital into a beneficial resource. It needs to be emphasized that this discussion in no way detracts from the vital importance of formal institutional resources for resettlement, including avenues to help the immigrants to regularize their legal status. In fact, it further illustrates the effects of a lack of formal infrastructure for resettlement, which in turn curtails the availability of resources that immigrants could muster based on informal ties with friends and relatives.

Alejandro M. once told me that he wanted to investigate the possibility of entering a nursing program or any other health-related field in the United States because he is well aware that it would be impossible to try to enter medical school in this country to finish his degree. He speaks passable English, as he spent one semester in a language school in Florida, but is concerned about the lack of information that he is able to obtain, and complained that he "doesn't know anybody." When I asked what he meant, his response was:

Well, I don't know the right people. I know a lot of people, of course, but everyone is like, you know, our people are not well informed here, most don't have enough education, and they come here to work hard, with their hands. I admire them, don't take me wrong. What I'm telling you is that it doesn't do me any good. I need to enter other circles. You know, when I came here to learn English some years ago, I was in a completely different world. I was in Miami [laughs]. So I can tell differences. People I have met here have helped me with information, and they're very good-hearted people. But they know where to find a dishwashing job, or where I can go to paint a house. But nobody knows how I can apply to medical school, for instance.

Even if Alejandro were able to maintain close ties with others around him, these would only allow him to access the limited resources in their surroundings, which reflect the immediacy of need in which many of these immigrants live. For example, instead of channeling him in the direction of revalidating his experience as an advanced medical school student, his ties direct him to jobs at the bottom of the economy with little potential for mobility. In the conceptualization of Jeremy Boissevain (1974), Alejandro's ties lack multiplexity; that is, his network is composed of people with the same social status, and it does not provide links to other fields of activity. Alejandro is not alone in this respect. Other informants, particularly those with some college education, spoke in similar terms. Evelyn S., another former medical student who had not been able to locate any jobs beyond the usual housekeeping or baby-sitting ones, mentioned, "I don't even think of my life back there [in El Salvador] because everything I did went out the window. I can get a job here, a job there. A lady in BART told me, oh, you should apply to get some food stamps, another told me to go to get food [at the food distribution program]. Everything is important; without this information, I would not survive. But the information is just to get by, day by day. Not to think, oh, I will live here nicely, with a good future as a professional."

Lolita Q., who has a degree in psychology and philosophy from the National University of El Salvador, cleans houses every day. She said that she would not even know where to start to access information relevant to obtaining a professional job. As she explained, "I can make sense, understand scientifically, you know, the situation in which our compatriots live. I am educated, I have traveled in Europe doing political work — but this is where I came to, this is my world now. I sweep and mop like the rest because I don't know anybody, and I can't stop to look around because I have to earn so that I can eat. Nobody is in a better situation here. Sure I'd like to work in my profession, but how?" When Alejandro, Evelyn, and Lolita spoke of "everybody," of "nobody," they meant, of course, everybody around them, everybody who lived in the same precarious situation they did — as Lolita said, in "my world." Their contacts could generate only the social capital needed to survive in their immediate surroundings, to access poor and limited resources and unstable and low-paid jobs, which are not at all commensurate to these immigrants' human capital and offer little opportunity for mobility. Their ties do not allow them to reach benefits and information that could translate into a modicum of mobility.[14] Without social capital, these immigrants' human capital cannot be translated into benefits.

The "surroundings" mentioned in these cases and the access to benefits that these people can muster in their immediate environments contrast sharply with the situation of Enzo M., an upper-middle-class graduate student in his early thirties originally from a city in western El Salvador. When Enzo migrated to the United States, he entered a vastly different world from that of his compatriots. His case, an exception among my informants in terms of social class extraction and of the reception he encountered in the United States, reveals the importance of these factors in generating social capital. Enzo comes from a family of coffee growers with close ties to the United States. His family had long-established links here, as his grandmother married a high-ranking U.S. official and his mother attended private schools in the United States. Enzo, his parents, and his siblings traveled regularly to the United States to vacation in Florida while he was growing up. Through his relatives, Enzo, like his parents and siblings, had obtained U.S. permanent residence status before migrating to live in San Francisco in the mid-1980s. Enzo enrolled in a private college in the United States, but as the war progressed in El Salvador, his family's economic situation deteriorated, and they could no longer afford his U.S. education. As a permanent resident, however, Enzo had access to a range of resources, including student loans and scholarships, which allowed him to finish an undergraduate degree in physics and mathematics and to go to graduate school.

When Enzo found out about my research project, he was eager to hear about it. In a trendy café, where all the dishwashers were Salvadoran (we ended up having a conversation with one of them), we talked over biscotti and espresso about what I was researching, and especially about the lives of my informants. He was astonished because this was all new to him — a world he never knew existed in the United States. In contrast to Alejandro, Evelyn, and Lolita, Enzo observed,

Where do these people find jobs? Can you explain to me, if I wanted to work as a day laborer, how I would go about getting a job like that? And you, how do you meet all these people? Where do you go? I am amazed at their lives. They're brave. How do they do it? To tell you the truth, I had never known what a coyote was or what such a person does. If my *mommy* didn't buy my plane ticket to Miami, I wouldn't have the faintest idea of how to get to the United States.

Enzo too, in Lolita's conceptualization, "belonged in a different world"; that is, his incorporation in U.S. society and the ties that emerged from it placed him in an entirely different social milieu, with access to goods and benefits unknown to most of my informants.

At this point I would like to introduce a case that depicts the flip side of Alejandro, Evelyn, and Lolita, for a handful of my informants (in addition to Enzo) had access to desirable goods and information. The most spectacular is that of Joaquín M., the ex-guerrilla combatant introduced earlier. Joaquín's membership in particular networks generated the kind of social capital that translated into benefits for him. In Boissevain's (1974) conceptualization, Joaquín's network has a high degree of multiplexity, or in Granovetter's (1995), it reflects the strength of weak ties. Joaquín grew up in a working-class neighborhood of San Salvador and began to participate in opposition groups while a student in junior high school. As he grew more active in an umbrella organization for students who were supporters of the guerrilla movement, he started having problems at home, because his family was afraid of the potential consequences that Joaquín's activities might have for them. Eventually, when he finished high school, Joaquín left his house and went underground. After approximately six years of fighting in the guerrilla forces, he was seriously injured in a confrontation and subsequently had both legs amputated. Under these conditions, he could not continue to fight, but he was also unable to return to his family because the government army was already after him. His "contacts" came to the rescue.

Joaquín explained that people in the movement obtained safe passage through the International Red Cross for him to leave for Mexico, "ironically, not as our people go through Mexico, but in a very different situation, as an exile, with open doors." However, the Salvadoran government refused to issue him a passport to travel as an exile, so he could not leave. Next his people organized his migration to the United States via Puerto Rico. Joaquín explained:

The guys in the Red Cross said, don't worry, this is something international that your government can't violate and you have to get out. They got me an official passport to go with a delegation to Puerto Rico, as a member of the special-games basketball team. Well, my uncle worked at the immigration office, so he helped there, to get my passport. Remember, I couldn't show up in any government office, I'd have been arrested. Everything was arranged for me, I didn't have to go anywhere. So when I arrived in San Juan, I separated from the group and went with a man who was waiting for me. From

there, they put me in a plane to Miami. The people had already rented a
room for me there. I was very happy to hear that I was going to be among
Spanish-speaking people and that they were Cubans, revolutionaries, I
thought. But what a surprise! I was in the middle of all the Cuban exiles! It
was a shock. After a few months there, without people to talk to, kind of isolated, I wanted to leave because I couldn't identify with anyone there. So my
contacts, my friends, got me out of there quickly. First, they said, we'll start
with contacts in North Carolina, but then the contacts in Berkeley said okay
first. I thought, yes, Berkeley, yes, better than the politics of Miami. They
immediately put me in touch with people in San Francisco. So they arranged
for me to come to the Bay Area.

When Joaquín arrived in the Bay Area, his "contacts" in political
circles mobilized resources for him to apply for political asylum, which
he eventually received. He explained, "It was risky for me to apply for
asylum because Salvadorans don't get it, but my friends said, don't
worry, there are people in Canada if you don't get to stay here. By this
time I had met lawyers and a lot of Americans, people who understood the role of their government in our [Salvadoran] conflict and
were opposed to it. So my lawyer said, 'Look, we'll win your case, we'll
even take it to the Supreme Court if necessary.' But we won it
quickly." In addition, his contacts arranged housing and, through
friends of friends, learned about English-language classes. Later
Joaquín enrolled in vocational training to learn wheelchair design and,
on completing the course, went to work with a North American man
he met at a political rally who made wheelchairs and sold them around
the world. Through his contacts (and his contacts' contacts), Joaquín
had secured a place in the United States, had won political asylum,
had learned functional English, and had finished a vocational course
that brought him a well-paying job. Most of these things were out of
the reach of the majority of people I met. In fact, of all the Salvadoran
newcomers I came across in my study, Joaquín was the most "successful." Indeed, he came closest to the immigrant that the HBO producer's assistant I wrote about in chapter 1 was looking for, because
Joaquín was a legal resident, spoke functional English, and had established a business (and a successful one at that), all in a relatively short
time. But because of his political convictions and deeply held beliefs
about social justice, he downplayed his own achievements and instead
spoke of the plight of the majority of his compatriots: "For every one

like me, there may be one thousand who are suffering injustices here. I can't be happy about that. I may be an exception because I was lucky to know the right people, but what about the rest?" Joaquín's case contrasts sharply with that of Alejandro M. Alejandro comes from a higher-class background, has more years of formal education and work experience in El Salvador than does Joaquín, and even spoke better English than Joaquín when he arrived in the United States. But Alejandro lacked access to the *kinds* of contacts that helped Joaquín.[15] Joaquín's case exemplifies the benefits that social capital can generate when people in a network have access to desirable resources and information. Elsewhere (Menjívar 1995, 1997b) I have compared how the structure of opportunities affects the availability of resources among Vietnamese, Mexicans, and Salvadorans. Although the informants in all three groups were poor, the Vietnamese had access to resources that they then could share with one another, including state assistance that they could piece together to make ends meet. Mexicans had access to more mature networks established through a long immigration history, but Salvadorans lacked both and thus ended up resource poor and with weaker informal networks. Luis, Joaquín's roommate, summarized Joaquín's remarkable experience in the saying "Al que a buen árbol se arrima, buena sombra le cobija," the one who stands by a good tree gets good shade.

Conclusion: Material Conditions and Informal Exchanges

Informal exchanges among immigrants occur in varied, multifaceted ways. Networks of assistance cannot be assumed to be straightforward, smooth interactions that always behave in expected ways. Immigrants do not automatically assist each other simply because they are relatives or friends; having relatives and friends at the place of destination should not be equated with assistance in the settlement process. Exchanging assistance among poor immigrants is a complex, often contentious process that may produce contradictory results. The image that emerges from my work shows networks not as fixed structures — or even attributes — but as representing processes in flux, which thus generate a plurality of experiences.

The receiving context affects the fate of the immigrants in fundamental ways. It determines if they will have access to the goods and services of society, or if they will become some of its most vulnerable members. The material conditions that immigrants encounter permeate their social relationships, specifically informal exchanges, and dictate their new social standing; such conditions determine what, if any, resources the immigrants will have available to assist one another. An impoverished context of reception, such as that encountered by many Salvadorans, inhibits the immigrants' ability to uphold norms of reciprocity and socially accepted expectations of assistance, and it impinges on the process through which immigrants help one another. When physical and material conditions prevent immigrants from engaging in regular informal exchanges because they do not have much to share, informal networks will weaken. This has implications for the potential social capital that these immigrants can muster based on kinship and friendship ties. Social capital may be drained under extreme conditions of poverty, because exchanges with friends and relatives become highly irregular. But even if immigrants manage to maintain close ties, the social capital that could potentially be generated from these ties and the benefits usually associated with them cannot be actualized under extreme conditions of marginality. When all members of one's network live in highly constrained conditions, links to multiple social fields that could create social capital are practically nonexistent.

People need a minimum of resources to help others; otherwise they simply have nothing to share. Thus our attention should shift from reifying the notion that immigrants achieve benefits through informal exchanges with relatives and friends toward examining the structure of opportunities that determines if immigrants will have the means (and what kind) to help one another in the first place. The assumption that extended social networks represent a "survival strategy" to ameliorate the effects of poverty needs to be reexamined, perhaps even reversed, for the very conditions that informal networks supposedly mitigate may impede resource-strapped people from assisting one another.

Chapter 6

Gendered Networks

Since I was very little I have always known that women and men
do different things, they are supposed to do different things, so
it's not just one thing, it's many. Look, Ceci, we all know that
what men do, women don't, and what women do, men don't.
Men and women were born to do different things. Just look at an
old man and an old woman; they are different, don't you think? A
Salvadoran man and a Salvadoran woman are different. Even
undocumented women and undocumented men are different
[laughs]. So, of course, our lives here [as immigrants] are going to
be very different, even though we're all in the same situation.

Paula A.

The Salvadorans in this study may all face an impoverished context of
reception, but within this general situation, gender affects informal
exchanges in important ways. More often than not, participation in
informal exchanges reflects not only access to goods and benefits and
the social insertion of the people that engage in them but other characteristics as well, including gender. Men and women are positioned
differently vis-à-vis the state and the economy and thus have different
domains of interest and control. As Fernández-Kelly (1990, 184)
notes, gender is political because it contributes to unequal access to
goods on the basis of sexual difference. Thus macrostructural forces
may delineate the constraints and opportunities that immigrants face,
but gender relations shape the way immigrants respond to them
(Hondagneu-Sotelo 1994a). Moreover, cultural norms that regulate
both gender relations and gender-appropriate behavior shape in fundamental ways the informal exchanges of men and women within the
parameters their opportunities afford.

Men and women derive dissimilar benefits from their membership
in networks. Mariken Vaa, Sally E. Findley, and Assitan Diallo (1989)
found in their study of Malians that there were qualitative and quan-
titative differences between what men and women exchanged. The

very nature of networks between men and women has been found to differ. For instance, Karen L. S. Muir (1988) observed among Lao refugees that men tended to create networks in a patron-client fashion, whereas women accomplished everyday tasks without focusing on power or competition but rather on cooperation. Among Finnish women in Canada, Varpu Lindström-Best (1988) found that women tended to form stronger networks than men do; the networks proved invaluable in the women's lives. And Mercedes González de la Rocha (1994, 215) observed among the working-class Mexicans in her Guadalajara study that men's networks are primarily with co-workers and are specialized in the world of work; women's networks, however, are primarily composed of "local" ties, such as neighbors and close relatives, and are aimed at everyday subsistence.

There is also research that documents unequal benefits from networks built along gender lines, with women getting a smaller share of the benefits. For instance, research on the Cuban and Chinese enclaves that controls for gender (Portes and Jensen 1989; Zhou 1992) has revealed that women derive fewer economic advantages from networks with coethnics than do their male counterparts. Furthermore, because women have different access to goods and benefits, they end up with different, often not so highly desirable, resources to help others. And, because of gender ideologies, expectations of help differ for men and women. Informal exchanges thus become gendered processes. In the long run, as Jacqueline Maria Hagan (1998) observes, differences in network dynamics may account for divergences in the social, economic, and legal incorporation of immigrant women and men.

Researchers have documented the highly developed networks among immigrant men, particularly Mexicans (Gamio 1930; Massey et al. 1987; Mines 1981). Also, researchers have long acknowledged the presence of female-centered networks among immigrants, minorities, and impoverished groups (Bott 1957; di Leonardo 1987; Lamphere et al. 1993; Stack 1974; Wetherell, Plakans, and Wellman 1994; Yanagisako 1977). Women have been depicted as the keepers of kin (Wetherell, Plakans, and Wellman 1994, 649) or as performing what Micaela di Leonardo (1987) calls "kinship work." However, observing network dynamics through a gendered lens allows for contrasts that address important questions about the different access to social resources that immigrant men and women have (see Hagan 1998; Ho 1993; and Hondagneu-Sotelo 1994a for gender-inflected research on immigrant social networks).

To assess the fundamentally gendered nature of informal exchanges (not only to analyze the effects of gender as a variable; see Pedraza 1991), it is important first to examine giving and receiving help across genders — between related and unrelated men and women — and within gender, and second to focus on expectations and norms of behavior that govern these exchanges. Also, there are immigration-induced changes with potential effects on how women and men provide and receive help. Although the first deals with the different forms that gender-informed exchanges take and the second with new household arrangements and reconfigurations in families, they both concern how immigrant men and women contribute dissimilarly to and derive different benefits from informal networks of assistance.

Giving and Receiving as Defined by Gender

Relying on already overburdened friends and relatives often led to resentment, and experiences in obtaining and giving assistance frequently turned contentious. As Hondagneu-Sotelo (1994a, 189) observes, "Immigrant social networks are highly contested social resources, and they are not always shared, even within the same family." We have seen that networks are highly specialized; different forms of assistance are expected and come from different people. This is also the case when networks are examined through the lens of gender. Distance of relationship matters here as well; it determines the gender-specific expectations and obligations people have.

I divide the kinds of goods and services that circulated among my informants into two general categories that help us to discern gender differences in these exchanges: those that directly or indirectly involved money (such as loans or gifts or lodging), or services that *became* monetized (such as child care or transportation); and those that required an investment of time but not money (such as information, teaching others the informal requirements of a job or the ropes of daily life in San Francisco, and emotional and moral support).

Cross-Gender Exchanges

Investigating cross-gender exchanges provides a unique opportunity
to capture the different access that men and women have to goods and
services and how gender ideologies shape informal exchanges. The
most salient difference in these exchanges occurs between men and
women who are related to each other, on the one hand, and between
unrelated men and women, on the other. Assistance of different types
(involving both money and time) is expected and actually exchanged
between related men and women. For instance, brothers and sisters
and parents and children expect to (and do) exchange material, financial, and emotional support with one another. In contrast, exchanges
between unrelated men and women (including compadres) generally
are limited to those that have become monetized. For instance,
Amparo A. and her sister Anabel regularly borrow from and lend
money to their brother, who in turn baby-sits for Amparo or gives both
women rides to work if he is available. But Amparo makes it clear that
she could not ask a man who is not a relative for a favor for which she
could not pay because it could lead to serious misunderstandings.

I can't ask my friend from work, even if we are close, to lend me money
because our friendship would be ruined. He would think that I could pay him
back in another way, you know, by having something [a relationship] with
him. So one needs to be careful. Especially me, a single woman, I can't ask
favors from men who are not in my family. Even the godfather of my baby, I
can't ask him for a favor. He gives me rides to take the baby to the sitter. And
I pay him for this because I don't want to owe him anything. I don't care, I
just don't want to owe any men anything. Men take advantage of any little
thing to get what they want.

Virginia M. made it clear to me that she only had female friends.
"Amigas sí, amigos no," she said when I asked her if she had friends in
the area with whom she exchanged favors. When I posed the same
question to Alicia N., she inadvertently said simply, "Yes," but quickly
offered a similar clarification. Amparo, Virginia, and Alicia are not
alone in feeling this way.

On my weekly visit to the food distribution program, I was
approached often by women asking me to give them rides home. The
bundles of food they received were too heavy to carry on the bus

because many of them usually had children and other packages to juggle. I also noticed that there were several men around, most of whom seemed to have their own transportation. I wondered why these women would not ask the men for a ride, and Paula A. explained: "Because those men have other intentions. Look, Ceci, I'll be honest with you. You know how these men [Salvadorans] are. You ask them for a ride, and they want to stay in your house and go to your room. No, it's true. I don't exaggerate. They think that women can pay a favor in another way, you know, by going to bed. I don't ever ask a favor from any of these [men], even if they say they're my friends." Marcela Q. expressed the same distrust, adding, "That's why I told you, I always try to pay for a ride, and if I don't have money, I'd rather walk home, but I won't accept a free ride. Men don't give anything for free."

Thus a favor *needed to become* monetized between unrelated men and women. This was not simply because compatriots with some resources try to make money off others who do not have any (as Mahler [1995a] described, and which also happened in this study) but to avoid unsolicited sexual advances. Paying in cash for a service put both parties on equal footing and assured the women that the men would not use the favor as a bargaining chip. Such expectations permeated practically all transactions between unrelated men and women, even among the married ones, in this context. To avoid any misunderstandings, women would do their best to limit or even avoid altogether accepting favors from unrelated men. Those who did not, as Paula explained, "know what they're getting into. Receiving a favor means agreeing to do something else. Whether they [women] need to or they like it, they know well the consequences of receiving favors from these men."

Linked to this issue was gossip, one of the most widespread forms of social control that hindered exchanges between unrelated men and women. Although it has been argued that gossip may help to maintain and even strengthen friendships (Coates 1989), it can be destructive.[1] For instance, several women expressed concern that if they accepted rides, a loan of money, or emotional support from unrelated men, others would "talk." (I will return to the issue of gossip later in this chapter, when I discuss women-to-women networks, but because gossip also affected exchanges between men and women, it is important in this context also.) Gossip was especially problematic if the threat existed that it could reach relatives (particularly a husband or in-laws) in El Salvador. Marcela Q. said that she tried not to talk with men at all, for fear that people would spread lies about her and ruin her reputation. Her friend Matilde A. was particularly concerned about gossip because her own marriage had been in jeopardy when her husband in El Salvador heard that she was "going around with men here," that she was "loose." Her husband, who had not planned to migrate, decided to make an emergency trip to the United States, only to find out that she was living in a shelter run by nuns and had on occasion asked men to help her move heavy bundles. Matilde explained,

My husband was furious when he was told that I had been seen with men here. He thought that I had become a prostitute and the money I was sending was from my new business. So he felt that he had to come to fix the problem. But I wasn't doing anything wrong. People talk because they have tongues, or they have nothing to do, just watch others and try to harm people. I can't tell you that all women are being good here because there are some that are really loose and go around with men. But I guess one pays for what others do.

The problem in establishing informal networks of assistance between unrelated men and women has to do in part with the limited capacity of women to generate a surplus that would allow them to possess the resources to help others. Although women often work more than men do, they generally earn less than men and consequently have less extra money (and material goods) with which to return favors. Another important aspect of the women's inability to establish reciprocal relations with unrelated men is the cultural prescriptions regarding gender relations that limit women's space of interaction. For women, the expected (and easiest) way to reciprocate a favor is to provide a service such as baby-sitting or doing household chores, sharing information, or even giving moral support; but all these activities require spending time with the person who receives the favor. In this cultural context, when a woman spends time with an unrelated man — whether it is to reciprocate a favor or not — it is not considered "proper" behavior and is sanctioned because it can be easily interpreted as insinuating intimacy.[2]

The men had good bargaining chips in exchanges and were aware of it. They had desirable resources to exchange as well as in-kind services. Generally the men tended to own cars, to have slightly more discretionary income, and, often, to have one of the most precious resources around: legal documents (there were more men than women with some form of documents). Some men openly discussed their advantages when it came time to reciprocate favors with women. Don David M., Chentía A.'s husband, is a case in point.[3] The first time I talked with the couple, they seemed sincerely to care for each other. I had lunch with them in their house, and over the meal they talked as if everything were going well. A couple of months later I saw them at a Christmas party sponsored by a community organization, and again they seemed happy. However, when I had a chance to talk with Chentía alone, she invited me to the house but specifically told me that I should come when Don David was not home. This time Chentía spoke openly about her marriage. It turns out that Chentía had married Don David, twenty-four years her senior, to obtain her residence papers. She had made a previous attempt to get her green card through marriage, but it had failed miserably. This time Chentía thought it would work because she was sure that Don David was a U.S. citizen. Six months into the marriage, however, she discovered that he was a permanent resident (in which case it takes longer to obtain residence documents through marriage). Furthermore, he had already sponsored several family members to get their documents, which Chentía thought would jeopardize her own chances to become legal through him. From there on the marriage took an irreversible turn, and two years later it ended in divorce.

Chentía felt cheated and upset, but Don David, quite sure that he had more bargaining power than Chentía, acted as if he did not care. He warned Chentía that if she left him, there were other young women around who were desperate for a green card, and he could get any of them. In a conversation I had with Don David, he confirmed this and, making a point that there were many women available, added:

I told her, you married me for the papers, not for love. So now you're going to leave without love and without the papers because I will stop the process with the Immigration [INS]. I'll tell them that we're not married anymore, so she won't get her green card. I'll have her deported, you'll see. Me? No, I am in a good position here. I am legal. I have a job, a good truck. I can get married tomorrow if I want to. Women abound here. And I may be old, but I am a good candidate.

However, things did not turn out exactly as Don David had predicted. Chentía was able to apply for and obtain Temporary Protected Status. She also left and divorced Don David and ended up marrying a man ten years her junior, with whom Don David had earlier suspected she had an affair.

Observations and conversations with the men tended to corroborate the women's stories. Some spoke of owning a car as an asset to "get women"; others mentioned that whatever favor they did for women might open up an opportunity to have an affair. It must be remembered that these men's resources did not amount to much, but they were enough to give them some bargaining power in any informal exchanges. I came across one extreme case. One morning, at a community organization, a social worker and I were talking about this situation, and she agreed that it was commonplace and serious. She said that they had found out about a man in his early fifties who would hang out on Mission Street preying on young women who seemed a little disoriented. He would offer them help with locating a job, finding an agency where they could get legal information, or seeking out a clinic (whatever the women's concerns were). He would then take them to his apartment and attempt to rape them. In another case, a friend of Amparo A. told me that she (along with several other young women) had been promised jobs by men who pretended to be their friends. It had turned out that the jobs were as "dance girls" at local bars. Apparently these men were hiring young women to dance with men who frequented the bars alone, and the women would get paid 50 cents per song. However, in this cultural context, the dance sessions were meant to open up opportunities for the men, who expected much more than simply a dance.

The result of all this is that it becomes difficult for women, particularly single ones, to establish the kinds of ties with men — namely, with the other half of the community that commands relatively more resources — that would be beneficial to them. But as we will see later, being unable to obtain assistance from this group provides opportunities, or perhaps even incentives, for women to forge informal ties with others, particularly with other women, and with a wider variety of people, including non-Latinos, through the community organizations. This proves crucial for the women, as these networks allow them access to a wider variety of resources.

The type of domestic work these women perform affects the ties they are able to forge beyond their immediate group. Hagan (1998) observed among the Guatemalan Maya that live-in domestic work confined the women to a limited set of personal networks, and thus their pool of resources decreased. The women in my study who held domestic jobs were not live-in domestics and thus were not cut off from community ties, particularly with local organizations. Another work-related factor that contributes to these women being able to create networks with people in a wider variety of fields was their different labor force experiences, compared to men. One of the most important occurrences in this group, one that carries important repercussions for networks of assistance, is that women tended to find work more easily than men did. It is noteworthy, however, that these women's economic activities represent more continuity than change, for they had been wage earners in El Salvador before they migrated.[4] But the fact that the women were able to find work when the men could not posed serious problems; it represented a situation at odds with expectations of men's and women's financial contributions. It needs to be emphasized, however, that generally women did not earn more than their partners did, because when both men and women worked, the men earned more. Nor is it that women worked full-time — they were seldom able to put together enough hours to earn a full-time income. Also, women's jobs were not stable; that is, the flexibility inherent in the kind of work these women performed often translated into instability. As Victoria O. explained, "Yes, one can get jobs, but it's temporary. Sometimes I work every day, but other times I only work one day a week. Now, for instance, I'm doing well, but if we had talked a year ago, you'd have had a different impression. Can you imagine that I moved three times in five months because I didn't have money to pay for rent? It was awful. So, yes, I have work now, but I have to find more hours. Who knows what will happen next." As Victoria's words illustrate, the ability to find a job does not automatically translate into keeping a job or higher pay. Women can find work with relative ease, but just as easily they can be told not to come back. What is noteworthy, however, is that women are often the major contributors to the family, or even the sole earners (for brief or sometimes extended periods), because men cannot procure stable, well-paid jobs and therefore make only irregular contributions. Of course,

Salvadorans are not an exception here. Instances of women's increasing economic contributions when men's contributions decline have been observed among other immigrant groups (Diner 1983; Kibria 1994; Lamphere 1986). In some cases this has led to conflict in the household (Kibria 1993; Kudat 1982; Lamphere 1987), but my concern here is with the consequences this has for networks of support.

Some of the men in this study, already feeling constrained by their inability to command adequate earnings, and aware of the women's potential to support the household, had responded by diminishing their financial responsibilities. As the men's financial contributions lessened or became highly irregular, the women turned to others, notably to their own informal networks, for help. The women's networks consisted mainly of members of their own family, friends, acquaintances, and, of special importance, wider contacts, such as personalized ties they forged through community organizations or public offices. The case of Chentía A. illustrates how the declining, often erratic contributions of men affected in important ways how women went about creating networks of support. It may also indicate what several women confessed: when men become aware of women's increased financial potential, they willingly decrease their own contributions so as to "get back at them." According to Chentía, her husband, Don David, was taking advantage of her well-paying job ($11 per hour plus benefits) cleaning offices and had decided to leave her on her own financially. Chentía worked the night shift and often needed a ride home at two o'clock in the morning. Don David gave her a ride but always charged her for the gasoline. He would not give her any money for the household expenses, much less any funds to help Chentía's grown children, who were not his. Don David claimed that Chentía had married him "for the papers, not for love," so he felt somewhat entitled to the financial perks of being married to her.

But Chentía, who, in spite of having a more stable (and in her case, a better-paying) job than her current and former husbands, complained that she could not make ends meet and that in the absence of this support she had turned to others, including acquaintances. In her words:

He [Don David] thinks that I can earn, that I have a good job, so he wants me to support him. I always pay him for rides, for anything that should be a favor.

Even if he goes with me to an office or a bank, afterwards, I have to pay for gas, parking, or sometimes he even wants me to invite him to lunch and things like that. So I'm left with nothing. And I have many people who depend on me. I have my children here — they are grown up, but if they need something, I'm here for them. I also have another boy in El Salvador. So I'm always looking here and there for opportunities, for chances to improve, not to just sit with my arms crossed and wait. *Me informo* [I find information]. I learn about jobs, about the food distribution [program], you know, things like that. Just by asking around when I go out, which is not too much, of course.

Her daughter Amparo also complained about men's perceived irresponsibility:

Here they [the men] think, oh, she can [earn] so I don't have to. Why should I help her if she can live on what she makes? It's bad for us women, because one counts on the men's help, but they don't help out. You know, we're poor, any little bit of help is important. But one cannot just sit around looking at the ceiling waiting for the men to help, because one may grow old waiting. I left two children in El Salvador, and they don't ask if I have money or not. They need the money, and it's my responsibility to see where I get it. And my *mommy* always repeats that saying, God says, help yourself, and I will help you. So I try. I look for ways to get ahead. The other day, as I was waiting at the clinic on 24th Street — remember that one? — I started a conversation with the lady who takes information there. And she told me that hotels near the airport need chambermaids. So I went there, and that's where I got a job.

The case of Ana Graciela C. further illustrates this point. Ana Graciela, a shy woman in her mid-twenties, could not study past the fifth grade in her small town in central El Salvador because the teachers had all been kidnapped and disappeared. She had been abandoned in the second trimester of pregnancy by her partner in New York and spoke bitterly about "men's irresponsibility."

It'd be different in El Salvador. He [the partner] wouldn't have left me like this because men are responsible there. Here they don't help out. They behave like children here. One has to take care of them, to help them, instead of the other way around. But, luckily, my cousins told me to come to San Francisco, and they're helping me. And one way I can help them a little bit is by cleaning around the house — you know, they're men — and by bringing this food [from the distribution] every Friday. This has helped me, because the people here [at the food distribution] informed me about WIC and about how I need to take care of myself during my pregnancy. Also, other [women] told me about an apartment that is not as expensive as the one where we now

live, so we'll move in soon. But you have to talk, to ask, to meet others. I'm
not one who goes around chatting with everyone. I don't like to talk too
much, but I know that if I don't ask around, *si no me informo* [if I don't find
out information], things will go very bad for me.

It is possible that the obviously difficult time that both Amparo A.
and Ana Graciela C. are facing might taint their comparisons of how
men behave in El Salvador and in the United States. "Irresponsible
paternity," a term commonly used in El Salvador to refer to the men's
refusal to provide for their out-of-wedlock (sometimes even legiti-
mate, in cases when the parents are divorced) children, has long been
recognized as a serious problem that many women in El Salvador
experience (see Baires et al. 1996). But as these cases indicate, as
women are more pressured to search for "opportunities," they in the
process establish informal ties that will be of benefit to themselves and
to their families as well.

An indirect consequence of the women's increased ability to find
work is that sometimes men turn to drinking, and sometimes it leads
the men to abandon the women. This has a negative impact on the
women's ability to obtain assistance, not only directly from the men,
but also from the men's network of friends and relatives. The case of
Amparo A.'s roommate Rosa is an example of this. Rosa's partner had
resumed drinking. He refused Rosa's plea to join Alcoholics Anonymous, abandoned her in the fifth month of her pregnancy, did not let
her know his whereabouts, and requested that she not bother any of
his friends or relatives. Out of frustration, it seems, because he could
not find a stable job, he had resorted to drinking. Here is how Rosa
interpreted his behavior:

Well, his problem is that I always manage to work. I clean a house here and
there, baby-sit, and sometimes I even help this lady to sell clothes. I do whatever I can. And even if it's little, I earn to be able to buy tortillas, milk, you
know, otherwise we'd go hungry. I go to the food distribution once a week,
and I'm always trying to find ways so that we don't go hungry. He doesn't. He
gets depressed and angry that we came here because we're not doing what
we came here for, to work hard, as we thought. So what does he do? He
drinks, so it's even worse. Tell me, who's going to hire a drunken, ugly man
[laughs]? His brothers used to help us a little, and a friend from our town
[in El Salvador] let us stay with him for a while. But this coward [her partner]
is embarrassed that they'll find out that I'm, yes, supporting him, that he

doesn't have a job, that he can't bring money to the house, that he doesn't give me a hand. So he doesn't want me to contact them. Can you imagine how stupid a man who drinks can get?

Over all, however, the women did not blame the men for their unwillingness to help out but linked their irresponsibility to the lack of economic opportunities they had encountered in the United States. The men, for their part, were not so quick to point out that part of the problem had to do with their own inability to find jobs. They tended to blame the increased "self-assurance" that, according to them, women had gained from living in the United States. They spoke of women becoming libertines, of women shunning the men in their quest to earn more money, of women "not behaving as women should," and of women "having a lot of people to help them." For instance, Don David, Chentía A.'s husband, obviously resentful of Chentía's prospects, had a few bitter words to say about her.

At first, I gave her anything she wanted, but she's capricious. She wants this and that. You know, women become too important here, and they don't want what you give them, they want more and more. In El Salvador women are content with what one gives them, but here no. Here they demand things. So I said [to her], go to hell. I don't give her anything now. Besides, from what I can see, she earns good money and knows a lot of people. In case she's in need, she can go to them. Most of what she wants is things to make her look young, anyway. She's coquettish and wants to impress younger men. I'm not stupid. I wasn't born yesterday. I know what she's up to. I'm not going to help her to do that.

Lilian M.'s son Edwin complained that women become "independent and loose because they think they can do it all on their own." "I don't even think of marrying here," he continued. "Even a decent Salvadoran woman may remain decent for a while, but after three months, they start working, they have money to go out with their friends, and that's the end, they become spoiled. Because they can support themselves, they think they own the world. Plus, this country teaches them bad habits. And so they don't take men seriously. They are self-sufficient, at least they think they are." Priscilla F.'s cousin Rogelio said that when his partner, Marta, and he moved into a studio apartment by themselves, they were not sure they would be able to shoulder the household financial responsibilities alone. But he made an arrangement with Marta. They would go back to share a two-bedroom apartment with his family if the separate living arrangement got too expensive for them, rather than have Marta work more hours. Unfortunately for Rogelio, Marta was not convinced, and as soon as she saw that they could not make it financially, she took up two more houses to clean. This brought Marta's contributions to the household to more than half, which Rogelio did not welcome.

I had talked with her, and I thought it was clear. But no, she became so full of herself that she wouldn't even listen to me. So do you know what I did? I said to her, you want to be on your own? Then do it. And she started to pay for everything. Then she found friends who probably told her that she didn't need me, so she became very busy, working all the time. And then do you know what she did? She told me that since I wasn't helping with the expenses, she didn't see a reason for me to stay with her. So she, the ingrate, she asked me to leave. That's how she paid me for my efforts.

When I met Marta, however, her explanation was different. She said that she never wanted to move back to live with her in-laws because living with them had been hell and that, when it seemed as though they would have to move back with them, she decided to do whatever it would take to avoid it. She went to the job cooperative at a community organization, where she got a job and in addition a contact through which she applied for subsidized housing. Also, and important, through this organization she found a woman's advocacy group that provided her with substantial information about her rights in the United States. She explained, "As a woman, one has rights in this country, over there [in El Salvador] that's a joke. Can you imagine calling the police [in El Salvador] to complain about a husband beating you? It's ridiculous." This information, together with her new job, gave her a sense of security that she was not going to be alone if she needed help: "Women get help here easily. People respond when one is in need. It's different from back there [in El Salvador]."[5] In her eyes, Rogelio was upset because she had humiliated him by establishing an informal network that had permitted her to survive on her own.

Although men and women had different ideas about why men were not more forthcoming with assistance, in my view they might both be right. Women have more economic opportunities in large part as a result of how their legal instability plays out in the local labor market. Women's improved economic position poses a double threat to the men; it undermines the men's social role as the breadwinner and lends more authority to women to make their own decisions. Significantly, women gain knowledge about different institutions and services — often unavailable to men — that further undermines men's status. Men respond (willingly or unwillingly) by diminishing their contributions to women, which further reinforces transformations in gender relations. In these situations, as Patricia Fernández-Kelly and Anna M. García (1990) note, such changes have more to do with the economic vulnerability of men than with the increased economic potential of women. The end result is that women are placed in positions where they become engaged actively in procuring help from others and in establishing efficient networks of support. This benefits the women themselves, as well as others in their families. As the cases above illustrate, the women's networks were composed of a wide variety of people, some with influence and knowledge that proved crucial for these women's lives. Fernández-Kelly (1994) observes that a plurality of linkages increases institutional overlap. Thus the increased heterogeneity in the women's networks proved beneficial in accessing crucial goods and services. Had they relied solely on immediate sources of support, these women might have been cut off from access to key resources for such transformations in their lives.

A related characteristic of these informal ties is that social networks may or may not be shared by the man and the woman. For instance, Bott (1957) proposes that couples may share a social network (and perceive each other as partners) in direct relation to how they divide tasks at home. In the cases I came across, I did not observe this relationship directly, but I did notice a greater tendency among couples who were legally married to talk more about (and use) common networks than among those in consensual unions, regardless of the distribution of household tasks. With some exceptions, partners who were married would sometimes point out that a person had helped *them*, or that *they* did not want to bother someone else with a favor, or would use phrases such as "We need a ride for so and so." This may be a way to express the oneness that is expected in a conjugal unit, and being in a legal one — which carries social prestige associated with middle-class standing — these women might have wished to get this point across. Among couples in consensual unions, these forms of speech were less common.

Women's Networks

Extensive research has revealed that poor women engage in intricate networks of exchange that provide them with crucial means of support (Bott 1957; González de la Rocha 1994; Joseph 1983; Lamphere, Silva, and Sousa 1980; Lomnitz 1985; Nelson 1978–1979; Obbo 1980; O'Connor 1990; Stack 1979). As the cases discussed earlier demonstrate, many of the women I met engaged in enduring informal exchanges with other women, both relatives and friends.

There were differences in the kinds of assistance that were expected and actually exchanged between related and unrelated women, as more material and financial help was expected (and received) from relatives.[6] But often these forms of help were also exchanged between friends. Thus women, related and unrelated alike, loaned each other money, shared housing, looked after other women's children, and informed one another about matters that ranged from job tips to housing vacancies and legal and health services. For instance, Amparo A. told me that without her mother's help, both material and moral, she felt she could not survive in the United States. "It is natural that I would find so much support in her, she's my mother. She's my *paño de lágrimas* [literally, the handkerchief on which I shed my tears]. And she's with me in good and in bad times." She added that she could not have expected the same level of support from another woman, particularly if they were not related. Ileana A. and her sister Carolina (whose older sister sponsored their legal immigration) also expressed the same views and said that they felt much closer to their sister than to their brother. "For us, our sister is like our mother, we're very close and open with her. We confide in her. You know, she's a woman too. We can tell her things that we can't tell our brother. It's different with him. But no, not just because she's a woman, but she's our sister too, and whatever we tell her, it'll stay in the family. We can't be like this with a stranger."

Notwithstanding these views about the importance of assistance within the family, unrelated women shared resources with other women, and they were quick to establish reciprocal ties. Invariably, at the food distribution program, at the job cooperative, at legalization workshops, outside church, or any other place where women had an opportunity to gather and talk, they would engage in informative conversations about different topics and would actually exchange favors. At the food distribution, while waiting their turn to get their food, Chentía A. and her daughter Amparo got information about legal services that eventually led them to obtain Temporary Protected Status. Marcela Q. found a place to live in a shelter run by nuns for her friend Matilde A. and asked me for a ride to take her to apply for WIC. And I overheard Amparo encouraging Ana Graciela C. to apply for WIC while she was pregnant, emphasizing the importance of good nutrition for a pregnant woman. Amparo A.'s roommate confided that often she shared her prescribed birth control pills with those who cannot afford them; she usually had enough to give out because she — and the friends she gave the pills to — would only take them on days they had sex. Lety R. and her sister coached Matilde A. on how to use San Francisco's transportation system more efficiently and cheaply. At the community organizations, while waiting their turn to speak with assistance workers, women also made informal arrangements for baby-sitting.

Often women offered each other unsolicited advice too. The women Elvira M. met at a community organization — two of them eventually became her housemates — while waiting to speak with a case worker had done just that. Elvira is a woman in her thirties who came from a rural town in eastern El Salvador (she is the only illiterate person in this study). She was determined to deliver her baby at home and without anyone's help, as she had done with her previous four children in El Salvador. "It's too embarrassing for me to have people watching me have a baby — that's a private thing for a woman. I don't let anyone watch me," she explained to me. Her friends insisted that she go to a hospital this time, particularly because the doctor had told her that she had slightly high blood pressure and therefore might have complications with the birth. Although the doctor could not convince Elvira, the female friends she met at the community organization finally did, and she delivered the baby in the hospital.

As demonstrated in earlier research (O'Connor 1990; Porter Benson 1983; Zavella 1985), women's networks are particularly efficient for job-related matters. Many times women would recommend each other to prospective employers for cleaning or baby-sitting jobs,

share tips on how to do the job and negotiate the terms of employment, and warn one another about employers' practices that they
found somewhat peculiar or undesirable.[7] These informal networks,
similar to those of the sales clerks in Susan Porter Benson's (1983)
study, socialized the women into the work culture. For instance, during the baptism celebration of Marcela Q.'s daughter, Claudia, I overheard her cousin Sonia and one of Marcela's friends discussing at
length how to make a house look "cleaner than it actually is," in effect,
how to make a good impression. "This," Sonia assured the woman,
"will get you a raise, but better yet, another house [to clean] because
they recommend you that way, they go by what they see you do. You
won't kill yourself cleaning, you'll just make it look as if you do. It's
your best job recommendation." She added that the woman needed to
be careful with the detergents and other cleaning aids. "You'll see the
409, that's how they call it — that's for cleaning, not for washing. The
first time I ever used it, I washed the lady's socks with it. She
screamed no, no, no! I don't know what she said, but she was laughing.
Remember that." On another occasion, Amparo A. shared stories
about her life as a live-in domestic with her next-door neighbor, who
was preparing to leave for her own new job as a live-in.

At the house of the Indians, I didn't like their food. I lost like twenty-five
pounds there. It's better to bring your own food because you never know
what they eat. Then I worked for an American couple, and I thought, oh, they
eat food that I know, like hamburgers. But no, all they ate was these leaves —
they were vegetarian! Imagine! So I tell people [women], be careful.
Americans are nice; they smile when you don't understand them. They don't
get upset, but they are delicate. So you have to see what they like and what
they don't like. I always advise people [women] who work in houses.
Especially the new ones [newcomers] because they know nothing about how
Americans live.

For all the sharing that went on among women, their interactions
cannot be romanticized, for friction and conflict often accompanied
their relationships, which illustrates the complexity of these networks;
they may provide grounds for cooperation but at the same time breed
conflict. This tended to happen when women became aware of the
power that came from having more experience in the United States —
in terms of knowledge about work and of daily life in general. Similar
to the Mexican women who were apprentices of other Mexicans in

Hondagneu-Sotelo's study (1994b), some of my informants experienced exploitation from more seasoned compatriots. For instance, a veteran of domestic work in San Francisco had promised Rosa María B., who had arrived a few months before, that she would "give her a couple of houses to clean" in exchange for a week's work. This woman had made it sound very appealing and had told Rosa María that she would also learn the ropes of domestic work, which according to this woman was "very difficult and serious." At the end of a week's work, Rosa María was disheartened because the woman told her that she was "unfit for domestic work because people who get tired can't do this kind of work." Rosa María explained that she was indeed quite exhausted because it had been a grueling ten-hour-a-day workweek, and she felt this woman had taken advantage of her. Rosa María asked the woman for some monetary compensation because the woman had refused to "give her the houses." However, the woman said that paying had never been part of the deal. Lety R.'s story is similar. Her subcontractor had taken Lety to live in her house but had her sleep on the floor and pay for her own food. At the end of the week Lety got paid, but only $10 a day instead of the $35 she had been promised.

An important aspect of exchanges among women was the moral and emotional support they obtained from them. More than men, women, it seemed, had license to share personal concerns and worries with each other. But this was a very delicate issue, as it could quickly turn into an opportunity for gossip, which permeated women's relations and sometimes interfered with their ability to establish enduring networks of support.[8] For instance, Marcela Q.'s friendship with Amparo A. was temporarily disrupted because Amparo had heard that Marcela was spreading rumors about Amparo's new boyfriend, who had been Marcela's suitor at an earlier point. Amparo and Marcela would exchange baby-sitting occasionally. So, during their rift, Marcela was left with no one to turn to for this kind of help because she said she did not trust anyone else with her baby (most of these women only trusted relatives or people they knew well with their children). Her neighbor Doña Berta had started to charge her for baby-sitting, which Marcela could not afford and was upset about. Paula A. had broken her friendship with a neighbor with whom she had a good relationship; they had regularly done favors for each other. They had taken care of each other's children, and the woman had even lent Paula a bus pass when she did not have money for the fare. According to Paula, the woman had found what seemed to be birth control pills on Paula's side of the kitchen counter at the shelter and had spread the rumor that Paula was probably engaged in a sexual relationship, which Paula vehemently denied, particularly because her boyfriend was in Canada. This, Paula said, infuriated her. It led her to break all ties with this woman, even though she recognized that she would lose an important source of support. Other women had similar experiences, and some went so far as to assure me that they had no friends at all. Chentía A. told me that she did not know anyone in her apartment complex, that she only said "hola y adiós" (hello and good-bye) to people, mostly to avoid gossip. At one point Chentía's daughter Amparo had suggested to her that to complement their incomes they could sell Avon products to friends or neighbors. Chentía refused on the grounds that "one doesn't do business with friends, *uno termina peleado* [one ends up having a dispute], one loses both the business and the friendship." Besides, she argued, she had no friends to sell the products to. Several others acknowledged that although avoiding ties with other women would probably mean (they were not always sure) losing support, they preferred the tranquility of living without gossip. Interestingly both Barton J. Hirsch (1979) and Brian L. Wilcox (1981) found that lower-density networks (i.e., less interconnectedness among network members) are associated with positive adjustment among women who are undergoing major life transitions.

Although the women made a point of letting me know that they used their free time at home alone or with their families, in reality they spent quite a bit of time in public places. I often saw them taking their children to clinics (an activity commonly relegated to women) and frequenting assistance centers to obtain food, clothing, and information about housing and community programs, among other things. The women often phrased their activities as "I'm not a person who likes to be out on the street," or "Estoy acostumbrada a estar en la casa" (I'm used to being at home), or "It's not me to be out" and "No me hallo en la calle" (I feel uncomfortable to be out in the street). As other researchers have noted, these notions equate women with the "private" and men with the "public" (Georges 1990, 20; Pessar 1995, 40; Rouse 1989, 134) and are linked to cultural norms governing sexuality (Prieto 1992, 197). In the Salvadoran immigrants' cultural milieu, it was important to reaffirm the women's position at home, as if to counteract reality, because in fact they spent a substantial amount of time outside the home either working or dealing with their own or their families' matters.

Public places provided ample opportunities for women to talk with one another, to exchange information and advice,[9] even to console and comfort one another, but also to gossip. Because these women were in regular contact with community organizations and other public places, it also gave them access to information beyond their immediate surroundings. Invariably, the women mentioned that they had heard, through word of mouth or just by being around these places, information about job networks and about many aspects of their lives, including their legal rights. Alicia N. had heard that her daughter could obtain prenatal care at a local clinic, though she lacked documents. Lolita Q. and Lety R. had located "North American" employers there, who put them in touch with friends in the "Avenues,"[10] who later hired them as live-in domestics. Amparo A. and Marcela Q. also learned quite a lot about their legal rights (or in Edwin M.'s view, the "bad habits" that the United States teaches women).[11] Although she is undocumented, Amparo exercised her legal rights and took her partner (whom she later married) to court because he had not provided child support in several months. Marcela Q. threatened to take her landlord to court when she demanded a full month's rent despite the fact that the electricity had been out for most of the month in the garage that she was renting. In fact, Marcela and Lolita had found so much informal help in community organizations that they assured me — echoing others — that "it's easier for women to be helped in this country. One doesn't go hungry here, there's always help for women."

Women actively sought resources in community organizations because they were often in charge of those family needs for which the community organizations could provide assistance. In turn, these contacts increased considerably the women's informal network of assistance, and they became particularly adept at using outside resources. Kibria (1993) observed a similar situation among Vietnamese-Americans, among whom women's networks became diversified as a result of their newly assumed responsibilities in resettlement. Indeed, I would argue, as Hondagneu-Sotelo (1994a, 174) does, that women are drawn into various organizations and social interactions because of their families and become key players in different forms of community building.

Men's Networks

Although my observations about the networks of men are more limited, I had several conversations with men that allow me to sketch their informal exchanges. Similar to the women, men (friends and relatives) also engaged in enduring exchanges with other men. They too taught one another about life in the United States, informed one another about jobs and housing, and, in general, shared vital resources. But there are some important differences between men and women that point to segmented access to goods and benefits. As in the case of women, gender ideologies shape in important ways how men exchange favors with one another. For instance, whereas men would talk about how they had either lent or borrowed money from other men or had allowed other men to stay in an apartment during hard times, they rarely mentioned issues related to moral or emotional support. This was especially interesting because in our conversations they usually talked openly about such matters and would tell me that at times they had felt depressed, nostalgic, or simply lonely.[12] But they also intimated that although they did not talk frankly about these feelings with male friends or relatives, they had often sought their company in the hope that doing something together would dissipate their pain. Marvin C. explained it as follows:

It's tough to be here, one feels lonely, [one] gets depressed, sad, very sad, and one gets a feeling from deep down that makes you want to give up everything. So what I do is read my Bible or I go out, go visit cousins or friends. And we watch TV together — a good soccer match gets your mind off of things [laughs]. One gets distracted that way. But no, I'm not going to talk like in a soap opera about what I feel, that sometimes I have cried when I'm alone. No, that'll be terrible. They [my friends] will think that there's something wrong with me, you know, that I'm from the other team [gay].

Others said that although they sometimes told their friends they were nostalgic, they tried not to dwell on it, so that they would not be perceived as weak.

Through their male friends and relatives, many of the men had access to resources that the women did not. Unlike the women, men could often obtain favors from other men without having to pay for the service.[13] In part, this had to do with the fact that men had control over relatively more material resources than women did, which allowed them to exchange goods with others. It also can be linked to gender ideologies that do not permit women to exchange favors with men openly. For instance, the nature of compensation that was expected when an exchange took place between unrelated people of the same gender was different when it happened across genders. This served to build enduring networks, albeit of a different kind, among men. Thus, in terms of transportation (a highly desirable and "typically" men's resource), the men who owned cars could give rides to other men and in return obtain a valuable favor.[14] Or they could even lend their cars to others and obtain an even more desirable favor in return. Ricardo R.'s cousin owned a pickup truck and would often give rides to Ricardo and a friend who worked at a nearby Burger King. Ricardo's cousin never charged them, but when he needed a favor, he knew he could count on Ricardo (at least) for help, especially when it was a favor that had to do with the pickup, like running out of gas or locking himself out. On two such occasions Ricardo and his friend went to his rescue. They would also help out when the pickup needed repairs. Ricardo told me (and I had the opportunity to observe) that they could easily spend an entire afternoon working on the car, which, according to him, was also a form of pastime. From what I observed and heard, these "work sessions" also served to strengthen bonds between men because they provided them with opportunities to talk, to exchange information, and to meet others.

As in the case of women, men also obtained information about jobs from other men, which proved to be quite beneficial. For instance, Roberto C. was in a desperate situation because he had been out of work for three months, and his family in El Salvador kept asking him for money so that his children could buy school supplies and uniforms. "Chepe," a Salvadoran friend, was working as a cook at an Italian restaurant and told Roberto that he should learn how to cook in case someone quit. On slow days and when the owners of the restaurant were not around, Roberto dutifully learned how to make pasta. One day, after about three weeks of off-and-on informal training, one of the Mexican cooks called in sick, and Chepe told the owners that he had a friend who could fill in. The owners were so impressed that Roberto already knew how to "make pasta in seventy different ways" (as Roberto explained) that they hired him (at a slightly lower hourly rate) and let the ill cook go.[15]

Roberto confessed that he would always be grateful to Chepe, and whenever Chepe needed a favor he would always be there to help. Indeed, Roberto has already reciprocated; he has been a good friend who has listened to Chepe's problems and complaints and tried to give him advice. Gilberto F.'s brother-in-law introduced him to a German landlord who hired him as a handyman. In addition, this brother-in-law provided Gilberto with some important tips about the trade, plus advice on how to deal with pay (they worked on a day basis) and over-time. A Salvadoran friend of Ricardo R.'s recommended him for a job washing dishes in a cafeteria where the friend worked. In addition, this man taught Ricardo how to do the job and a little bit about "American culture," which, Ricardo was certain, greatly facilitated his dealings with both bosses and patrons at the cafeteria. And a Nicara-guan friend of Marcela Q.'s husband told him about an opening as a helper in a nearby Italian bakery.

Informal ties between men also have an underside — the potential to become abusive. The practice of finding apprentices, as with women, tends to benefit those who subcontract more than those who are hired. For instance, a friend recruited Alejandro M. to work on a construction team. Alejandro worked as a "helper" painting empty apartments, but in spite of ten- to twelve-hour workdays, he could only command $20 per day. Alejandro quit after ten days on the job and lost the friendship as well. In the case of José C., a friendly man with an eighth-grade education from a city in western El Salvador, a friend of his brother-in-law — whose brother owned an auto body shop — took him to work. He was given a one-month "probationary period," during which he was supposed to work without earning.[16] He was eventually hired but recognized that the owner, a Nicaraguan, was taking advantage of him. In his words: "This is the only job that I have had, and the owner knows that I need it, so he makes me work; *me saca el jugo* [lit., he squeezes me, meaning he gets his money's worth]. I install car stereos, I repair signs, I paint cars, and when I'm finished, I have to clean the whole place. I can't complain because without papers there's not much I can do, and, besides, the situation [for jobs] here doesn't allow for one to be too choosy." In addition, he said he felt that other Latinos, including his compatriots, were taking advantage of newcomers and that it was a practice that might be perpetuated. "At first I lied, I told him [the boss] that I had been here for some time, because if I had told him that I came a few months ago, it'd be even worse. They treat us [newcomers] like garbage, because we don't know what's going on. The problem is that one may feel the same way and treat more recent [newcomers] like this, and on and on. It'll never stop. We Latinos don't care. If one gets ahead, who cares about the others? That's how we are."

Whereas many of the women who were either out of a job and looking for work or working part-time would frequent community organizations, many of the men in the same predicament spent time at "corners" — with other day laborers — looking for jobs. These places allowed the men to exchange important information about jobs, housing, and daily life in San Francisco. These were also places where men from the same hometown would run into each other, not always a pleasant surprise. Such encounters sometimes proved embarrassing, because searching for work at "the corner" was usually seen as a last resort. Also, from what I learned, these corners were far from being bastions of camaraderie, as there was sometimes fierce competition for jobs. To be sure, there were informal agreements and intricate arrangements on how to negotiate jobs, so as not to upset the delicate balance at these sites, and the process was far from utter disarray and chaos. Nonetheless, the men competed and would sometimes undermine one another's dealings with prospective employers in ways that would sometimes cost them jobs.

An efficient way for men to establish networks with other men was through sports clubs, which, as researchers have suggested, provides one of the most important mechanisms of community integration in the United States (Massey et al. 1987). Soccer and baseball clubs provide male members with a range of assistance, from information about housing and jobs to arrangements for sharing rides to even moral support. Marvin C.'s roommate got in touch with a baseball team made up of Nicaraguans, Salvadorans, and a few Puerto Ricans through a Salvadoran friend he had met at the English-language school. When Marvin needed a job, this roommate asked his teammates, and one of them put him in touch with a Salvadoran man who owned a business repairing hardwood floors. Edwin M. also was introduced to a soccer team through a classmate at the language school. In his case, the team opened up opportunities to socialize, which Edwin had been missing since he arrived in the United States, even though he came to join his immediate family. He spends time with his teammates; they watch sports on TV together, invite each other to parties, and "hang out" on weekends. Mauricio A. found a good deal on a used car (and later help to repair it) through his teammates in a soccer club. And José C. found housing to share with a teammate in a soccer club. José's family, with whom he was living, had to move into a smaller apartment and told him that he could not go with them. Although the teammate lived in a two-bedroom apartment with six others, José was invited to move in too. "Since we're all men, it doesn't matter how many share a room," he explained.

Although men have several channels through which they can establish enduring informal networks with other men and they have access to somewhat more desirable resources, which allows them to more readily reciprocate favors, most of these networks are composed of compatriots or other Latino men living in the same ambit. Consequently, these networks do not allow them access to goods and services beyond their immediate group. These networks are homogeneous; everyone seemed to be in the same situation and had access to the same kinds of information and resources. The information they exchanged allowed them to survive — often by finding jobs — on a day-to-day basis, but it did not serve to establish links through which they, or their families, could obtain access to goods that in the long run might prove more useful. As the case of Rosa indicated, sometimes these men's networks had an unintended negative consequence for other family members. Whereas these ties provided the men with material and emotional help, they also opened up ample opportunities for the men to get together to drink — which the women (as well as other family members) despised.

New Families in the United States and Networks of Assistance

The Salvadorans with whom I came in contact had gone through many changes in their lives. The new context posed challenges not only to their identity as individuals but also to their identity as members of their immediate social groups. As a result of immigration, families sometimes disintegrate, but in their place new ones are formed. In fact, it has been observed that the changes in the structure of the family that occur with migration may not be directly related to a "change in values" but to the separation of families (Keefe 1979). Thus my informants assumed positions as mothers, fathers, children, siblings, and in-laws in newly reconfigured families. Such arrangements and rearrangements have important repercussions for networks of assistance — particularly those based on kinship — with dissimilar consequences for men and women. As the family composition changes, so do the people who constitute networks of assistance and the goods to which they have access.

To be sure, the changes among the families that I discuss here are not unique to this group. Ever since Thomas and Znaniecki (1927) explored issues of social disorganization among Polish immigrants, researchers have devoted considerable time to this topic. However, I am not talking about the kind of "social disorganization" that Thomas and Znaniecki observed, but about particular social formations that emerge as a result of immigration. A central point here is the immigration-specific circumstances that have prompted many of these immigrants to establish different family arrangements in the United States. For many Salvadorans, it is still difficult to travel back and forth regularly to visit family back home. This is related to their legal instability in the United States, further aggravated by the perilous and costly journeys they would have to undertake as undocumented immigrants. Although the immigrants' presence is constantly felt in their homes in El Salvador through the substantial remittances and gifts they send, through letters, telephone calls, and lately even through video conferences, families are still physically separated for undetermined periods. These circumstances have facilitated the creation or rearrangement of families in the new context. During this time of separation, it is not uncommon for these immigrants to form new unions in the United States, mostly *acompañándose* (cohabiting) with partners who often have children from previous unions. This practice is slightly more common among people who are in consensual unions than among the legally married. Notably, this pattern might not have first emerged in the United States. As discussed in chapter 2, historically, among rural, poor (mostly landless) men in El Salvador who made a living as seasonal agricultural workers, it was not uncommon to form new unions in the places where they went to work, given the difficulty of uprooting entire families (Menjívar 1992).

Although by no means all Salvadoran families undergo profound transformation that leads to rearrangement or dissolution, these instances come up with enough frequency to warrant discussion (more than one-third of my informants were, or had been at some point, in a U.S.-reestablished union). The consequences of these rearrangements are not limited to kinship networks but extend to the access (or lack thereof) that men and women have to sources outside the family through networks with kin. Priscilla F. is a case in point. Joining her mother in San Francisco, she confirmed what she had been told back home. Her mother and father were no longer together, and her mother was living with a new partner. Priscilla's family on her father's side was upset at Priscilla's mother, because in their eyes she should have made a greater effort to maintain the relationship with Priscilla's father. As a result, this side of Priscilla's family was estranged, and when she arrived she could not easily get in touch with them. She was particularly disappointed because on her father's side she had several cousins and other relatives who had been in the United States for a long time and, according to Priscilla, were in a good position to at least guide her in San Francisco.

After many attempts, Priscilla obtained the telephone number of one of her cousins from her grandmother in El Salvador. Although these relatives did not respond as Priscilla had expected, they at least gave her very useful information. One cousin told her about an English-language school (where I met her), and another one told her about a waitress job opening at a Mexican restaurant. Priscilla thought that if it had been her brother requesting their help, they would have responded differently. "They would have given him more help because he's my father's only son, and they want him to be on good terms with them. With me it's different. But at least they helped me in finding a job and a school. So I'm grateful." Ironically, when Priscilla's brother arrived, it was she who taught him about daily life in San Francisco and supported him for a while, partly because the brother did not get along with her mother's new partner, but also because Priscilla felt she had gained the experience necessary to guide him.

In Elvira M.'s case, her immediate network changed radically when she decided not to accompany her husband to Washington, D.C., when he moved there. Although Elvira was pregnant, she opted for staying behind, arguing that she would not like the weather in Washington; she had heard that it snowed there. Though not completely surprised, I still found this reason a bit peculiar. The next time I saw her I pressed a bit more to find out why she had stayed and the consequences this would have for her. Without discarding her fear of the snow, she expressed a more powerful reason. She explained that she had been able to obtain baby-sitting jobs through an employer she had met at a community organization, and she felt she could support herself and be able to remit a little if she kept working at about the same pace after her baby was born. "Why would I want to venture in other places when I am more or less established here? I've heard that it snows there. I don't know if I can survive that. He's leaving because he can't find work here and he's been told that it's easier to get a job in Washington without papers. I don't know about that, I don't know why he's so sure. So I'm staying. I think he'll be back because he won't find what he's been told." Staying behind meant that Elvira would not have access to her husband's network of relatives and friends, but it also meant that she would reinforce the ones she had established on her own. She was sharing an apartment with three other Salvadoran women, one of whom she had met in one of the houses where she worked; they let Elvira stay there for free, and Elvira looked after the women's children in exchange.

The case of María del Carmen C. further illustrates the effects of long-term separation on networks of support and the double standard to which Priscilla F. alluded. María del Carmen, a woman in her late twenties who only managed to finish the first grade in her village in eastern El Salvador, arrived in San Francisco to meet her husband, whom she had not seen in almost three years. Her trip had been paid for by her husband, who had labored hard to save the necessary $1,800. But the journey had been particularly taxing for María del Carmen because she was four months pregnant when she traveled. Obviously, María del Carmen's husband was not the father of the baby and was furious about her pregnancy. María del Carmen explained, "I never thought I'd ever see him again, because since he left he only sent money three times, at the beginning, and I even thought that he had died. So I accepted this other man who was after me." Her husband asked María del Carmen to leave his house, but she had no one to turn to in San Francisco, except for relatives of her husband. One of his cousins let her stay with her, but when this cousin found out that María del Carmen's husband "had nothing to do with the pregnancy," she told her that she was welcome to stay but that she had to sleep on the floor. This proved very uncomfortable because María del Carmen was seven months pregnant by then. She was only able to stand this situation for two weeks.

One morning María del Carmen met a neighbor on the steps of the building where she was staying, who told her about the food distribution program, where María del Carmen met, among other people, Marcela Q. Marcela eventually put María del Carmen in touch with nuns who ran a shelter for single mothers (this was the second person that Marcela had referred to the nuns). María del Carmen had the baby while she stayed at the shelter, and though she had found a few supportive people along the way, she still was at a loss about what she would do next. She especially missed her husband's family because they had always lent her a hand. But she recognized that she had done something "that a woman is not forgiven for." She added, "If I were a man, it'd be different because that's acceptable in a man, to have children with other women. They do that all the time. But a woman, no, one makes a mistake like that and one is dead. Nobody wants to have anything to do with you anymore. But believe it or not, I feel that my conscience is clean; it may seem crazy, but it's true. It's not all my fault."

Virginia M.'s niece Regina's story is a bit different, for in her case a new kinship network gave her access to more benefits. Regina, a thirty-year-old from San Salvador with a high school diploma, had been married for four years when her husband left for the United States because he had been active as a union organizer and had received death threats. Regina and their baby daughter stayed behind, but she had regular contact with her husband during the two years they were separated. Her husband, Tulio, also a high school graduate in his thirties, used to send money sporadically, as he had a hard time trying to pay off the debts he incurred for the trip and for his bail (he had been detained by the INS). At Regina's insistence, Tulio agreed that she and their little girl would come to join him in San Francisco.

When Regina arrived in San Francisco and saw Tulio's lifestyle, she became upset, for he was living with several men in a small apartment and drank regularly in their company. She demanded that they move out; she was particularly concerned about the little girl living in that place "with all those men." Although Tulio disagreed, he did not expect that Regina would take the initiative to move out. Regina was especially vexed with Tulio's drinking and wanted him to join Alcoholics Anonymous, but Tulio categorically refused. She moved into an apartment that she shared with a family, and she cleaned and baby-sat for them. On weekends she also cleaned other houses.

Later Regina met a Nicaraguan man who offered to help her legalize her status and to provide financial support for her toddler daughter. Eventually they married. In retrospect, Regina said that she would not have been able to do much with Tulio because he did not want to stop his drinking and make future plans.

He lives in the past, he thinks that getting together with a bunch of drunken guys on weekends is the good life. With him [the new husband] it is different. He is *emprendedor* [enterprising], and we'll do something in this country. Look, for example, through his mother I got a job in the store; now I don't clean houses, I am a sales clerk. I will also *arreglar mis papeles* [fix my papers, meaning legalize her status] because he's a [permanent] resident. So I'm providing a better future for my girl. It's not just me benefiting, it's also her. [His] sister is teaching me a little bit of English and will lend me her cassettes [from a mail-order English-language course] to learn more. She has told me that she'll show me where the girl can go to school. I'm much better now than I was with Tulio. I feel different. I feel as if I have entered a different world.

It is worth noting that the women depicted in these stories were pivotal in procuring assistance for others in their families. As their marital unions faded, they forged new relationships and formed new networks that put benefits within reach of other family members. It was the women who actively sought to establish new contacts and create new informal arrangements for exchanges. These were not, however, exclusively women-to-women networks — which are not uncommon among immigrants (Kossoudji and Ranney 1984) — because the ties these women established made opportunities available to both men and women in their families. Interestingly too, the new arrangements that women initiated did not challenge gender stereotypes. Thus, even though Priscilla succeeded in her contacts with her father's side of the family and later helped her brother, Elvira opted not to join her husband, and Regina's decisions eventually led to more options for her family, these actions did not fundamentally alter gender ideologies within their families. Within the limits that gender ideology imposes, however, women forged vital ties for the good of their families.

Although women often created important ties through which family members benefited, it should not be inferred that they acted altruistically and were always available to help anyone around them. Sometimes, if the women perceived that helping someone out would eventually result in a negative outcome for them, they would do what it took to stop it. For instance, when Paula A. discovered that her fiancé was thinking about lending $250 to a cousin for the purchase of a used truck, she immediately stopped it. She said that a problem with her fiancé was that he was very *confiado* (trusted others easily), which is why she thought he could never save money for them.

> Can you believe it? He said, oh, so and so needs money, and I want to lend it to him because he doesn't have anyone else. And I said to him, and you, do you have anyone else, do you have people to lend you money whenever you feel like borrowing? No, right? So what do you think you're doing? He'll never pay you back because he [the cousin] is as *acabado* [without any money] as we are. He [my fiancé] sometimes tells me that I'm bad, that I don't want to help. I'm not a bad person, I'm just careful.

Union dissolution and family reconstitution also had important effects on the lives of men. For instance, Carlos R.'s wife went back to El Salvador because there they had left a daughter who was epileptic and needed more care. The wife's plan was that she would go back only temporarily, but due to more difficult conditions of travel and more expensive trips by land, she ended up staying there for much longer than anticipated. Meanwhile, Carlos remitted regularly to his family. But as time passed and his wife did not return, Carlos *se acompañó* — he started cohabiting with another woman — and they eventually married. One important, though not the only, consideration for Carlos was that this woman was a legal resident and he needed to regularize his status. His new partner had been in the United States for a long time, but her children were still in El Salvador in the care of her mother. Carlos and his new wife kept their finances strictly separate, mostly because of their responsibilities to their own families. In

Carlos's perception, this new wife had many advantages over his previous one. His new wife was not only a legal resident, but because she was "chatty and would get into everything, meet people, very sociable," she also had been able to establish a good network that was useful for job contacts and information about assistance from community organizations. Thus, through her, Carlos was able to obtain permanent residence, and whenever he was out of work, his wife would mobilize her contacts to find him a job. Also, she would bring food from the distribution program, which was invaluable help when their financial problems were acute. One of her employers advised Carlos to collect recyclable materials and sell them to increase his income. Carlos undoubtedly benefited from the networks that his new wife had created.

Carlos's first wife, however, was anxious to return to the United States. She was unaware of her husband's new wife, as Carlos kept on remitting and communicating with her regularly, never mentioning his situation. Carlos and his second wife had constant disagreements, some arising from their separate financial obligations, so when he was sure that his first wife was indeed planning to return, he decided to leave his second wife. As he said, "My true wife was going to come back, and I would have been in major trouble if she had found out I was living with, well, married [laughs] to someone else. The one from here was good, but the mother of my children is more important. I feel more secure with the one I've been with for most of my life." When Carlos's "true wife" returned, she was able to begin the process of regularizing her status because Carlos was now legal. In addition, she took advantage of the network of information that Carlos had been able to access through his second wife. He had met a couple of families who used to collect soda cans and glass bottles for him. One of these families hired his first wife to clean their house. Carlos's "true wife" later found out about his relationship in her absence, and though she initially was beside herself, she eventually accepted it as an inevitable consequence of leaving a man on his own for a long time. Besides, Carlos had managed to convince her that the marriage had been purely a business agreement for him to obtain a green card, an explanation that Carlos confessed was only partially true.

Carlos's story points out an important aspect of these arrangements. Usually when partners had children from a previous union their obligations and responsibilities would pull them in different directions. This certainly runs contrary to idealized notions of immigrant — or sometimes of poor — families in which members supposedly pool incomes for the benefit of all. Marcela Q., who has three children from a previous marriage, married Ramón, who had two children of his own. When Marcela needs an emergency loan (usually to send money to her two children still in El Salvador), she hesitates to ask Ramón because she is well aware of his difficult financial situation. She cannot borrow from her cousins because their help has been so erratic and qualified that she does not feel comfortable asking them for a favor, so she usually ends up borrowing the money from a good friend. Lolita Q.'s roommate's new partner does not care much for her family, which further complicates her efforts to help them. She tries to remit on a regular basis, but when her brother asked her for help to come to the United States, her partner said no. Despite his opposition, she sent her brother money so that he could make the trip, but the brother now lives in Los Angeles with other relatives and not in San Francisco with his sister, as they both would have preferred.

Sometimes informal ties with in-laws were not severed as a result of a separation, and these people continued to provide help. Rosa María B. said she gets along much better with her (female) in-laws now than when she was with her partner. Her former sister-in-law, who had gossiped about Rosa María when she was acompañada with her brother, even allowed her to stay with her when she was threatened with eviction for not having paid the rent on time. Rosa María's former mother-in-law, whom she used to detest, now baby-sits for her when she needs such help. Rosa María says that things are much easier now because her former partner is not involved in their negotiations. She and her in-laws can talk directly to each other instead of through him, which, in her eyes, facilitates all forms of communication and assistance. In addition, Rosa María stressed, "They see what a hard worker I am, they see my efforts and sacrifices, and they see that I am a decent woman." This was an important point to make, for if her former partner's family had suspected that she was dating another man or even just going out with friends, they would not have behaved in the same way.

In other cases, networks with a partner's, or a husband's, extended families disintegrated as conjugal units faded. For instance, Marcela

Q. did not keep in touch with her ex-husband's family, although eventually she and her first husband reestablished an amicable relationship, "because of the children."[17] For a while her relationship with her in-laws was soured, as she made it clear to them that she would not go back to her husband. They slandered her and accused her of infidelity. This angered Marcela because in fact she had been the victim of adultery, which eventually led to her divorce. This hurt Marcela profoundly for, as she put it, "I was married, really married, not just *acompañada.*" In her view, these rumors had been an excuse for her ex-husband's sister not to repay a debt she had incurred when Marcela was still married to this man. Marcela added, "Because they had talked about me like that, that I was a loose one, their friends didn't want anything to do with me, even those I considered my friends. Can you imagine how I felt? [Marcela is very angry and has tears in her eyes.] They closed the doors to me. But this taught me who my real friends were and who were hypocrites. All those were a bunch of hypocrites."

Whereas the women sometimes stood to benefit, just as often they experienced losses as their unions dissolved and were rearranged after migration. In general, men tended not to be so adversely affected. Usually men were able to establish new unions with relatively fewer losses to their networks of support. Further, whereas men even benefited from the networks of their partners, this was not always the case for women, particularly if there was a suspicion of infidelity or "loose behavior" on the part of the women. These two situations rarely, if ever, affected men's networks negatively, even if some men were quite open about their unfaithfulness. Thus the double standard in gender ideologies that control sexuality had dissimilar consequences for the networks of men and women.

Conclusion

Although the immigrants in this study faced a structure of opportunities that limited the resources they had available to assist one another, men and women confronted the situation in different ways because gender mediated the effects of larger structures on these individuals' informal networks of exchange.

In general, women have fewer financial and material resources with which to help others, and this places them at a disadvantage in exchanges of financial or material help. However, women tend to dispose of more in-kind resources to exchange with others. Also, women are frequently in charge of seeking out the assistance of community organizations and other local institutions to fulfill the needs of their families; this increases opportunities for expanding their networks with other women in similar situations, as well as for personalizing ties with those who run the organizations. Furthermore, as women spend more time in these places, they gain crucial knowledge, which becomes an important resource that they can share with others and helps them maintain and create informal networks of support. Women's participation in the public sphere allows them to establish networks independent from those of men. Their networks are key in disseminating information ranging from employment to housing to various institutions in the host society. Thus, whereas it is easier for men to engage in exchanges with others around them (mainly because they have more material resources at their disposal, which tends to solidify ties with compatriot co-workers and friends), women are better positioned to establish ties beyond their immediate ambit. In a way this increases their social capital, for these links provide them access to a wider range of resources in different fields of activity. The nature of networks that women and men establish vary, for in cases in which women establish ties — however tenuous, hierarchical, or temporary — with non-Latinas they meet at community organizations, such ties are more akin to patron-client relationships than the ties they forge with women in their same predicament.

Informal exchanges are shaped by cultural norms and practices that govern gender relations, including sexuality, which in many ways preclude women from deriving benefits from exchanges with men. This may be offset by the women's wider-reaching networks, which unlike those of men, often go beyond their immediate milieu. When families are realigned by migration, cultural practices also shape the ways in which men and women create and re-create informal networks of support, often facilitating men's access to goods and services, even through the informal ties that women create. In the end, women and men derive dissimilar benefits from informal networks, and go about establishing these linkages in different ways, because the social process of creating and transforming such ties remains fundamentally gendered.

In the process of procuring assistance for themselves and their families — and of actively building community — immigrant women acquire knowledge about their rights in the host society, which is often reinforced by witnessing the relatively more egalitarian behavior of their mostly middle-class employers. This carries great potential to alter gender relations. In fact, the cases of these Salvadorans may attest to the powerful impact that immigration has on gender relations — often transforming them to the benefit of women but at times affirming orthodox practices (Menjívar 1999a). As the great majority of these women had earned incomes in El Salvador, paid employment or migration *alone* may not promote changes in gender relations; what matters is that they occur in conjunction, in a different social, economic, political, and cultural environment. Moreover, simply getting a wage does not automatically translate into advantages for women. But new developments in the lives of these women serve as catalysts for important transformations in gender relations as a result of migration. These transformations within the marginalized context in which these immigrants live may affect their overall incorporation into U.S. society; it remains an important question what impact they will have on the socioeconomic mobility of these immigrants.

Chapter 7

Informal Exchanges and Intergenerational Relations

One Sunday afternoon, as I was sitting in the small living room of the apartment where Marvin C. and his family live, I had the opportunity to listen to their views on family relationships. Marvin, his cousin Hernán and his wife, Ana María, and their children were there; Hernán's mother had left for church, so they felt at ease conversing about these matters more openly. While they all agreed that in principle they owed a lot to their parents and needed to instill in the children the same gratitude and respect, Hernán said, "It'd be ridiculous to expect that we should behave toward our parents exactly as if we were in El Salvador. We need to adjust to the customs of this country. But I would like my children to respect me, to obey me, and to remember me in my old age." Ana María interrupted: "Listen to him, he expects from his children what he won't do for his parents. But the children in this country are like adults; they have rights. Back there they're treated like children, you know, as if they know nothing. Here they know more than we do, so, of course, I think that they occupy a different place in the family, whether we [parents] like it or not [laughs]. Yes, on the other hand, our poor parents know less and less about things here and feel useless, yes, like they're good for nothing. So, of course, even though we love them dearly, the situation forces us to, well, to not pay much attention to them, to treat them different than if we were there."

As this family's conversation illustrates, expectations about help from informal networks are affected by the immigrants' position in the life cycle. Structural conditions, sociocultural patterns that govern age roles, and immigration itself shape the way in which generation affects networks of assistance. The Salvadoran families in this study, like other minority families in the United States, may be limited in their ability to adequately meet the needs of all generations by their lack of financial and human capital (Burton 1991, cited in Hogan, Eggebeen, and Clogg 1993). Also, their sociocultural traditions shape age expectations, needs, and resources, and all these vary as individuals go through the life cycle. Older members of the family, for instance, may be expected to help with child care and household chores as their financial potential decreases through diminished participation in the labor force. Children may be counted on to provide in-kind help also, as they do not yet possess the necessary financial and material goods to cooperate in other areas.

But immigration alters age-related expectations, for it reshapes access to the resources, albeit scarce, that people have available. Thus such expectations and the dynamics in which they are embedded are not static. As Kibria (1997) reminds us, the character of family traditions and orientations is shaped by a number of factors, such as the time of arrival and the socioeconomic background that internally differentiates immigrant groups. Even though kin play a strategic role in assisting families and individuals in need over the entire life course (Eggebeen and Hogan 1990), the sociocultural expectations that mold these exchanges are conditioned by the material resources that immigrants have at hand. In fact, norms may operate only within the constraints and opportunities that those social structures provide (Wellman 1988, 34). Thus the conditions that immigrants face are crucial in shaping new roles and responsibilities for the members of a family, for age-appropriate behaviors may become irrelevant and often may be reversed. Poor immigrants may be overburdened with trying to make ends meet, leaving them with little time to spend with their parents or to supervise children at home. Children may take on responsibilities normally reserved for adults. Older members may feel isolated as their roles in the family become increasingly more ambiguous. Thus, whereas expectations for giving and receiving help may be rooted in sociocultural norms, they are not detached from the material and social conditions that immigrants confront.

Although this study does not include many elderly people and children were not participants, intergenerational issues regularly surfaced in conversations with my informants. Therefore, with some exceptions, I approach this subject from the point of view of the "middle group." And although I frame informal exchanges mostly within the context of the family — this is where they were manifested more frequently — their pertinence is broader, because not only the elderly but also the children often engage in networks of assistance with friends and acquaintances. Such exchanges often occur through a person in the middle group and affect people beyond the immediate family.

To capture the social processes embedded in intergenerational relations, it is necessary to locate the immigrants in the age hierarchy, without strictly categorizing them according to specific age groups. This means that there will be conceptual overlap, as a person may be simultaneously a parent and a child. In general, however, the different generations roughly correspond to the age groups "older," "parent," and "younger," which reflect the interactions that take place among them.

"Here One Feels Like *Estorbo*": The Grandparents and Parents

Immigration is accompanied more often than not by significant transformations for the parents' generation. Here this group includes immigrants who are still able to participate actively in the labor force and those who can no longer do so. These two subgroups share important concerns in their dealings with the children's generation, particularly in relation to matters of authority and discipline. But they also experience important differences.

The Grandparents

In addition to facing the stress of life in a new context, grandparents' social status has been diminished and their socially expected roles often reversed. Older immigrants, particularly those who are no longer physically able to endure the long hours of backbreaking labor that consume the lives of many of the Salvadorans in my study, often feel out of place. Sometimes their presence is more a burden than a welcome addition. But, according to cultural norms, it is expected that the children will take care of parents and that a measure of obedience and respect will accompany such filial obligations. However, the new context often curtails the children's (as well as other family members') wishes to fulfill these expectations. The relatives are not always in a financial position to provide such assistance. As Elisa Facio (1996) observes, the literature that emphasizes an ideal image of Hispanic elderly—always relying on family for financial, emotional, and social support—ignores the reality of the conditions in which the relatives live. Controlling for ethnicity, Eggebeen and Hogan (1990) find that poverty reduces assistance given between generations. Thus the material conditions of the relatives shape exchanges with older immigrants in important ways.

Marvin C.'s cousin Hernán is a forty-year-old man originally from a city in central El Salvador and an accountant by training. He lives with his wife, two children, and mother and says that he cannot provide for his mother's needs, even though he is expected to and would like to. He works as a dishwasher on weekdays and as a parking lot attendant on weekends, and when he gets an afternoon off, he spends it helping at a construction site. His wife landed a job at a packing factory and often works twelve-hour shifts but earns less than the minimum wage and no overtime. Sometimes she helps a neighbor sell cosmetics and accessories, from which she earns a small commission. Hernán is especially worried that his mother's arthritis has worsened as a result of San Francisco's damp climate. She does not have health coverage because she has not worked in the United States and cannot obtain Medicaid because, she was told, she needs to be a legal resident to apply for it. Hernán cannot afford to pay for her treatment because he works for an employer who does not provide health insurance even for him. According to him,

I felt bad for her, you know, being by herself in El Salvador. So I told her, come here, and we'll see how we can make it. Besides, it was too dangerous for her to be there by herself. But now that she's here, I wonder if it wasn't better if she had stayed there. It's almost impossible to have her here with me. She's nice, and she is company for us, and she's my mother. But this country is not for the elderly. This country is for the strong and young, with energy to work. I can't give my mother what she needs here. It's worse than with the children because her needs are more expensive.

When I spoke with Hernán's seventy-year-old mother, Doña Tulita, she expressed the same concern.

I have never depended on anyone, but here I can't work because of my hands, and if there aren't enough jobs for the young ones, how is there going to be a job for me? Who's going to want to hire me? I try to help out in whatever way I can. I help them [Hernán and his wife] cook, clean, I pick up the little girl from school. You know, I do what I can. And my son is good, he kills himself working, and look at his wife, they almost never see each other. But if there's an emergency, God forbid, where are we going to get money? I worry and then I get sick. *Me pongo mal de los nervios* [I get tense]. I feel as if because of me they will end up begging in the streets.

The high cost of health care is of general concern for the elderly, but for these immigrants, who lack access to health benefits and other means to treat themselves, it has become a serious problem. Many have labored hard in their home country but are not guaranteed security in old age either there or in the United States. Declining health exacerbates their vulnerability. Like Hernán, other informants worried that their parents would be unable to obtain adequate treatment if they fell ill. But they also worried about who would take care of these parents, for the children could neither afford nor conceive of placing their parents in a nursing home. Amparo A.'s friend Ana Ruth A. said that if her mother got seriously ill she would send her back to El Salvador.

What would I do with her here? Take her around with me like a baby when I go to work? No, I can't. I can't stay and take care of her at home, because we'd all die of hunger if I don't work. And I can't do what Americans do, you know, go leave them in those homes where they never visit them. Besides, I couldn't afford it. I've just heard that it's what Americans do. But they are practical people, which is good. It has helped this country. We're different. We cannot abandon our parents like that. But yes, to El Salvador, that's where I'd send her. It's better than here.

Others echoed Ana Ruth's words. In fact, the majority of my informants said that they would rather spend their old age back in their home country because they have seen how older immigrants fare in the United States. As one put it, "The United States does not like old [people]. It's good to work, but not to get old here."[1]

The story of Marcela Q.'s neighbor Doña Berta, whom I did not include in my original group of informants (she arrived in the United States in 1974), reveals important and disturbing aspects of growing old amid the poverty in which many of these immigrants live. Originally from San Salvador, Doña Berta arrived at the age of forty-eight with only a fourth-grade education and cleaned houses until she was sixty-four. Her health deteriorated, and she could not work as much as she had in the past. She is a legal resident, but because she worked through informal arrangements, now she does not have access to a pension or other retirement benefits. I met her at the food distribution program, and when I discovered that she had been in San Francisco for almost twenty years — and still needed donated food and clothing — I became intrigued. Her children had been in the United States for more than a decade but were not doing well financially because they had been laid off for more than a year from a paint factory. They had to move out of a rented house into a cheaper one-bedroom apartment, but there was no room for Doña Berta in the new apartment. She moved in with a couple of nieces who let her sleep in their living room in exchange for baby-sitting. The building where they lived was so dilapidated that it should have been condemned. Once Doña Berta complained that she had to sleep on the kitchen floor because after a heavy rain the roof in the living room had collapsed. As a result, she caught pneumonia. With her increasingly frail health, she could not take much more. Her nieces were busy working and could not look after her. But a neighbor for whom Doña Berta had baby-sat helped her out. Doña Berta recounted, "She [the neighbor] and her husband took me to San Francisco General, and the doctor said that I was very ill. I didn't know. I just felt weak. To tell you the truth, I was scared because I don't have health insurance or anything. And when doctors say that you're very ill, it usually means that they want to charge a lot of money. So I worried. But he just prescribed some medications and told me to rest a lot."

Although it is not expected that they assist others financially, older people are counted on to help in other ways. Women such as Doña Tulita take care of the children and do other household chores. Sometimes, to make a little money, they take in other children for baby-sitting, something Doña Tulita does once in a while. She explained that since she is already looking after her youngest grandson, she welcomes other children because it is an opportunity to earn some cash. Both her neighbors and friends of her son, Hernán, bring their children. Sometimes she does not charge, and when she "accepts payment" it is only a small amount. She told me that she could not charge her neighbors or her son's friends all the time because they often do favors for her, like taking her shopping or to church on

Sunday when Hernán is working. She said that this tires her because a couple of the children are rowdy, but she has little choice; she needs to earn in order to be able to purchase her own medicines at least. On one occasion she asked me for a ride to the nearby laundromat so that she could do her family's laundry. She stressed that she needed a ride not because the bundle was too heavy, which it was, but because it was raining and quite cold. When we returned she wanted to invite me to eat, as if compensating me for taking her to do the laundry in the rain, but also because she wanted some company. She prepared a Salvadoran-style stew — not as rich as she would have liked it, she pointed out, because she could not afford all the right ingredients — and we shared it with her granddaughter, whom we picked up from school on our way back from the laundromat.

For older women, it is easier to find ways to contribute to their families and others around them because they usually pitch in with activities that are extensions of their previously prescribed roles, like babysitting and household chores. For older men, however, these new roles represent a departure from what is traditionally expected of them. In the new context there are not many culturally appropriate tasks that older men can carry out, and so they engage in what older women do. For these men, this involves a substantial dissonance, for they end up taking care of grandchildren and sometimes even cooking and helping with other household chores. For them, both culturally expected age and gender roles are reversed. Don Mario M., who is in his early seventies, says that he accepts his new role: "It's a new country, new customs, new everything. So I am a *niñera* [nanny] now [laughs]. Who would tell me this? I enjoy the company of my grandchildren, but taking care of them as my main occupation is a different story. I even help with household things. Look what I'm doing at my age! But I can't complain because my daughter needs this. I have to accommodate. Besides [laughs], nobody knows me here, so it doesn't look ridiculous."

For Don Armando Q., immigration turned the world upside down. He was a teacher in a working-class suburb of San Salvador. A group of heavily armed men took him out of his house at night, but his life was miraculously spared.

The men came looking for me because they wanted information about an acquaintance who had been rumored to have dealings with the guerrillas. I had no idea I even knew someone in that position. I never went around asking people what they did with their lives. The men made me kneel on the pavement, and when one of them was about to shoot me, like this [pointing as if with a gun to his temple], a boy delivering bread turned the corner. He saved my life because the men quickly got in their jeep and drove away. But one of them said to me, "We'll be back one of these days." One doesn't wait for heavily armed men to come take you out of your house in the middle of the night. So I had no choice but to leave the country. Can you imagine, at my age, to start all over again?

Don Armando's trip was not quite as dangerous as some. He received help from the Catholic church and a refugee organization in Mexico City, where he even saw a psychiatrist for the psychological trauma he had experienced in El Salvador. He continued to the United States because his sons live in Virginia, but the coyote dropped him off in Los Angeles, and he only had enough money to get to San Francisco, where some of his sons' in-laws live.

Don Armando does not receive much support from his sons because he does not ask them for it. He says that he does not want to bother them; he knows that they are financially strapped, so he lives on the little he manages to earn. His sons' in-laws have allowed him to live in a large flat that he shares with five others; he is immensely grateful for this help. But there are problems, he explains: "They are nice, they're good people. Because my sons are married to their daughters, you know, they treat me as family. Just by giving me a roof over my head, it's a tremendous help. But, you know, at my age, with my life almost over, I can't start again like a young person. I feel like I'm living a bad nightmare and it'll be all over soon. But the next day, I wake up, and it's the same. My emotional, mental state is not very stable. I don't feel well in this area."

There are other special needs that concern older immigrants and particular ways in which their children respond. As the cases above indicate, paying for their own housing, for instance, is often beyond the reach of many older people. One way for the children of elderly immigrants to help their parents is by providing housing. However, as in Facio's (1996) study, housing assistance often has contradictory consequences. Although it would make more sense economically, sometimes neither the older people nor their children want to live together. For example, Doña Hilda A., a delightful woman in her mid-seventies who finished the sixth grade in her small town in western El Salvador, said that she wishes to live a peaceful life, which could be compromised if she lived with her daughter. Doña Hilda told me, "My son-in-law gave me bad looks, and I said I better leave, to avoid serious problems." So she preferred to rent a room in the house of her daughter's ex-sister-in-law. Also, she used to be asked to look after her grandchildren, but they were terribly misbehaved and she did not want to be held responsible if anything should happen to them. Virginia M. said that she now lives with her son but does not expect this arrangement to continue much longer because she often feels unappreciated, even though she does whatever she can to help out. Doña Berta also said that she is not happy with her living arrangement. "Here one feels like *estorbo* [an annoyance]," she said.

Some of the older people seemed to need more social and emotional support than younger immigrants did. This included accompanying them to shop, to a clinic, or to church; or simply sitting down to converse with them. But life in the United States, especially given the work schedules of the younger immigrants, is not conducive to long hours of visiting and socializing. Older immigrants lack the opportunity to socialize with others their age because they are needed at home to help out. For example, Meredith Minkler, Kathleen M. Roe, and Relda J. Robertson-Beckley (1994) found that sometimes elderly people must reduce their networks of friends because their responsibilities with child care do not leave enough time to socialize. Because most of the older immigrants do not speak the language, they do not feel secure enough to go around on their own; their families often worry about it too. Doña Tulita, for instance, would often invite me to stop by because she said that she did not have people with whom she could talk; she appreciated that I was always willing to listen. Her son and daughter-in-law were so busy working that she often felt forgotten. Carlos R., who has three adult children in the Bay Area, complained that his children do not visit him as much as he would like. "I only see them once a month even though they live on the other side of the Bay Bridge [in Oakland]."

When I first interviewed Don Mario M., he confessed that he migrated because his children insisted, not because he was particularly enthusiastic about it. He felt that his social world had collapsed since he arrived in the United States. My first interview with him was much longer than anticipated; I suspect he had not had an opportunity to talk at length about himself in his approximately one year in this country. He said that even his marriage had deteriorated, because his wife — who is much younger than he is — had taken a job and he only saw her briefly in the mornings and at night. "My life is nowhere near what it was back there. There people knew me. I'd go out and talk with people. Here, there are days when I don't even open my mouth. And I don't know the language. Even my own family, they don't have time for anything, not even for a cup of coffee with me. And my wife, oh well, she's almost a stranger; with all my respect for you because you're a lady, I can only tell you this, we're only married in the eyes of God now." Don Mario even joined an Alcoholics Anonymous group that a friend took him to, simply because it offered an opportunity to socialize. "It makes you feel recognized," he said. "You know, they call you by your first name and everything. I don't have a problem with alcohol or anything, but it feels good to go there because people know who I am and they treat me with respect. It's truly very nice."

Doña Hilda A., who had befriended several Spanish-speaking people at her doctor's clinic, would show up at the clinic even though she did not have an appointment or was not ill. She explained,

I am enchanted with them. Oh, the doctors are beautiful. I don't mean physically or because they're young, but because of the way they treat me. My doctor is from where Julio Iglesias comes from, yes, Spain. He is so kind. He says, "Let's see Señora Hilda, how are you feeling?" And he talks to me and sits with me and doesn't rush. And he tells me that he'll take care of me if I do what he recommends. And I say, yes, of course, but he talks and tells me that I'm pretty, that I'm still young, that I need to keep healthy, and this and that. I feel very happy when I leave.

In addition to having developed ties through which she obtains social support at the clinic, stopping there regularly has also allowed Doña Hilda to establish contacts that provide access to other sources of help. For instance, one of the nurses she has befriended routinely gives her free samples of the very expensive medications she needs. A staff person in charge of a program for older people with diabetes had Doña Hilda enrolled in the program, which included weekly exercises and group meetings once a month. Even though Doña Hilda's diabetes had been under control for several years and she did not need to participate in the sessions, this staff person kept her in the program because she had mentioned that she enjoyed it. Doña Hilda, like other

older informants, pointed out that back in their home country older
adults did not feel isolated because there was always someone around
to be asked to accompany them on an errand, to listen to their advice,
or simply to sit down with them to talk.

But Doña Hilda also mentioned that the only "true" consolation she
finds is in her religion, a sentiment expressed by others in the parents'
generation as well. She said that when she feels lonely, which she does
regularly, she prays. "My only true friend is Santa Marta de Bethania,
patron saint of the impossible. I have a little image of her, I light a little candle to her, and I place a glass of water by her, and I pray — like
a conversation. I tell her with frankness, look Martita, you are my only
true friend, my only saint, you can get to where God is — speak to Him
for me, please. I feel better when I know she's taking care of my worries." Virginia M. also said that she finds great consolation in her
church. In her case it is mostly the congregation and her "brothers
in Christ," as she called the members of her Evangelical church.
According to her, she has found in them the support that her own children cannot provide her, and she appreciates that her pastor visited
her more often than her own daughter did.

One of the most vexing transformations for this group does not
arise from their reduced economic role. (Research has found that the
socioeconomic disadvantage of Latinas persists in old age, but it often
worsens; they have the lowest median income of all age groups
[Torrez 1997].) In fact, even back in their own country, older people
are not expected to support themselves when they reach a certain age,
provided that the children have a degree of economic stability to assist
them. The most important negative change for this group stems from
their diminished sense of authority, particularly in the areas of discipline and advice, where it is expected that they will make their most
important contributions as older adults.[2] For instance, one of the reasons Doña Hilda did not want to live with her children was that she
thought they had no respect for her (a common complaint this group
shares with the younger, parents' generation). She tried to give her
children advice on a variety of issues, ranging from health to weight
loss to marriage counseling. She particularly resented that they did not
heed her advice in matters in which she thought she had more authority, like how to raise and discipline children and what treatments were
needed for specific illnesses. In short, the culturally expected contri-

butions from her role as a "healer of mind and body" (Facio 1996, 91) were considerably diminished. One day Doña Hilda was especially annoyed. Not only had her grandchildren ridiculed the home remedies she had prescribed for them, but they were also mocking her for using them herself.

I don't know who these children think they are. They think they know everything because they were born here and speak English and I don't. They think that I'm a child. How dare they laugh because I prepare my arthritis medicine, oh, it's rosemary with avocado seed and alcohol together. I rub that on my knees, and I drink cactus water for the same thing. For constipation it's linseed tea with honey. I prepare it for them, and they won't touch it, they make fun. They say that it doesn't help. I say, if it doesn't help, it won't kill you either. But they think that only what you buy at the pharmacy cures.

The situation of older immigrants was aggravated by the fact that they could not do things that would be normal for their age. This was due in part to their lack of English-language skills, but also to the diminished standing of older adults in the United States. They needed assistance with tasks such as going to a doctor or a government office, with translations, and with many other daily activities. They also needed to deal with people in public places who "did not know" them and did not show the culturally expected deference for older adults. Their relatives would worry if they ventured in the streets by themselves, because of the dangers of inner-city neighborhoods. As Doña Hilda pointed out, "I feel like a little girl who hasn't learned how to talk yet. My daughter took me to school the other day, the English school. And she said to me, stay here, you need to learn. No more TV, soap operas, you know, only school. And I stayed like a girl in kindergarten. I'm old. I shouldn't be treated like this. I know they want to help me, but it makes me feel like an invalid." Doña Hilda also took issue with her grown children's changed behavior. With much effort, Doña Hilda had managed to obtain a Salvadoran delicacy of dried, salted meat, which she remembers her daughters enjoyed eating when they lived in El Salvador. But, much to her surprise, her daughters refused to eat it now because they considered it "unsanitary, fattening, and dirty." Doña Hilda was deeply hurt; she was trying to please them, and as there were few things around with which she could do that, she felt that they were rejecting her thoughtfulness.

Research points out that widowed, aging parents receive more assistance from their children than do married parents (Lopata 1979; Rossi and Rossi 1990). However, as the experiences of the older Salvadorans discussed here show, the financial and material conditions of the children are crucial. As the cases of Doña Tulita and Doña Berta (and to a certain extent Don Armando too) demonstrate, even if the children would like to assist their aging parents more, their material conditions preclude them from fulfilling these important obligations. The result is frustration on the part of the children and disappointment on the part of the parents, with repercussions for the potential to assist each other.

The Parents

The parents' generation — on whose experiences I have concentrated in previous chapters — were very much caught in the middle. They were the main providers of material and financial support for their parents and for their children, and often felt suffocated by the weight of their obligations to both. Their Herculean efforts to balance their already complicated lives between the demands of their jobs, their children, and their parents often left them drained physically and emotionally, but they had little time to even think about their weariness. Whether their parents live in El Salvador or in the United States, they worry because they cannot afford to help them financially as much as they would like. If their parents live in the United States, life becomes further complicated, for they cannot afford the time to take care of them. They frequently feel guilty because they do not give as much as is culturally prescribed to those who depend on them, or they resent the fact that they do. Some feel that their sacrifices are in vain; neither their aging parents nor their children reciprocate with what they want the most: some appreciation for their efforts and, once in a while, a little helping hand. And no matter how much they do for their parents or children, it always seems that it is not enough, or that it is not timed right.

This group shares an important concern with the grandparents' generation. The issue of children's discipline was perhaps the area that equally concerned all my informants who had children or grandchildren or who were members of a generation of parents. They complained about the "liberal" ways of children in the United States, about a lack of discipline, and especially about the restrictions on disciplining children. They expressed serious concerns about the state's protection of children and thought that "letting the law interfere in private matters," as one put it, was counterproductive. Chentía A. observed that "there is so much delinquency in this country because the government gets involved in *corregir* [mending the behavior of] the children, when that should be uniquely and exclusively the parents' right." That immigrant parents have these kinds of complaints is not new (see Pleck 1983; Waters 1997), but it is noteworthy because of the importance this has for informal networks within and outside the family.

As in the case of Doña Hilda, who did not want to live with her grandchildren, there were other adults who preferred to live with friends, or even alone, rather than to stay with relatives who had children, particularly adolescents. Since living under one roof facilitated many informal exchanges, residing elsewhere significantly diminished these opportunities. Also, moving out under these circumstances was usually accompanied by tension resulting from a problem that involved the children—which further exacerbated a weakening of these informal ties. For instance, Lolita Q. simply could not stand her niece and nephew and moved out of her brother's apartment. In El Salvador Lolita had been jailed and tortured for several days because of her political activism. She was released as part of an agreement with the International Red Cross and was given forty-eight hours to leave the country. She arrived in San Francisco at the invitation of her brother, who knew of her political activities and had offered her his help in case she needed to flee El Salvador. She lived with her brother, his wife, and their two children for a few months. She would clean houses occasionally to earn money to help out her brother and to send to her one-year-old daughter, who was in the care of her mother in El Salvador.

During the time she lived with her brother, Lolita observed that her niece and nephew were "unos malcriados y desobedientes [some spoiled and disobedient children]" and tried to help out. She did not anticipate the outcome. She explained,

My brother and my sister-in-law, they are good people, but the problem there is the children. The children have bad manners. The parents work all the time. She works days and he works nights and on weekends too, so those children are growing up alone. And when the parents want to correct the children's behavior, it's too late. One is ten years old, the other twelve. The boy who is twelve once told me that he was going to call the police on me if I tried to reprimand him. I guess that's what children do in this country, call the authorities. But because he knows of my problems there [in El Salvador], he said, "And they'll take you to jail, where you have been before, and then I'll have you deported if you keep bugging me" — because he knows that I'm here illegally. Can you imagine what kind of monsters these are? What are these children going to do to their parents when they grow up? What can one expect from them? My brother is frustrated with them. He drinks a lot and comes home very late. I was trying to help, to improve them [the children], but it's impossible because here the laws say that one must not talk bad to children. The law doesn't let you educate them, and at the schools, where they are supposed to learn at least something, they're the problem to begin with. These guys only go there to learn bad things. I think that what they know about being bad, they learn it at school. No, it's true. So I try to avoid those kids and only visit my brother once in a while, when those spoiled monsters are not home.

Lety R. brought one of her daughters from El Salvador to live with her because this daughter insisted that she no longer wanted to stay with her four siblings in the care of their grandmother. Lety used to work *encerrada* (as a live-in domestic), but since her fourteen-year-old daughter arrived, she can only work during the day because she wants to be at home with her daughter as much as she can. But she simply cannot afford to live on the income she earns from one job. She often works half days on weekends too, for she needs to send money back to El Salvador. Lety was growing suspicious that her daughter was not attending school and was upset at the girl because she had refused to help around the house. One day Lety asked me if I would accompany her to talk with the teacher and interpret for her. When I arrived for our appointment, Lety did not want to go because her daughter had threatened her. The girl had announced that no one could tell her anything about her behavior because she "was free," and in addition she would accuse anyone who tried to stop her of child abuse, including her mother, if necessary.

Knowing that Lety and the rest of the family were apprehensive of anything that had to do with the law due to their undocumented status, the girl (who lacked documents herself) had made it clear that beating an underage person was considered child abuse, punishable by law in the United States. Thus she threatened to accuse them of beating her and was willing to harm herself to produce the necessary bruises as evidence to get her family in trouble. Lety was sobbing and insisted that the child would go back to El Salvador as soon as she could collect enough money to send her. "Can you imagine, if tomorrow I need something, she'll kick me and tell me to go to hell. This is what I'll get if I let her grow up here." Lety's cousin Aracely's case was similar but had escalated to a much bigger problem. After several suspensions from school, Aracely's daughter was taken by Child Protective Services. They deemed Aracely an unfit mother mainly because she worked about seventy hours a week and consequently had little time left to oversee her daughter. Aracely was devastated and could not understand why she could not simply send her daughter to live with her brother in Los Angeles: "It's a family affair, no one should get into this. I don't know why the authorities have to intervene here."

Given such circumstances, some of the people in this group were ambivalent about raising children in the United States. They pointed to the advantages that the children have in the United States, the better educational opportunities and jobs and, in general, a higher standard of living. Whenever they talked about these perceived benefits, however, they would qualify them by mentioning the downside of raising children in this country. They mainly talked about the lack of respect for older adults and about the "exaggerated" freedom of U.S. children. Afraid of the children's prospects in the United States, some had sent them back to El Salvador, even those who had been born in the United States. This decision was very painful for Priscilla F., but she thought it was the best thing to do. Although her daughter was born in the United States, Priscilla was terribly concerned about "what may happen to her when she starts going to school." "She's only two," Priscilla explained, "but I couldn't sleep at night thinking about the things that could happen to her here — at the baby-sitter's, at school, you never know. So with *el dolor de mi alma* [pain in my soul], I had to send her back. I know she'll be better there. Here children only learn to disrespect parents and pay you back with bad behavior." And Estela Z., who had never brought her children to live with her, said,

It's better that I work here like a donkey and send them money so that they can live comfortably there. For instance, with what I send them, they can even go to a nice school, buy uniforms, books. But here, what would I do? I can't look after them because I'm always working, and with what I earn I can only afford to send them to Mission High. What for? So that they learn how to use drugs and join a gang? They become disobedient, undisciplined. Tell me, what makes more sense, to keep them there or bring them here? Besides, one never knows, tomorrow we may be deported, and what about the kids?

Like Estela and Priscilla, a few of my informants preferred, when possible, to support their children in El Salvador instead of having them in the United States. In Estela's and other cases, it must be noted that their own legal instability plays an important role in considering whether to send for their children. They worry that their children also will be undocumented, which in the long run may impede their access to the perceived benefits of living in the United States. And when the children were in El Salvador and the parents in San Francisco, the parents worried constantly about the well-being of their children. These mothers experienced the painful consequences of what Pierrette Hondagneu-Sotelo and Ernestine Avila (1997) call "transnational motherhood." For instance, Marcela Q. frequently brought up the fact that her two older boys each stayed with a grandmother back in El Salvador, and she had no idea how they were faring.

I live *angustiada* [anguished] because I don't know if they eat or not, if they are clothed or not, if they get sick, will they get good treatment. [Her voice breaking] It's the most horrible torture for a human being, not knowing how your children are, if they're suffering. Sometimes I want to abandon everything and go home to see my boys. But then I think, I have a daughter here and I have put up with this life for a while already, so I better stay put so that they can, God willing, benefit more in the future. It's my only consolation.

Parents were also concerned about the best way to keep their children from becoming "too Americanized," meaning to keep them from losing respect for older adults and to teach them obedience and a sense of obligation to parents. These parents worried that their children would become too independent and detached from them, that they would be unable to educate them as they themselves had been educated, and that they would not be able to instill in them the values that they considered fundamental for families to survive. These values included a sense of respect, duty, and obligation to the parents, particularly in the parents' old age. For instance, Amparo A., who is a daughter and a mother, explained her perspective from both sides.

Hopefully I'll be able to raise my baby like I was raised, you know, with respect for our parents. I think it's good to know that parents know better. I won't keep her from learning what's good in this country, but I want her to learn the values that I was taught. Look at me. I'm twenty-eight years old, and whenever I go out, to a party or just out with friends, I always tell my mommy, who lives upstairs. We don't even live in the same apartment, but we live in the same building, and I want her to know where I am. We all tell her where we go and with whom. It's appropriate. Sometimes I even ask her permission to see if it's okay to go out. Regardless of your age, your parents are your parents, and that's that. And when my mommy is old, it's my obligation to look after her. She's my mother. I want to teach this to my baby too.

Younger immigrants did not always share those views, and the expectations of older immigrants did not make much sense to them. Roberto C., a twenty-year-old high school graduate who has lived in the United States for five years and recently visited El Salvador, told me that there he did not see what older people in his family had been talking about so much.

They used to say, oh, in El Salvador you wouldn't do this or that or, oh, back there is not like here. For them everything was so much better and different there. The problem with them [the parents] is that they left a long time ago, and things have changed a lot there. It's like they have in their heads a country that doesn't exist anymore, except in their imagination. It's like a made-up country with made-up customs that they try to teach me about and then expect me to behave like that. But nothing is the way they see it — neither there nor here. So it doesn't make sense for me to try to behave according to something that no longer exists.

But no matter how preoccupied older immigrants were with their youngsters' perceived "Americanization" or loss of respect for parents, these older ones still expected, somehow, that the children (particularly the U.S.-born) would take advantage of the benefits that the United States offered. They wished that the children would become educated and that they would feel at least a little obligation to the parents and, if possible, to other relatives. For instance, Rosa María B. said that she knew her children would never grow up like children do in El Salvador. However, she tried to teach them important values that would help them in the future. Especially such values as "if tomorrow they find a person in conditions worse than theirs, especially if it's their own blood, they have to help out because God lives in our neighbor, and in helping others, you give back to God." Marcela Q. said,

I have put my hopes in Claudia [her daughter]. Because she's an American citizen and won't have to struggle with documents, doors will open to her. And she's intelligent, so I want her to go to the university [smiling]. I never thought about these things before, I had never talked about universities in my life, but I want Claudia to educate herself and be someone here, so that her brothers will also have a better future. She knows that she's not alone. She has to see that her brothers are not suffering. She's six years old, but she already knows that. I am educating her as a responsible human being with a good heart.

In general, the parents' generation had mixed feelings about their dealings with the children's generation. Although they recognized the increased advantages for children in the United States (in terms of improvements in status within the family and of future opportunities), these parents were also cognizant of the negative consequences the children's newfound rights and freedom would have for their own families, as well as for their networks of support. The parents worried that the family would lose the authority that it traditionally held over the children and that, as a result, these ties would weaken; they were especially concerned about the perceived interference of the law in the private affairs of the family. In a sense these parents had to deal with a situation that worked against them in two ways. First, the law restricted them from disciplining the children; thus it assured the children their rights at the cost of diminishing those of the parents. Second, and more important, these parents lacked the social ties in the community that would enforce informal rules of behavior for the children. The parents' long work hours prevented them from watching their children closely, and there was no one around in the immediate community to do so either. San Francisco is not the kind of place where neighbors are going to mind each other's children, particularly in low-income areas such as the Mission District, where crime has skyrocketed in recent years and people try to avoid spending time in the street.[3] Informal means to enforce parental supervision are, as we shall see later, quite important. A study of Central American moth-

ers of young children in Washington, D.C., found that a deficit in support from contextual sources increased the levels of parental stress
and affected a parent's ability to cope with parenting tasks (Borrero
1992).

"Here I Do What I Please and No One Can Control Me": The Children

The "children" also experience their share of transformations.
Immigration has positioned the younger group in situations in which
expectations of them have changed dramatically and their culturally
expected roles have frequently been reversed. While the position of
authority of the older immigrants has been threatened and even
diminished with immigration, the social role of the younger group has
been expanded and strengthened and their status enhanced. In many
ways they have assumed positions of authority previously occupied by
adults. The younger group is more likely to be in contact with (and to
gain more knowledge about) the host society — or at least of the milieu
they inhabit — and with those surroundings where adults may be too
timid to venture (mostly because of language barriers). The children's
contact with a wider social field has important implications for networks of support and for the consequences that these may have for the
future of this group.

One of the most important transformations comes from children's
increased contact with their environment. This happens because they
often acquire knowledge of English before others in their families and
become more familiar with the culture of their immediate environment. It must be stressed that these youngsters acquire a great deal of
knowledge of their *immediate* ambit, not of the wider society or of
"American" culture at large.[4] Nonetheless, this knowledge makes
them adept at dealings with the wider society and at forging links
between their families and local institutions, and they assume the role
of "cultural brokers" (Buriel and De Ment 1997, 189), which also happens among other groups (see Gold 1992 for the Jewish case). In these
cases the children acquire power and authority within the family (and
to some extent within the community at large) that they previously did
not hold. This new role is accompanied by hopes that they will assist
their families and sometimes other unrelated adults in ways that are at

variance with the youngsters' culturally prescribed roles. The imbalance often leads to tension. As research has pointed out, when the parents' or other adults' authority is eroded by migration, intergenerational conflict follows (Huang 1989; Kibria 1993; Rumbaut 1995b). Although these are general experiences, gender matters, as daughters tend to experience a wider gap with their parents than sons do, as a result of the more numerous changes in their roles after arriving in the United States (Nguyen and Williams 1989). Thus, whereas the children acquire important resources to help their parents and other adults, the process is hardly a smooth one devoid of conflict.

Take the case of Doña Hilda A. She told me that whenever she goes to "important meetings" with a doctor, a social worker, or the like, she always takes someone with her to serve as an interpreter, preferably her daughter, although her grandchildren have accompanied her on occasion. However, she complains, "I'm putting myself in the hands of these kids who know nothing and I have to confide everything to them. I don't like it that they find out so much about me. It's not good that at their young age they know so much about adult matters." One day she was furious that her irreverent grandchildren had divulged what they considered humorous facts about her — they had been privy to the information when they translated for her during a visit to the doctor's office. She said that this is not likely to happen with her daughters, but when her own children are not available, she has to rely on her grandchildren for this important service.

Sometimes the children's translation services help the parents in indirect ways. For instance, if a neighbor or a friend needs a translator, a parent can "lend" a child and, in return, the friend or neighbor would feel indebted to the parent. On numerous occasions Doña Hilda's granddaughter had helped a neighbor with translating government documents. In exchange, the neighbor sometimes cooked a special dish for the girl's family or shared with them delicacies that she received from El Salvador. Doña Hilda said that it was only natural that the neighbor would feel obligated to the parents and not to the girl: "Children are under our dominion, and we can tell the girl to help or not to help. It's basically our decision, not the girl's, because she's only a child and can't make a decision on her own." This demonstrates the contradiction between recognizing the children's increased social status due to their language ability and the efforts on the part of adults to neutralize the youngsters' enhanced position by continuing to treat them as dependents or even "possessions" of the family.

Asking younger people to translate sometimes has serious consequences, for instance, when the children feel empowered by it — or perhaps tired of the difficult task at hand — and take the liberty of making decisions for the older immigrants. Lolita Q. was incensed when she discovered that her twelve-year-old nephew and translator had answered questions for her during an interview with a legal caseworker. The nephew had assumed that he knew when and under what conditions his aunt had arrived in the United States, if she had ever been deported, and if she had a criminal record in the United States. To her dismay he had portrayed her as a felon who smuggled people across the border as her main occupation. He had mistaken her political imprisonment in El Salvador for U.S. criminal incarceration, and because he had heard that his aunt tried to enter the United States more than once, he concluded that it was a routine activity. Lolita was unsure if her nephew had done this because he was inattentive and rushed through the interview or because he was trying to get back at her for reprimanding him the day before, when he had been disrepectful to his parents.

But Lolita was not alone. Others had similar complaints and linked them to the increased authority of youngsters in the United States. They were frustrated by having to put important matters into the hands of children and by the fact that this gave the children an increased sense of decision-making authority. Milagro V. found out that on several occasions her Chinese landlord had tried to let her know that the badly needed repairs to her apartment's bathroom were finally going to be done. But her daughter Dinorah had dismissed the landlord's messages as unimportant, and consequently Milagro was not home when the landlord dropped by with the repair crew. One day, as I was leaving the apartment building, I heard Milagro shouting, asking me to go back to her place. The landlord was there, and I was able to explain to Milagro what had been going on. The landlord told me that Dinorah had always acted in a "self-sufficient" way and that he had similar problems with other children in the building. From then on, when the landlord saw me around the building, he called on me to help him communicate with his tenants, most of whom were either Salvadoran or Nicaraguan. He addressed me as "Doctor" and reminded me that he preferred my services, even though they were irregular. He explained, "Those kids are ill-intentioned, they're pests. I feel bad for those hardworking parents."[5]

Sometimes children manipulated important information with negative consequences for themselves. This happened when school officials or teachers made attempts to get in touch with the parents (usually because of a problem with the children), and the children did not inform their parents or distorted the information. For instance, Milagro V. had no idea that Dinorah had been skipping classes and had been in trouble for displaying the clothing colors and style of a local gang. Milagro only found out about Dinorah's problems when, on her day off, she noticed that Dinorah did not get up early to go to school. It turned out that Dinorah had already been expelled. She had told the school staff that her mother was back in El Salvador and that she lived with relatives who refused to meet with the school officials because they were too busy working. She was partly right. Milagro was extremely busy — working two jobs to give Dinorah what she needed so that the girl would not have to work, and sending money back to Milagro's mother in El Salvador. But Milagro was in the United States, sad and profoundly disappointed, because she had expected Dinorah to get the schooling that she could not get in El Salvador and had thought that, with the many opportunities in the United States, this would be easier to accomplish here. The school officials told Milagro that if she had been in touch with them when they first summoned her, Dinorah's dismissal could have been prevented.

A disturbing issue having to do with the U.S. upbringing of these children further complicates the important task of mediating between the parents and the non-Spanish speakers in the community. I noticed that sometimes it was not the children's mischief that got in the way of the translations but rather a crucial aspect of their life in the United States. Translations were haphazard or incorrect mainly because the children did not speak either language correctly. It has been reported that to acquire a new language children should have a firm knowledge of their mother tongue (Paulston 1978). However, even if these children arrive in the United States with a decent command of Spanish, they tend to lose it because they have limited interaction with Spanish-speaking adults, who are home very little. And when the children are at home with adults, they spend their time either watching

English-language television or speaking in English with siblings rather than interacting with adults. Alejandro Portes and Richard Schauffler (1994) observe that the children of immigrants demonstrate an unambiguous preference for English, so what is at risk is the preservation of the parents' language. In the cases that I observed (and heard about), which were all of children born in El Salvador, as the children started to make progress in English, it became their language of choice. Importantly, it conveyed more prestige. For instance, Rosa María B. recognized that to transmit the values she considered important for her children — but also to know what they were up to — she needed to learn basic English. "My children don't want to speak Spanish. Look at them, they refuse to speak it, so I need to learn at least a little bit of English if I want to understand what they're saying and what they're doing, so as to be able to tell them what's right from wrong."[6] These parents firmly believed that the key to their children's success in the United States was to learn English. In fact, in a recent survey (NALEO 1998), parents of Salvadoran children expressed frustration with the slow pace at which their children learn English in the schools. And even though their incomes are quite low (in this survey, a quarter of the respondents earn less than $9,999 annually and only a small percentage more than $19,999), the parents said they were willing to pay higher taxes to improve the delivery of school services.

A troubling matter I observed is that it is not proper English that I heard these children speak but the English they had learned from peers (both in and outside school), which was limited and not always correct. Their version of English was reinforced because they spent more time socializing with friends than with adults, a problem that may afflict other immigrant communities as well, as Fernández-Kelly and Schauffler (1994) found among Nicaraguans in Florida. Besides the obvious consequences for the lives of these young immigrants, this problem plagues their interactions with the adults in their family and community. With time, they grow distant from the adults with whom they can no longer communicate well, and they increase their interactions and reinforce networks with their peers, which in a way buttresses the subculture that the parents try so hard to counteract.[7] Finally, it decreases their chances in the wider society because it makes problematic the accumulation of cultural capital that they need to succeed (see also Bourdieu 1986; Stanton-Salazar 1997).[8] The children, however, do not see the benefits of speaking Spanish, for it is associated with poverty, undesirable occupations, and, very likely, undocumented status and recency of arrival.

Alongside their role as cultural brokers, which the children fulfill with varying degrees of efficiency (and tension), they contribute in other tangible ways to their families. A few of the children earned incomes. These were not the occasional part-time jobs that many U.S. youngsters take in order to purchase the trinkets that their parents are unable or unwilling to buy for them. The work that the Salvadoran children often do is difficult and labor-intensive. Their incomes were often used to supplement their parents' meager earnings.[9] The many demands on parental income often did not leave enough money to sustain the family, much less to purchase the material goods that the children needed, wished for, or even demanded. For instance, Anabel, Chentía A.'s teenage daughter, enrolled in the tenth grade when she arrived in the United States, but for her it was more imperative to earn money than to stay in school. A friend informed her about job openings at a nearby McDonald's, where she was hired to work full-time. Gilberto F.'s and Alicia N.'s three older children[10]— Yanira, Roberto, and Miguel—got jobs at a local laundromat when they were fifteen, thirteen, and eleven years old respectively. They worked twelve hours a day on Saturdays and Sundays and four hours each day the rest of the week. But they quit because the owner of the laundromat ended up giving them each $10 for twelve hours of work and not $2 per hour as agreed. They then decided to take turns helping their mother clean houses, and although they did not receive a cash payment, they could ask their mother for a treat at a later point, such as an item of clothing or money for the video arcade. Rosa María B. took her daughter Sonia, who is ten, to work with her because Sonia helped her clean, but the girl also baby-sat one of her bosses' children, for which she would get $5 for the six hours that it took Rosa María to clean this person's house.

Parents with working children spoke proudly of their children's work ethic. However, the practice of children earning incomes had unintended negative consequences. As in Anabel A.'s case, some of the children decided to quit school in order to work full-time and increase their families' inadequate incomes. Also, given the conditions in the lives of these immigrants, the children's view of the future was not particularly encouraging, which made full-time work an attractive option. Their own (and their parents') undocumented status did not assure them that they could reach an educational level beyond high school or achieve any of the perceived benefits of living in the United States. In addition, this environment did not provide them with role models. As María Eugenia Matute-Bianchi (1986) observes, the living quarters, places of leisure and entertainment, local businesses, and schools have a powerful impact on the children's prospects. The decision to quit school to work full-time makes sense when one looks at the alternatives these children have.[11] They live in an environment where only a handful can escape the deleterious effects of poverty and where high school graduates do not become successful college graduates; the fortunate ones who get jobs end up working as menial laborers in the small businesses in the neighborhood.

For instance, a few months after Yanira F. turned fifteen, she announced that she was quitting school because she did not see any purpose in it. Alicia, her mother, was dismayed at the idea, because she could not figure out why Yanira was giving up the educational opportunities that the United States had to offer. To Yanira, the answer was simple. She explained that she was not about to continue wasting her time in school. All she was going to be able to do was get a job at Walgreen's on the corner, or Woolworth's on Mission, or El Pollo Supremo down the street—where those who graduated from her high school were most likely to find work. (In contrast, the daughter of the Salvadoran couple I discuss in chapter 4 got a job as a clerk in a downtown office when she finished high school twenty-five years ago.) Besides, she pointed out, with her undocumented status she might not even be able to get those jobs in the future, as restrictions on undocumented workers have gotten stiffer with time. Yanira reasoned that it was better to find a job now, when it was still possible, than to continue with school, which only offered tenuous benefits for an unspecified future, when she might not even be in the United States any longer. Two years later her brother Roberto reached the same decision, and on his fifteenth birthday he received his first full-time paycheck as an assistant at a construction site. Their younger brother, Miguel, did not want to quit school, but he kept on saying that he "was being forced to." His mother explained that Miguel had grown apathetic toward everything that had to do with school and in the mornings would make all kinds of excuses not to go. When his mother questioned him and his siblings about it, she discovered, to her disappointment, that he was afraid to go to school. At the school, it seems, he was being pressured to join a gang and constantly harassed (and at one point seriously threatened) for refusing to do so. His parents were at a loss; they had no alternative but to continue sending him to that school or take him out altogether, for any other schools were far beyond their economic means. And it is not that these children did not have the intellectual capacity to do well in school. Roberto excelled in algebra and demonstrated an exceptional capacity for analytical thought and problem solving. Yanira's photographic memory allowed her to memorize entire poems, paragraphs from textbooks, and numbers from the telephone directory, which her family would use to test her ability. And Miguel, because of his English-language facility and penchant for talking and asking "difficult" questions, was teased that he would become a lawyer, about which he admitted he had fantasized.

The poverty and legal instability of these children cast a dim light on their vision of the future, and education seemed almost out of place in such conditions. They learned that they had to survive, and to do this they had to earn incomes and work hard at an early age. In a different context, taking a job as a teenager might have served to instill a work ethic that would be beneficial in the future. But for these children, working at this young age meant survival and an immediate alternative to the uncertain benefits that education might bring.

In the children's quest to help their families, too often they suffer the consequences of assuming adult responsibilities prematurely (Athey and Ahearn 1991). They become overburdened with adult duties that sometimes interfere with their schooling and emotional development. This issue is particularly troubling because often their childhood has been marred by psychological trauma during the civil war in El Salvador (Espino 1991) and the indelible scars they still bear. These children experienced adult-sized violence, for example, witnessing the abduction or murder of family members, seeing tortured bodies in the streets, bombings, crossfire, and the generalized terror that reigned in El Salvador for most of their lives. In addition, many children, some as young as twelve, were forcibly recruited by combatant groups (Urrutia-Rojas and Rodríguez 1997). One day,

Alicia N.'s then eleven-year-old son, Miguel, and I were talking about music and John Lennon's death came up. Miguel was very intrigued, asking me if Lennon had been the victim of a bomb or if he had been taken out of his house at night — two common forms of death in the El Salvador of Miguel's memory. Miguel's brother Roberto quickly corrected him, saying that there are other ways of dying, but then Roberto started asking me if the singer had been tortured for long or if he had been killed right away.[12] The traumatized condition in which many of these children arrived in the United States has been manifested in some instances in learning disorders and delinquent behavior during adolescence (Arroyo 1985, cited in Espino 1991).[13] Frightening experiences in their home country were often exacerbated during their harrowing journeys to the United States, as the children were exposed to the same experiences as the adults. Once in the United States, these children usually join the inner-city working poor, with the added anxiety of being undocumented (Espino 1991, 122).

Like the vast majority of Salvadoran immigrants, the trip for Alicia N. and her children was long and arduous. After leaving Guatemala, their journey to the United States took about two months to complete. They often went hungry, walked for many hours at a time in desolated regions, and hid in back alleys and under trucks to avoid detection by Mexican authorities. They also experienced traumatic events. They saw human remains, conceivably of compatriots who had perished in the Sonoran Desert trying to reach the United States. They were assaulted and robbed several times and heard stories recounted by women who had been raped by bandits who prey on *transmigrantes*. To cross over to the United States they had to wake up at 1:00 A.M., so that by the time the sun was up, they would be on the U.S. side. They arrived in Los Angeles — the drop-off point for the group — drowsy and hungry, in a van with twenty-two people on board.

Alicia's daughter Yanira never talked about her ordeal, about what she went through back in El Salvador or during the journey. Alicia said, "There's nothing in this world that'll make her say a word about anything [she experienced]; it looks as if she's forgotten it all." But Yanira, it seems, never forgot anything. One day Alicia was very worried because Yanira had stopped talking altogether. She "went mute from night to day," her mother said to me. For no physically apparent reason, Yanira did not utter a single word for almost two months.

Later Alicia explained, "Just as she stopped talking, she started again. From night to day, just like that. But we don't know why or what happened to her. And she doesn't say anything, except that she just couldn't talk; she says that words couldn't come out from her throat. I don't know what happened to her. The counselor [at school] says that it's probably because they tried to ask her about her country and her experiences back there. [At school] they wanted to know about the war and all that. I don't know. Maybe he's right." Also, Yanira would cry for no apparent reason, and her parents and brothers would simply say "así es ella" (that's how she is). The day she turned fifteen years old, I stopped by, and she was sad because her parents did not have money to buy her a cake. I went to the bakery to get her one, and when I came back and set it on the kitchen table, without saying a word, Yanira sat in front of it with her eyes fixed on the candles, and tears rolled down her cheeks. Her mother said to me that the school counselor had told them on repeated occasions that Yanira needed a lot of emotional support at home. But Alicia and Gilberto were torn because they had to choose either to spend many hours outside the home (working or looking for jobs) or to spend time with Yanira, but they could not do both. The fruits of the parents' labor are supposed to make these children's lives more comfortable, but often the children are shortchanged (see Waters 1997). First, the parents' meager paychecks are seldom enough to provide the material and financial comforts that the youngsters require or sometimes demand. Second, because the parents must spend so much time working, they cannot provide the children with badly needed emotional support.

Another issue that further complicates intergenerational relations is the experiences of these children when they reunite with their parents in the United States after a long separation. Too often the parents and children feel very much like strangers when they see each other again. As Leigh A. Leslie (1993, 201) points out, sometimes Central Americans cope with separation by fantasizing about the good life when the family is reunited, a strategy that sets up unrealistic expectations that lead to disappointments when family members arrive. Some of my informants recalled times when their own children have reproached them for "abandoning" them in El Salvador, when the parents were in fact working hard in the United States for their benefit. In some instances they do not even recognize each other physically when they finally meet. Chentía A. laughed endlessly when she recounted how she had hugged and kissed the wrong (and bewildered) man when she went to meet her son at the coyote's drop-off house in Los Angeles. Sometimes family reunifications did not work out smoothly because new families had been formed in the United States, particularly when step- and half-sibling combinations had been created. These problems were exacerbated when newcomers had to join U.S. relatives in overcrowded homes ridden with tension. As a result, the volatile environment prevented people from reestablishing ties that would have allowed them to fulfill expectations of assistance. Priscilla F. moved in with an aunt because of her mother's new husband. Several points of contention now prevent Priscilla and her mother from relying on each other for help. First, Priscilla wants her mother to leave her husband, which her mother is not prepared to do. Second, Priscilla and her mother need to find excuses to talk with each other because her mother's husband does not let her communicate with Priscilla; he is afraid that Priscilla will one day convince her mother to leave him. When she needs someone to talk to, Priscilla turns to others, mainly her aunt, friends, and even her two-year-old toddler when she was still in the United States.

Relationships across generations are affected when the families in the United States and in El Salvador have been exposed to widely divergent experiences. This happens more frequently among young persons who have participated in political or religious activities in El Salvador, in which their U.S. families either do not share or of which they do not approve. For instance, as mentioned earlier, Joaquín M.'s roommates, Luis, Tony, and Armando, had all been politically active in El Salvador and came to San Francisco to join their families. On arrival, however, they discovered that they did not have much in common with their families and that their political ideology got in the way of establishing congenial relations with their relatives. Armando told me why he was upset: "My sisters have become materialists, all they care about is their appearance and money, and I get upset at them, I reprimand them, but they don't listen." Tony was disillusioned because his relatives did not approve of his political beliefs and wanted him to go to business or law school instead of organizing political rallies. Luis was disappointed with his family's political views and engaged in heated debates to "make them face the reality in which we live." When the three men moved in with Joaquín, their ties with one another became stronger, but their relationships with their own families weakened.

In a similar case, Don Mario M.'s nephew Enrique, a young man in his early twenties, came to join his parents and two siblings in San Francisco. When he arrived he discovered that his family was "living in sin." Enrique had joined a Pentecostal Christian church in El Salvador and was appalled at the ways of his family in San Francisco. He had been separated from them for ten years, most of which he spent learning about his faith and "spreading the Word," as he put it. Enrique did not approve of his sister going out in short skirts or wearing makeup, and he despised his younger brother's penchant for parties and loud music. At first he resolutely tried to indoctrinate them, since he was convinced that God had put him in their path to guide them "to accept Christ as their savior." But when his repeated efforts failed and only served to antagonize everyone at home, he decided that he had to stay away from his family because he might be sinning if he shared a roof with them. And although he claimed rock-solid religious beliefs, he mentioned that avoiding temptation might have also played a role in his decision to move out. He turned to his pastor and the congregation for help, and they arranged for him to live with a "Christian brother" in a flat not far from his family. However, his contacts with his family diminished dramatically after he moved out.

When the children do not find the help they have hoped for from parents or other adult relatives, or when there is tension in their dealings with the older generation, they turn to other sources of support. They especially turn to people their own age, such as friends from school and from the neighborhood. In some instances these new arrangements provide them with the kind of help that is beneficial in the long run, as some of the previous cases demonstrate. However, in other instances, they turn to friends who may be supportive in the short run but whose help translates into questionable advantages for the future. The reasons that these children have for joining gangs, for instance, vary from searching for emotional support or "family" to looking for the material help that their families cannot provide to finding a place to "fit in."

Marcela Q.'s younger brother exemplifies this situation. He sought others for the material help he badly needed but instead ended up in a far worse predicament. Like Marcela, he had dropped out of the first grade. He arrived in San Francisco when he was fifteen years old to join his older sister, but he quickly discovered that she was in no position to give him the assistance he had expected (and needed). A few young men in the neighborhood befriended him, and soon I noticed that his appearance and demeanor began to change. It seemed that his new friends were involved in a business wherein they would produce on demand a variety of used goods for sale. I asked Marcela what her brother was doing for a living, because he seemed to be doing quite well. He was sporting an expensive pair of shoes, a thick gold chain, and a graduation ring that read in big letters simply "High School." Also he had given her a stereo and two color television sets (which she had to stack on top of each other because she had no room in her place to display them separately). At one point he mentioned that he could get a car stereo for me for very little money, but Marcela immediately asked him to stop peddling his merchandise to me. Although Marcela was embarrassed to tell me the truth, one day she called me to tell me that her younger brother had been arrested, but she was not sure if it was by immigration authorities or the police. It turned out that he had been engaged in illicit activities and that his accomplices had turned him in because they had quarreled. Marcela was beside herself; she was supposed to be in charge of him in the United States but had not been able to "control him." Crying, she explained, "It was the easiest way for him to survive here. I know he had a tough life here. One day he slept under a car because he had no place to go. But that's no excuse. I don't know if he's what they say he is, but I am ashamed of him. It hurts me, but the best thing would be to send him back to El Salvador, because here he'll end up in jail or being killed." Sadly, Marcela's younger brother went back to El Salvador but did not mend his ways. In fact, once there, he joined a ruthless gang (that bore the name of one with which he was familiar when he stayed in Los Angeles for a short time) and was eventually killed in a shooting.[14]

The case of Milagro V. and her daughter is less tragic but equally serious. Milagro's daughter Dinorah joined a local gang and eventually ran away from home to live with fellow gang members.[15] Milagro said that once when she had an argument with Dinorah, the girl said that she preferred to be with her peers because she felt at ease with them and that they were her family now. Milagro said that she had noticed that Dinorah's friends had given her money and clothes. In fact, Milagro felt she could not compete with the material gifts they had given Dinorah, because she simply could not afford them. In many cases I came across, the youngsters expected the parents to provide them with material comforts. As Mary Waters (1997) also found in her study of Caribbean children, these children's expectations were in part shaped by the parents' remittances before they were brought to this country. When Dinorah left the house, Milagro was terribly distraught and later confessed in a therapy session led by a volunteer psychologist at a community organization that she had been suicidal. She felt she had let her daughter down and not done a good job raising her and that it was entirely her fault that Dinorah was out of control. She was particularly upset because she could not conceive of "a daughter behaving like a [male] criminal."

In a similar case, Gilberto F. and Alicia N. were deeply saddened because they had not noticed "in time" that their daughter Yanira had become a gang member. They had suspected something was wrong when Yanira started wearing baggy clothes. "She dressed like a *chola* [female gang member], and she would wear the dark lipstick, you know, the kind that girls in gangs wear. And when she came home with this bracelet, we thought, there's something wrong here. But Yanira told us that we were old-fashioned and we didn't understand that it was fashionable. And we're always so careful with what the kids are doing, that this really took us by surprise." Unlike Milagro, who blamed herself for not taking the time to supervise Dinorah, Gilberto and Alicia believed they had always done their best to "know what the children were doing, at all times." Alicia said that because she spent so much time outside, either going to or coming back from work, or going to community organizations or a clinic, she would take these opportunities to ask people if they had seen any of her children around. "I especially asked about Yanira," she told me, "because she's a girl." In fact, aware of her parents' watchfulness, it seems, Yanira did not join a local gang but through friends in the South Bay became a member of one in Redwood City, some thirty miles south of where she lived. When I asked her why she went all the way to Redwood City when there were several gangs in her own neighborhood that she could have joined, she said that she had done so specifically to avoid being seen in the Mission District. Her mother had a lot of friends in the area who could recognize her and report back about her activities. Yanira eventually left the gang and married a young Salvadoran man who worked as a busboy and was not affiliated with any gangs. Alicia was delighted that her daughter's husband was a hard worker and did not drink — two of the most important qualities my informants valued in men (being a faithful partner was the third). At seventeen, Yanira gave birth to her first baby. However, Yanira's early motherhood should not be construed simply in negative terms or as a factor that may perpetuate poverty in this family, for as Kristin Luker (1996) observes, teen pregnancy has less effect on poverty than poverty on teen pregnancy. In her case, Yanira's new status as a mother placed her in a different situation vis-à-vis her parents. She moved in with her new family to a larger apartment that they would share with her parents and siblings. Alicia seemed happy with the arrangement because they now lived in a larger space. They could watch each other's children (Alicia's youngest is a toddler), and even though they earned little, they would all be able to contribute at least something to the household (either in-kind or financially), which could make their lives slightly more comfortable than before. (This observation is not meant to advocate teenage pregnancy; it merely points to some of the real consequences for the people who experience it.)

Some researchers have noted the importance of informal ties in helping parents to keep the children's behavior in check (Coleman 1988; Waters 1997). Dinorah's and Yanira's cases illustrate the importance of parents' contacts with neighbors and adults in the community where they live and the consequences when this important resource is not available.[16] Yanira's decision to join a gang in another neighborhood further underscores this point. By no means is it the only factor that prevents a youngster from joining a gang, but it is one that they may consider. The immediate neighborhoods where these youngsters live provide avenues for them to easily join gangs. In this context, adult supervision, not only by parents but also by other adults, may not arrest the process altogether, as the case of Yanira shows, but it makes it more cumbersome.

It should be underscored that it is not only a lack of parental supervision (which in this case is a side effect of poverty) but poverty itself that casts a dim light on the prospects of these youngsters. Recent research that has sought to answer the question of whether parental absence or poverty has more detrimental effects has concluded that both have negative effects but different outcomes. According to Sara McLanahan (1997), although the answer remains ambiguous, family structure may be more important than poverty in determining behavioral and psychological problems, but poverty may be more important in determining educational attainment.

Conclusion

Although age expectations shape the way in which help is exchanged, immigration itself significantly alters the social position of immigrants, and culturally prescribed age-expected roles are frequently inverted. Children may displace adults as they assume more adult responsibilities and older immigrants lose authority. The older immigrants' diminished position of authority stems in part from their decreased economic potential but also, and more important, from their limited communication skills and knowledge of the new culture, which places them in a dependent situation, particularly vis-à-vis the youngsters. The children's increased responsibilities and authority result from their exposure to the wider society (or at least the segment with which they come into contact) and from their early language acquisition, however limited their skills may be. This combination of factors shapes the resources available to people at different stages of the life cycle.

Older immigrants are no longer expected to help others by putting to use the knowledge they have acquired with age. Their expected (and actual) contributions are relegated to more ordinary tasks, such as help with household chores and child care. In turn, their children, or the parent group, are expected to provide for the older immigrants' material and financial needs. But these younger immigrants cannot always fulfill these obligations because of the extreme legal, financial, and material limitations in their lives. The situation is exacerbated by the undocumented status of the older immigrants and by the fact that they have labored outside the United States and thus are unable to qualify for formal means of support. Moreover, younger immigrants cannot always provide social and emotional support to the older generation. Older immigrants, accustomed to enjoying a certain degree of social interaction, require more social support than the time-strapped younger immigrants can provide. They turn to others, mainly friends and acquaintances made through community organizations and the church, for this vital form of support.

The children, in contrast, are expected to (and do) make their contributions mostly as intermediaries between their families (plus other adult immigrants) and local institutions. However, because of their families' scarce resources, they often take on financial responsibilities and contribute to their families as adults do. These children are uncertain about their future in the United States and about whether they will ever reap the fruits of going to school; the environment in which they live further contributes to a devaluation of education and diminishes expectations. Thus they become likely candidates for dropping out of school and taking up full-time jobs, or worse, becoming enticed by the easy money of drugs and other illicit activities. The parents try to provide the children with as much material comfort as they can by working longer hours, but this has the unintended consequence of leaving less time at home for the children. This is particularly problematic, as many of these children have suffered psychological trauma, either due to the war in their country or during their journey north. In the absence of the parents' tutelage and social and emotional support, the children, like the grandparents' generation, turn to friends for this important form of assistance. However, in the case of children, calling on friends to provide them with greatly needed social support sometimes has negative consequences, especially when they engage in dubious activities or join gangs.

Similar to the Central American students that Marcelo Suarez-Orozco (1989) depicted, several youngsters in this study framed their desires and aspirations in ways that would advance their families economically, both in the United States and in their home country, and in part to reciprocate their families' efforts. However, unlike the students in Suarez-Orozco's study, the young people I came across were generally disillusioned with their prospects in the United States. At some point they might have dreamed that through hard work and persevering study they would be able to help their families advance economically and socially, but reality dictated otherwise. The legal and financial instability in which these families live is a mighty obstacle that gets in the way of the youngsters' vision of their future. The experiences of these young immigrants resemble more closely those of children in inner cities — their poverty, troubled schools, exposure to the allure of easy money, and lower expectations of the future — than those of children of other immigrants with access to more and better resources. As Hondagneu-Sotelo and Avila (1997) observe for Central Americans, these adolescents confront the triple burden of simultaneously entering adolescence, a new society, and reconstituted families with little resemblance to those they knew before. It remains a question what effects their current predicament will have on their future and that of their families.

Chapter 8

Immigrant Social Networks
and the Receiving Context

The fact that these compatriots don't help one another shouldn't
be taken as something negative, something bad about these
immigrants, because it's not that they don't want to, it's that they
can't. So I don't think there's something wrong with them. Where
I think there's something wrong it's with the place that they come
to. No, not San Francisco specifically, of course not [smiles]. I'm
talking about the environment right now, at this particular time,
in which these poor things come to live.

Mireya C.

The assertion that immigrant social networks represent sources of
financial, material, and emotional support for newcomer immigrants
is understandable, given the emphasis placed on the functionality of
these ties as conduits for immigrant assimilation. The analysis presented in this study and Mireya's words above suggest otherwise, however. Arguably a deviant case, the Salvadoran networks are far from
being fixed, monolithic components of the immigrant experience; they
are fluid, contingent, and changing. This study set out to explain these
dynamics, and now I return to some questions posed in the beginning.
In doing so, I also assess the broader implications of these findings for
our understanding of immigrant social networks. This discussion highlights the benefit of examining in depth an anomalous case, for as
Howard Becker (1992) and Michael Burawoy (1991) remind us, such
cases present a unique opportunity to rework explanations of normal
ones.

Social Networks
and the Organization of Migration

The notion that immigrant newcomers rely on those who are
familiar — family, friends, and compatriots — in the place of arrival has

long been acknowledged. The crux of the argument is that social obligations that inhere in these ties allow immigrants to draw on them to
gain access to assistance at the point of destination, thus substantially
reducing the costs — financial and psychological — of migration. For
instance, the quantity and quality of social contacts that undocumented immigrants bring to the border are believed to shape their
eventual crossing, though these are constrained by U.S. enforcement
efforts (Singer and Massey 1998). As immigrants settle and their ties
mature, these also form the basis for solidarity and provide avenues
for successful incorporation into the host society. In essence, social
networks are presumed to protect immigrants from the vicissitudes of
the societies they enter. Thus these ties "function" to counteract the
detrimental effects of poverty or instability as well as to enhance the
immigrants' potential for success. In this view, social networks account
for immigrants' success in surviving the conditions they encounter and
for the prosperity that some immigrant groups have achieved. This
view also underscores important social aspects of immigrant life, as
individuals do not live in isolation but inhabit particular social
contexts.

Salvadorans left their country en masse during the twelve-year conflict there. The overwhelming majority of them left for reasons related
in some way to the civil war. Some were persecuted because of their
active membership in the wrong political group; others belonged to
social groups that the opposing armies deemed enemies and, thus,
feared for their lives; others were victims of the generalized violence
that reigned during those years. Therefore, the heterogeneous
Salvadoran population that arrived in the United States during the
1980s and into the 1990s included "activists," "targets," and "victims,"
in Aristide Zolberg, Astri Suhrke, and Sergio Aguayo's (1989, 269)
conceptualization of refugees. All three groups left their country
because of the immediate violence surrounding their everyday lives.
But this is why many left El Salvador; it is not why so many came to
the United States.

To enter the United States, the majority of these Salvadorans had to
cross two or three international borders, pay huge amounts of money,
and expose themselves to life-threatening dangers. They were able to
withstand the vicissitudes of the journey and eventually arrive in the
United States mainly because of the family and friends who awaited

them and often had helped them finance their trips. Thus the central organizing principle of Salvadoran migration to the United States has been the intricate web of social networks. The overwhelming majority of these immigrants had *contacts* in the United States — a family member who gave or lent them money, a friend who passed on essential information or a useful telephone number — who served as catalysts for migration. As has been the case for other immigrant groups, informal networks were key for Salvadorans.

The Salvadoran case further exemplifies what scholarship in the field has long noted: social networks bind migrants and nonmigrants in a complex web of interpersonal relations that over time perpetuate migratory flows (Massey et al. 1987). It also demonstrates, however, the key place of these ties in facilitating migration from politically conflictive regions. The relevance of social networks has been acknowledged in labor migration, particularly in efforts to correct explanations that favor macrostructural (at times overly deterministic) frameworks, and, of course, in family reunification. But more emphasis has been placed on the conditions of exit (or of reception) — of migration from war-torn areas — than on the social mechanisms that make migration possible. Conceptually, informal networks lose relevance for refugee migrations to countries of first asylum. The importance of social networks for this type of migration emerges when those involved cross several international borders — or oceans — to reach a safe haven. When refugee immigrants make use of social webs similar to those used by "regular" immigrants to reach their destinations, it becomes difficult to disentangle whether they are "political" or "economic" migrants. For Salvadorans, friends and family would represent the only potential source of support, as they cannot easily access goods and benefits necessary for their resettlement through formal channels.

Effects of the Receiving Context on Social Networks

When I began this study, it seemed reasonable — perhaps even expected — that Salvadoran newcomers would rely on informal networks of family, friends, and compatriots in San Francisco for different forms of assistance. They arrived in a city legendary for its tolerance, where there was a long-established Salvadoran community.

Also, they arrived to join relatives who had helped them to finance their trips north. And because newcomers are usually in great need of immediate necessities like housing, food, and jobs, I believed that their case presented a unique opportunity to capture the singular importance of informal assistance for immigrants.

Contrary to what the literature proposes, however, the family, friends, and compatriots on whom the newcomers had *expected* to rely did not rally to their support. The stories depicted in this study draw attention to several overlooked features of immigrant social networks. First, the social ties that immigrants make use of to migrate may weaken at the point of destination. The overwhelming majority of Salvadorans in this study made use of assistance from their U.S. relatives to migrate and expected this help to continue while they got a start here. On arrival in the United States, however, the hopes of many newcomers, as well as the hopes of their U.S. family members, were dashed. Thus a conceptual distinction between social networks as catalysts for migration and as resources in settlement may be necessary. Second, a strict characterization of these networks as either weak or strong does not capture accurately the inherent complexity in these ties. It should be recalled that the *same* people whom the participants in this study turned to for help at one time could not be of assistance at other times. Third, the same networks that are supportive at one point can be riddled with conflict at others; the viability of immigrant networks fluctuates with time and is affected by a multiplicity of place-specific factors. Fourth, giving and receiving help is a *process* that people create in their quotidian lives; even immigrants with access to strong ties do not always obtain assistance from the first person asked. Fifth, care must be exercised when the concept of immigrant social networks is used in relation to the term "social capital," as it is often assumed that the former will automatically result in the latter. Coleman (1988) observed that what makes social networks convertible into social capital is the obligations of trust and expectations that inhere in relationships. And as this study shows, social capital cannot be generated automatically when immigrants do not have access to desirable resources, because reciprocal obligations are undermined under these conditions. Sixth, a common background is not enough for cohesive ties among coethnics to flourish. Internal divisions within a group (e.g., along social class, time of arrival, political ideology) tend to be blurred when too much emphasis is placed on extolling ethnic solidarity — at the risk of simplifying formidable complexities. Salvadoran newcomers and their long-established compatriots did not interact much because more powerful social demarcations than a common birthplace acted to create important fissures among them. Seventh, the broader context of reception exerts a mighty influence on the dynamics of networks. These broader forces are not static; their effects on networks will vary, generating a plurality of experiences between and within immigrant groups. Thus, whereas cultural prescriptions are important, they are not the sole determinants of whether a particular group is going to be more or less prone to have supportive social networks. The results of this study are incongruent with accepted notions of immigrant families and of immigrants as always available to help compatriots in need, not so much because of cultural predicaments operating in this group but because a particular configuration of political and economic forces in the context of reception constrained the availability and quality of resources for assisting one another.

Although arguments about the efficacy of social networks in immigrant life seem reasonable — and they have gone a long way toward explaining different aspects of immigrant life, including assimilation — they tend to treat the existence of cohesive and immutable social networks as a given. The importance of social networks for immigrants, or for other groups, cannot be disputed of course, but the assumption that these ties are omnipresent and viable resources needs close scrutiny. This study suggests that a more fruitful approach to an examination of immigrant social networks is to begin by turning the argument around. Instead of focusing on the "function" of these ties as safeguarding immigrants from the effects of broader forces, the effects on social networks should be assessed first. This is not the only possible approach to examining the centrality of immigrant social networks; nonetheless, it is a useful one. It deflects attention from normative expectations about immigrant institutions that entangle what *should* take place with what *actually* takes place and brings into focus the preeminence of the context that immigrants face. As with other social relations, immigrant social networks are not impervious to the material and physical conditions within which they exist. Macrostructural forces can serve to facilitate exchanges among immigrants and thus can be conducive to enduring ties, but they can also impede people from helping one another. Examining the effects of broader forces on social networks, therefore, permits us to explain when these networks do in fact present viable sources of support and when they fail to do so, thus rendering a more complete picture of immigrant social life.

Extrapersonal factors such as immigration laws and the labor market shape the structure of opportunities for immigrants; they dictate whether immigrants have access to resources with which to assist one another and, when they do, to what kind. When these factors are favorable — meaning relaxed or even friendly immigration laws and a viable economy with abundant jobs — immigrants can muster the necessary resources. But when they are adverse, they have detrimental effects on informal networks. Immigrant laws restrict the movement of people into the country but make those who are already here with dubious legal status highly mobile. Labor market opportunities determine if participants in exchanges will have anything to give and whether and when those who receive will have the means to repay. A resource-poor community can curtail the goods that immigrants have available to assist one another. The practice of reciprocity and norms of exchange — which lie at the core of informal networks — are difficult to maintain in these circumstances, as material constraints interrupt the flow of exchanges and extend indefinitely the normative time within which favors should be returned.

Although these adverse factors taken individually can affect the viability of informal networks, it must be noted that it is the *confluence* of all three unfavorable conditions — stringent and hostile immigration laws, an economic downturn, and a resource-poor community reception — that has potentially deleterious repercussions on immigrants' informal networks, as the Salvadorans in this study indicate. Where one of these factors is present, immigrant networks would not necessarily be unstable (Menjívar 1997a). In a comparative study of immigrant networks among Vietnamese, Mexicans, and Salvadorans, I found that Salvadorans shared undocumented status with Mexicans, refugee characteristics with Vietnamese, and employment instability with both groups, but only the Salvadorans faced all three unfavorable conditions (Menjívar 1997b). The instability or weakening of the Salvadorans' ties was rooted in the singularly hostile context of reception that they faced. Barely surviving in the adverse environment they encountered, even in traditionally hospitable San Francisco, the Salvadorans in this study had too many demands on their meager resources. Often they were confronted with painful choices because they could not fulfill all their social obligations simultaneously.

An inhospitable context of reception creates instability in informal networks because even the poor need a minimum of resources to participate in reciprocal exchanges. Living conditions of extreme marginality can hamper the generation of social capital, which is created through active exchanges and interactions between individuals. This occurs in two ways. First, when people, by virtue of their material and social limitations, cannot participate in regular exchanges, ties weaken and the production of social capital is arrested. And second, even stable ties cannot be conducive to the formation of this social resource when the participants in exchanges only have access to the same limited resources, with little opportunity to reach goods and benefits beyond their immediate milieu. Bourdieu (1986, 249) observes that the volume of social capital that a person possesses depends on the size of the network that he or she can mobilize and on the volume of other forms of capital (economic, cultural) that each of those contacts has. A social network, though not a given, is necessary to produce and reproduce *lasting* useful relationships that will result in a material or symbolic profit (Bourdieu 1982). So when people are unable to regularly exchange favors, to produce and reproduce beneficial relationships, the generation of social capital may be suspended.

Social Position and Social Networks

Although macrostructural factors shape the structure of opportunities for immigrants and thus the resources people have available to assist one another, broader forces cannot fully account for the varied ways in which people actually go about reciprocating and helping out those who are close to them. Social class insertion (a combination of what immigrants bring in and the opportunities that await them) shapes the quality and quantity of resources that immigrants will have available to assist one another. Hierarchies of power dictate differential access to resources, however limited these may be. Differences in social position also result in dissimilar interests and obligations (both actual and expected). Thus gender and generation, for instance, shape reciprocal exchanges as these are delimited by constraints imposed by prescribed norms of behavior for men and women and for the young and old and mold their interactions. Within the general shrinking effect that poverty imposes on opportunities and resources, gender and generation inform informal exchanges in important ways.

Men and women are positioned differently vis-à-vis desirable resources, and cultural norms and practices that govern gender relations — including sexuality — affect men and women differently. Thus they derive dissimilar benefits from their informal networks and go about establishing these links differently. Cultural practices disfavor women by restricting their behavior and mobility, whereas they grant men more freedom of movement and action. Also, men tend to control relatively more material resources than women do. Hence men and women are positioned differently in informal exchanges. As the cases in this study show, men can access relatively stronger networks composed of compatriots and other coethnics, which may act as a disincentive to establishing wider-ranging ties. By contrast, women, in their efforts to procure goods for themselves and their families, are induced to forge ties with people beyond their immediate milieu. Whereas men's networks tend to be relatively stronger within their own group, those of women show a higher degree of "multiplexity" (in Boissevain's [1974] conceptualization). In a different scenario, the opposite may likely occur. For example, by virtue of their employment or geographic location, men's range of contacts could be wider while women's could be narrower. Also, cultural prescriptions that regulate gender relations are not fixed structures. As time elapses they will be altered — either becoming more egalitarian or reaffirming existing ones (Menjívar 1999b). But judging from this as well as other studies, I surmise that the actual process of giving and receiving may remain fundamentally gendered.

In the same vein, sociocultural ideologies that govern age roles shape age expectations, needs, and resources, and these vary as individuals go through the life cycle. Older immigrants are expected to help others by putting to use knowledge they have acquired with age, whereas children are expected to provide only in-kind help, as they do not yet possess the means to participate in other areas. But immigration itself plus the conditions immigrants face alter age-related expectations, for they reshape the resources — however scarce — that people have available; thus "traditional" age-appropriate behaviors often become irrelevant and are reversed. The Salvadoran children in this study often took on responsibilities that normally were handled by adults, just as older members often felt isolated because their roles in the family had become ambiguous and their status diminished.

The relative lack of knowledge of the new culture and diminished financial contributions of older immigrants undermine their "traditional" authority, whereas children's exposure to the larger society (at least that segment of it in which they live) and their early language acquisition increase their status and authority. Thus the immigrants' position in the life cycle at the time of migration, as it affects other important aspects of their experience, also impinges greatly on their informal exchanges.

Changes in Social Networks with Migration

A longitudinal approach to the study of social networks allows us to capture their potential for transformation in at least two ways — as time elapses in the United States and in relation to networks in the communities of origin. Although it is quite plausible that some immigrant groups always have access to enduring ties, it is equally plausible that social networks undergo changes, not only as a result of immigration itself, but also between initial arrival and later settlement. In the communities immigrants enter, social networks may be transformed over time because people face dissimilar conditions and have varying needs at different times; configurations of macrostructural factors fluctuate with time and place also. Thus social networks are seldom static structures that immigrants can always access. Moreover, not only do social networks differ from group to group, they also differ as waves of the same immigrant group — like the Salvadorans in this study — arrive at different historical junctures and so are exposed to dissimilar conditions. Thus, even for the same immigrant group, the receiving context makes a huge difference. This argument does not intend to downplay the importance of the immigrants' social class, for it definitely affects their prospects in the new society. Nor does it intend to downplay the powerful effect of cultural prescriptions, for these shape the immigrants' responses to the conditions they face. But when powerful structural forces are not propitious for networks to flourish, favorable individual characteristics are often diluted and socially prescribed norms of behavior become difficult to fulfill.

Social networks are also transformed by immigration because the contexts immigrants enter and those they exit sometimes vary profoundly. Often contemporary immigrants originate in social environments where close-knit, enduring ties of mutual assistance are the norm. In some cases immigrants may find that social obligations persist in the communities they enter, and they continue to offer opportunities to partake of resources with those that are familiar. In other cases the conditions in the receiving context are not propitious for the maintenance of such cohesive ties, and these become unstable and may even break down. This dual conceptualization, while useful for conveying a less "organic" image of social networks, may seem a bit simplistic, for reality is rarely so neatly compartmentalized. A characterization that emerges from this study, which avoids depicting social networks in such stark contrast, seems more in line with the complexity inherent in these ties.

It is noteworthy that even though many Salvadorans' social networks seemed to have weakened *on arrival* in the United States, there were indications that social relations based on trust could have already deteriorated *in El Salvador*, as people experienced poverty and extreme hardship there as well. Moreover, the war created competition for ever-scarcer resources, and distrust was fostered by the knowledge that close friends, co-workers, and neighbors might denounce people close to them. In addition, structural conditions, such as new capitalist forms of production, which drove families to separate to find work, might have taken a toll on informal ties even before migration. These study participants had hoped to receive help from friends or family members, especially close relatives such as parents or siblings, who had assisted them to migrate. Their expectations were not based on normative rules of behavior in their society of origin — which prescribe civility in social relations and govern assistance among families, friends, or even compatriots — but on very specific circumstances. So what was puzzling was that the *same* friends and family, sometimes a relative as close as a mother, who had helped them before through remittances and money or information to make the trip turned their backs on the newcomers. This indicates that it was the conditions of the receiving context that proved to powerfully effect transformations in the immigrants' networks of support.

The point of this study was not to portray immigrant social networks as uniformly weak or unstable. The Salvadorans seldom were left with no one to turn to, because they invariably sought family members, community agencies, or friends for help. In fact, while the stories depicted here at times might be sad and distressing, they should not be construed solely in those terms, or as a pessimistic assessment of immigrant social life. They make evident the formidable capacity of humans to transcend incalculably difficult circumstances. This case underscores the effects of a general lack of resources on the viability of immigrant social networks, and it illustrates the contingent, uneven nature of receiving and obtaining help. Thus the Salvadorans' experiences that I recount here challenge notions about the important "functions" that social networks play in immigrant life, as these may be suspended when the material and physical conditions in the receiving place are inadequate. This study provides a pragmatic counterbalance to overly romanticized notions of immigrant unity and solidarity that at times have proven counterproductive to the immigrants themselves.

Policy Recommendations

The assumption that poor immigrants — or the poor in general — rely on those who are familiar for help and comfort in trying times may need to be reassessed. In fact, those very conditions against which social networks presumably shield hinder the everyday exchanges that sustain social networks. This point carries important policy implications. Resources available to immigrants in the place of reception are crucial; immigrants who cannot count on much cannot be expected to help one another. Policies based on the assumption that because immigrants have strong networks — so often extrapolated from the mere fact that they have relatives in the United States — they can take care of one another need to be recast.

The general lack of access to such resources among the Salvadorans in this study had a powerful homogenizing effect. Even if their backgrounds were heterogeneous — ranging from street vendors to professionals, from rural poor to urban middle class, hailing from all corners of their homeland — in the United States they fared about the same. Barely able to survive in the inhospitable environment in which they lived, they lacked the means to prosper and thus were not in a position to help others, even if they wanted to. An infrastructure that would help immigrants resettle could create propitious conditions for networks to thrive and perhaps the potential for a community with real opportunities for economic advancement to develop. I am not speaking about a "government handout," which most immigrants would find demeaning because it goes against their strong work ethic and hopes for the future. By an infrastructure of resources for immigrants, I mean programs that would help newcomer immigrants translate their human capital into tangible socioeconomic gains. These include English-language classes. Short-term language instruction will enable those who arrive with professional training to work in their chosen fields; training or retraining will enable the less educated to obtain employment in the host country. In fact, perhaps the proponents of the recently passed English-only legislation in California would have seen their objectives better served by switching strategies. Rather than channel energies into promoting largely symbolic bills with strong negative messages to the immigrants, they could have lobbied to increase monies for English-language instruction for immigrants (for which the immigrants would have been profoundly grateful), which were drastically reduced by cuts in federal funding.

Also, as I have argued elsewhere (Menjívar 1994a), opportunities to regularize the Salvadoran immigrants' legal status are vital. In the current anti-immigrant climate these suggestions may seem ludicrous, but when put in a long-term perspective, they may begin to make sense. Here I refer to the "start-up" resources that would give them a better chance both to begin their lives in the United States and to acquire the resources to help others, which would allow them to become active members of society. This strategy may prove more effective in the long run. This study has demonstrated the negative consequences for the fate of immigrants starting out on the margins of society. In Lolita Q.'s words:

As you probably have noticed, we'll keep on coming to this country like we've been doing for a long time. That's the truth. No matter how much they'd like to throw us out, we'll be here. So, the only thing I'd like to add in this interview is to emphasize that we're here because we need to work to survive here and to support our families there. The war destroyed our lives, our livelihood.

So all we need is work, that's all, so that we can make a decent living, and not have to live the clandestine lives that we are forced to live. No, never to live off of these people. We could, because it was this government's money that supported the war. But, no, we're not going to remember those things. What's past is past. We're not bad people. It'd be enough to let us live here, as human beings. We only want to live in peace with them and with ourselves.

Appendix A

Crossing Boundaries:
A Personal Note on Research

Renato Rosaldo (1989) observed that the social analyst does not meet the informants as a blank slate; the latter are also analyzing subjects. Given the significance of the interaction between the "knower" and the "known," it is important to note not only what was said but also to whom and in what context. It is in this light that I wish to discuss how my own social characteristics might have influenced my relationship with my informants and thus shaped the nature of the data I gathered.

From the outset of the study, even though my informants were my compatriots, I knew that I would be crossing boundaries of age, class, education, and gender. For instance, because I was younger than many of my informants and was also a student at the time, I addressed everyone with the formal *usted*. I prefaced the names of all the women who were older than I with *niña* — the Salvadoran colloquial term for *señora* — or *doña*. (*Doña* conveys deference but sometimes distance; thus, in the context of informal conversations, *niña* is more appropriate. In the text I use *doña* and not *niña* to avoid confusion.) I addressed any man even slightly older than I as *don,* a term of respect. I did this in spite of having many more years of education than all but one — a graduate student — of my informants. As a Salvadoran, I had to communicate with them within a traditional age hierarchy. I also addressed everyone with these terms of respect in spite of the marked differences in our social class. My informants — all but two were urban working class or rural lower middle class — would quickly ascertain my middle-class standing when they heard the manner in which I spoke or learned where I lived or what school I attended. Also, our own immigrant trajectories were quite different. I was never an undocumented immigrant, never lived in the neighborhoods where my informants lived, never held the kinds of jobs they did, and never experienced most of what has shaped their lives.

At first I was afraid that this social difference would create a barrier between us and we would be unable to converse genuinely. However, I was surprised by my informants' openness and the ease with which they spoke to me about their lives. Only after conversing at length with them did I realize that there were class-bound aspects of their lives that were alien to me. Thus, in a sense, I was at times simultaneously an insider and an outsider. But I demonstrated a sincere interest in their lives and a genuine desire to understand them. My worries about the obstacle that our class differences would represent often were dissipated when my informants would joke and tease me about my inadequacies in dealing with the hypothetical situations they would sometimes pose to me, situations that were all too real in their daily lives — both past and present.

My informants often invited me to share with them the little they had, and occasionally I was asked to attend a special event, such as a wedding, a baptism, a birthday party, or even a funeral. Sometimes they would invite me to their homes when they had prepared a special Salvadoran dish that I had mentioned I particularly missed. On one occasion, Chentía A. had prepared *pupusas* (thick tortillas filled with cheese, pork, and/or beans), and as I was about to leave, she handed me three wrapped in foil paper, so that I would have "something to eat later." She was concerned that because I lived "among Americans" I would become nostalgic for these Salvadoran delicacies. Over the course of our meals my informants would talk about their lives both in the United States and in El Salvador and would take these opportunities to ask me about my own life. Something that always puzzled them was that even though I spoke English, had legal documents, had several years of graduate education, and "worked at the university" as a research assistant, I was not making much more money (and sometimes even less) than they were. It was during these moments of intimacy that I gained invaluable knowledge about their lives. In conversations filled with humor, teasing, gossip, and emotion, my informants shared with me the most telling moments of their relationships with one another. Marcela Q. explained to me that I had found such a warm reception because some of my informants probably expected me to reciprocate at some point in the future. She said that perhaps they did not necessarily want something material, just friendship with someone from a higher-class background. Indeed, some asked me for favors that needed immediate attention, whereas others asked me for longer-term commitments, such as being the godmother of a child, an obligation that I gladly accepted.

Another important social characteristic that shaped my interaction with my respondents was gender. My interactions with men and women were different. I would engage in more personal conversations with the women, even with the older ones, than with the men. I could meet with the women in their homes, even in their rooms, when they were alone; I could accompany them on errands and to visit relatives and friends, which provided unique opportunities for frank conversations. I could not interact in the same way with men; as a Salvadoran woman I simply could not cross these lines. Had I developed with the men the same level of closeness I had with the women, my reputation would have been compromised, and it would have been detrimental to my research. Such closeness would have been quickly construed as an invitation for a romantic relationship. Thus my conversations with men usually took place in more "businesslike" settings, such as my office at the language school or at the community organizations. I had to avoid conversing with the men alone, particularly given the personal nature of my conversations with my informants; otherwise I would not have been taken seriously by either the men or the women.

Unequal backgrounds and power relations unquestionably shaped exchanges with my informants, but our common nationality and language helped somewhat to counter — not to erase — those differences. My having been born and raised in El Salvador and my frequent travels and contacts with my family there brought me a little closer to my informants' personal worlds. Also, to some extent, because we were all in a foreign land, I was perceived as someone who could at least understand, if not share, their experiences. Undoubtedly our shared nationality and cultural derivatives were critical, but my participation in their world was also key to my research. It was not possible, or desirable, to keep distant or to abide by principles of detachment and neutrality when confronted with moving and at times paralyzing moments in my informants' existence. So I took part in their lives. I regularly encouraged and then transported pregnant women — many of them undocumented — to sign up for prenatal or other forms of medical care. I helped some of my informants, who were afraid to visit government offices, to locate suitable resources and to fill out the necessary paperwork. I helped to translate documents and to fill out immigration forms. I gave rides to my informants and their families and sometimes to their friends too. Thanks to donations from my own friends, I was able to take used clothes and household goods to my informants, and occasionally I even provided job contacts. In sum, my role as a researcher became an informal one, as my informants' networks temporarily expanded to include me as a potential source of assistance.

Ultimately what made field research possible was rapport with my informants, which I believe created an environment for sincere interactions and candid conversations. They shared with me information about their lives that could have placed them in a vulnerable situation had they not been fairly certain about my objectives. They would openly talk about and explain details of their and their families' undocumented status, about smuggling people across the border, about relatives engaged in crime, and about more personal matters such as rape, domestic violence, conjugal relations, and substance abuse in their families. I was perceived as someone who could be trusted but, most important, as someone who did not gossip. Thus my initial trepidation about the obstacles that my social characteristics might have presented eventually dissipated. My interactions with my informants, I believe, created opportunities for sincere conversations — both ways.

Study Participants

Name	Age	Education	Relationships
Ileana A.	20s	High school	Sister Carolina and two siblings
Julio A.	80s	6th grade	—
Mauricio A.	20s	High school	Aunt and uncle
María Alicia A.	20s	High school	—
Paula A.	20s	4th grade	Roommates at the shelter
Hilda A.	70s	6th grade	—
Chentía A.	40s	1st grade	Daughters Amparo (friend Ana Ruth A.) and Anabel (their roommate Rosa); husband David M.
Mayra B.	20s	Some college	Husband Ricardo R.
Rosa María B.	30s	6th grade	Daughter Sonia
Roberto C.	20s	High school	—
Marvin C.	20s	High school	Cousin Hernán and his mother, Doña Tulita; roommate
María del Carmen C.	20s	1st grade	—
Ana Graciela C.	20s	5th grade	—
José C.	30s	8th grade	—
Rosario E.	20s	6th grade	Cousins
Priscilla F.	20s	9th grade	Cousins Rogelio and Marta
Carlos G.	50s	High school	—
Lilian M.	50s	High school	Son Edwin
Virginia M.	50s	5th grade	Niece Regina and husband Tulio; son, nephew

Name	Age	Education	Relationships
Mario M.	70s	9th grade	Nephew Enrique
Joaquín M.	30s	High school	Roommates Luis, Tony, and Armando
Elvira M.	30s	None	Roommates
Alejandro M.	30s	5th yr. medical school	—
Enzo M.	30s	2d yr. graduate school	—
Alicia N.	30s	9th grade	Husband Gilberto F.; children Yanira, Roberto, and Miguel; mother-in-law Conchita F.
Victoria O.	30s	6th grade	—
Lolita Q.	30s	College	—
Marcela Q.	20s	1st grade	Daughter Claudia; brother; cousin Sonia; neighbor Doña Berta; friend Matilde A.
Armando Q.	60s	High school	—
Carlos R.	50s	11th grade	Wife; two grown sons
José R.	30s	High school	Roommate Roberto C.
Lety R.	40s	4th grade	Daughter; cousin Aracely
Evelyn S.	20s	2d yr. medical school	—
Carmen U.	20s	9th grade	—
Milagro V.	50s	6th grade	Daughter Dinorah
Estela Z.	40s	4th grade	Cousin María Luisa and her husband Humberto

Note: This is a list of the informants in this study, with relationships to other informants (the list has only 36 names because the other 14 informants are in one way or another related to the 36 and come from those in the list of "relationships"). In the relationships I only give a name if I spoke with that person at length and/or conducted a formal interview with him or her.

These names are all pseudonyms, even though when I showed my dissertation to some of my informants and they did not see their full names in print, they were disappointed. In the text I have also omitted the specific names of the towns from which my informants originated in El Salvador; I only mention the region from which they came. I have done this because in the case of Salvadorans who come from small towns or even cities, providing such information allows for relatively easy identification and thus would have compromised the confidentiality of the study participants. And I have used only an initial for the last name so as not to compromise the identity of a person who may have one of the pseudonyms as his or her real name.

"Education" refers to years of education at the time of the interview, whether the participant completed these years in El Salvador or in the United States. Since only three of these participants continued their education in the United States, this is an indication of the years of education that these immigrants had when they arrived. "High school" refers to high school or its equivalent, which for these Salvadorans is an accounting, secretarial, or teacher's degree.

Notes

Introduction

1. Societies have elaborate arrays of institutions and organizations, but daily life goes on, and societies themselves are structured through personal ties (Fischer 1982). Thus the relevance of an examination of social networks goes beyond immigrant life.

2. The approach one takes to the study of social networks is important. As Larner (1990, 181) wrote, "Viewed from a structural perspective, networks appear to be quite stable, but closer examination dissolves that stability into a myriad of counterbalanced changes — gains and losses, some gradual and others abrupt." For instance, in a study of informal support among Central American (mostly Salvadoran) immigrants, Leigh A. Leslie (1992) found that these immigrants enjoyed a great deal of support from kin. However, the study included only individuals living with at least one family member, leaving out those who might have had different experiences.

3. It is, of course, difficult to imagine a homogeneous U.S. culture, but the assumption that individuals should fend for themselves is prevalent in this country. However, even in an industrial, bureaucratized society such as the United States, success is related to "whom you know" (De Graaf and Flap 1988).

4. Ulloa (1998, 75) bases her estimates on figures from RENASAL (Red de Organizaciones Salvadoreñas en Estados Unidos), the Immigration and Naturalization Service, and the U.S. Census. She breaks them down as follows: 335,000 (32%) undocumented; 85,000 (8%) political asylum applicants; 260,000 (25%) ABC applicants; 319,597 (30%) permanent residents; and 50,000 (5%) U.S. citizens, for a total of 1,049,597.

5. The work of Hagan (1994, 1998) and Repak (1995) exemplifies how internal differentiation, particularly gender, affects these immigrants' incorporation into and long-term prospects in the United States.

6. On one occasion, when we went to the home of one of my informants for the interview, we found some of her relatives there, so she suggested that we talk in my car. I conducted two initial interviews in a Salvadoran restaurant, mainly because my informants had not had anything to eat that day (although in both cases they were pregnant).

7. Those with whom I lost contact might have had, in fact, more unstable situations — being forced to move more often — than those with whom I kept in touch for the duration of the study.

8. Even now, almost nine years after I met my informants, I still keep in touch with some of them.

9. Whereas I draw attention to the profiles in the tables when discussing the characteristics of the group in this study, comparisons should be drawn with caution for at least two reasons. First, the group in this study was not randomly selected in San Francisco, and so I make no claims regarding its representativeness. Second, the data presented in the tables do not differentiate by time of arrival; they are general data, and because those in the study were selected precisely because they were recent arrivals, disparities resulting from this selection should be kept in mind.

10. This, of course, reflects the fact that I contacted twenty-two of my informants at the language school.

11. These comparisons are not direct because the data presented in the tables do not distinguish consensual unions, an important marital arrangement among Salvadorans.

Chapter 1. The Structure of Opportunities, Social Networks, and Social Position

1. An important exception that comes to mind is Saskia Sassen's (Sassen-Koob 1984) conceptualization of international population movements where gender plays a central organizing role.

2. By this I mean the mathematically based approach to the study of networks.

3. There is also an extensive literature on social networks among the poor in the developing world (see Norris 1985 for Brazil; González de la Rocha 1994 for Mexico). Given the voluminous literature on the subject, I limit my discussion to a few that are representative of the main argument.

4. Lomnitz's study is based on research in Mexico City but has been used extensively to illustrate the efficiency of informal networks among the poor in other contexts.

5. In a study of informal networks among working-class families in Guadalajara, Mexico, González de la Rocha (1994, 228) observes that when "economic conditions deteriorate, social networks become fundamental tools for people to survive, as the sting of unemployment, the drop in real wages, and the lack of state support is less pungent when cushioning household arrangements are instrumented and social ties intensify." In contrast, Roberts (1973), in his study of poor families in Guatemala City, observed conflict and crises in social networks. An important distinction between the studies of González de la Rocha (and those of Lomnitz [1985] and Stack [1974] too)

and that of Roberts is that while she uses families or the household as her analytical units, Roberts departs from the individual level. Like Roberts, I approach the study of social networks using individuals — whose perceptions and experiences in network participation it is my task to understand — as my basic unit of analysis.

Chapter 2. Background to Migration

1. El Salvador, along with Guatemala, Honduras, Nicaragua, and Costa Rica, gained independence from Spain in 1821. However, for the next eighteen years they all existed as a single unified country, the United Provinces of Central America.

2. After about a hundred years of little attention to El Salvador, the United States strengthened its presence during this government. This marked the beginning of enduring U.S. influence on El Salvador's affairs (Murphy 1999).

3. The indigenous people of western El Salvador did not support President Araujo's election; they favored the candidate of the party in office. They eventually accepted Araujo, however, so as to demonstrate their unconditional loyalty to the government.

4. For instance, until recent years indigenous people were forced to live clandestine lives because any indication of indigenous culture — such as language or dress — could be interpreted as subversive. The irony is that General Maximiliano Hernández Martínez, who gave orders to carry out the massacre, was himself of indigenous background, and the country's elite, who never considered him one of their own, would refer to him as *el indio loco,* or the crazy Indian.

5. *Compadrazgo,* a social institution in Hispanicized countries, has roots in the Catholic sacraments of baptism, confirmation, marriage, and sometimes communion (although during pre-Columbian times, there existed similar institutions in Central America). Compadrazgo establishes close socioreligious relationships between a child, the parents, and the godparents, and it is assumed that if anything happens to the parents, the *padrinos* (godparents) will take care of the children.

6. These are large buildings located in poor sections of towns and cities where a person — often an entire family — rents a room and shares bathroom and kitchen facilities with the other tenants in the building. The rent for such a room can take up to one-third of the household income.

7. To be sure, landless and nearly landless peasants did not just passively accept the increasing trend in land concentration. As it had happened in the past, they often took over uncultivated lands and put them to use. Also as before, such actions were met with violence on the part of the landowners with help from the military (see Cabarrús P. 1983).

8. This conflict is sometimes known as the Hundred Hours War, or Soccer

War, because even though harassment against Salvadorans had already begun in Honduras, mass expulsions and looting of Salvadoran businesses started right after a soccer match between the two countries — won by El Salvador — in Honduras. The two countries took the matter of the border dispute to the International Court, which eventually ruled in favor of Honduras.

9. It is noteworthy that because out-of-wedlock children and free unions are so commonplace among Salvadoran poor families, they carry no stigma in this sector of Salvadoran society. This group, however, considers it prestigious to marry — especially through the Church — and have children within a marriage, as such practices are associated with middle-class standing. Among the middle and upper classes, in which women generally hold a more traditional position, out-of-wedlock childbearing does carry a negative stigma, and marriage — normally through the Church — is expected.

10. Recent estimates place the rate of female participation in informal activities at close to 40 percent; sometimes it is even higher than that of males (García and Gomáriz 1989, 115).

11. The important foreign support that opposition groups received throughout the civil conflict should also be recognized, for not only the government forces obtained extranational aid. In essence, the conflict was "internationalized" from its very beginning.

12. The Truth Commission, however, notes that close to 85 percent of the affected parties attributed violence to government forces.

13. The cousin of another informant shared the same view. He commented on how appalled he was at the "insensitivity" he had observed among the people in his hometown when the body of the newspaper boy was found in the town square with gunshot wounds through the eyes — an eerie warning that one should not see what one is not supposed to. Although people might have been shocked, they tried to ignore the incident and avoided talking about it openly for fear that doing so would be interpreted as disapproval, making them the next targets.

14. This suspicion was sometimes taken to extremes. One of my informants' relatives was detained and interrogated for several hours because he was suspected of collaborating with the guerrillas. The only evidence against him was that one day he had (unwittingly) occupied a parking space outside a government building that had just been vacated by someone who was suspected of collaborating with the guerrillas. Anyone who had any contact with the suspect — directly or indirectly as in the case of my informant's relative — was automatically a suspect as well.

Chapter 3. The Long Journey through Mexico

1. This cost can increase significantly if the coyote deems the case particularly complicated, such as smuggling children, the elderly, or a "nervous"

person. The cost also goes up substantially when border restrictions become enforced; sometimes the going rate for just bringing someone across the border may be $500 or $600.

2. Another example is Hondurans settling in New Orleans; this migration flow is tied to the banana companies based there that operated in Honduras.

3. As may be evident, the Salvadorans' reception in Mexico during this time and the debate over their presence there was not unlike the environment that undocumented immigrants faced when Proposition 187 was approved in California.

4. This case made the news back in the early 1980s; it called attention to the conditions of undocumented immigrants' travel.

5. Table 6 shows the relationship between land travel and the lack of a U.S. visa.

6. The cousin of one of my informants refused to learn anything about what she considered "Mexican politics." When the coyote, and eventually the rest of the group, desperately tried to convince her to memorize the names of Mexican politicians and political parties, she simply responded, "No, yo en política no me meto" — No, I don't get involved in politics. She was quite nervous about the entire operation because first she had to learn about political issues and then she had to withstand the authorities' interrogation. Her deep aversion to this situation had a very real basis back in her country, where she had learned to avoid even mentioning the word "politics."

7. Border restrictions may not necessarily reduce the flow of undocumented immigrants; they just make it riskier and more costly.

Chapter 4. The Context of Reception in the United States

1. The classic example of the relationship between foreign policy and refugee admission is the Cuban-Haitian case. Whereas thousands of Cubans are welcomed without close inspection of their motives for departure, Haitians have been systematically excluded and deemed deportable. Cuban émigrés became symbols that lent legitimacy to the U.S. position during the cold war, whereas Haitians served no such purpose. A similar paradoxical case involves the Chilean and Indo-Chinese émigrés in the mid-1970s.

2. This brought significant policy changes. It defined "refugee" according to the UN Convention and Protocol; it established the "normal flow" of refugees as 50,000 annually, up from the 17,400 limit established in 1965; and it gave refugees the opportunity to regularize their status to that of permanent residents after a certain period in the country (Lacey 1987, 27).

3. These definitions of "refugee" have never included gender-specific forms of persecution, an issue that is now being discussed in various forums. Some countries, notably Canada, are leading the initiative. The experiences

of the Salvadoran women with whom I spoke in San Francisco (Menjívar 1996) point to the importance of considering gender differences in refugees' motivations to leave conflictive regions.

4. This idea was quickly embraced in El Salvador, particularly among the middle and upper classes and the extreme right, who viewed it as their duty to contribute to the battle. A logo placed on bumper stickers and T-shirts during this time read *El Salvador: Apocalipse del comunismo* (El Salvador: Apocalypse of Communism).

5. One of the saddest legacies of this military buildup may be found in today's rampant crime and delinquency in El Salvador. Although the war ended and armies on both sides were ordered to relinquish their weapons, many soldiers did not comply. Also, promises of a land reform (included in the Peace Accords) that would give these (now unemployed) ex-combatants plots of their own have been largely unfulfilled. Such factors make up an explosive combination, as many of these unemployed and still heavily armed men have found alternative ways to make a living, that is, by engaging in criminal activities. Social programs to counteract the situation have been severely impaired because the U.S. government drastically reduced aid to El Salvador when the Peace Accords were signed, a time when such assistance was perhaps more needed than during the war.

6. Refugees are processed overseas and then admitted into the United States, whereas political asylum seekers apply for the status in the United States.

7. In addition, church (Sanctuary) workers who, as a matter of religious conscience, helped many Central American (mostly Guatemalan and Salvadoran) immigrants to come into the country were themselves indicted on charges of conspiracy to violate immigration laws and of smuggling and harboring illegal aliens (Loescher and Scanlan 1986).

8. Although these land trips were costly, they were more affordable than the minimum requirements for obtaining a visa.

9. I heard from two legal caseworkers that, based on their observations, former government army personnel had a better chance to obtain political asylum.

10. This figure includes the approximately 200,000 Salvadorans who applied in the first round for Temporary Protected Status. Lopez, Popkin, and Telles (1996, 287), using a larger estimate of the Salvadoran population in the United States, estimate this figure to be 49 percent. In any case, the percentage of undocumented Salvadorans is among the highest of any group.

11. Another important issue for these immigrants is the acquisition of English-language skills, which, if circumstances permitted, they were determined to obtain. Those who could not attend school went to great lengths to try to learn the language. For instance, Amparo A. and her family saved and pooled money to purchase a language course that they had seen advertised

on television. Invariably, however, my informants mentioned that the only thing that prevented them from attending English classes was their unpredictable work schedules or the lack of transportation at night. Thus, with more instruction available that would fit their schedules, these immigrants would not think twice about enrolling in classes.

12. The United States also granted TPS to people from Lebanon from March 1991 to March 1993; from Kuwait, from March 1991 to March 1992; and from Rwanda, from June 1994 to June 1995. Honduras and Nicaragua, Bosnia, Burundi, Kosovo Province in Yugoslavia, Liberia, Montserrat, Sierra Leone, Somalia, and Sudan are countries that as of December 1998 were designated for TPS.

13. NACARA has been unevenly implemented. For example, Nicaraguans, Cubans, and former Soviet applicants are granted permanent residence automatically, whereas Salvadorans (and Guatemalans) need to appear before an immigration judge. Also, whereas the cutoff for Nicaraguan applicants is December 1995, five years after a U.S.-backed Nicaraguan government was elected, the deadline for Salvadorans is 1990, when El Salvador was still mired in a civil war. Immigrant rights groups are now pressing the Clinton administration to establish the same cutoff date for Nicaraguans as for Salvadorans and Guatemalans and to relax the stringent requirements for the latter to be granted cancellation of removal. (There seem to be bipartisan efforts in Congress to make the cutoff date for Salvadorans and Haitians the same as that for Nicaraguans; and recently some have pressed for the inclusion of Peruvians and Colombians in the act.) The "extreme hardship" requirement may be particularly difficult to meet because, although it is assumed that the INS will infer "extreme hardship" from the situation in the immigrants' home countries, cases will still be evaluated individually.

14. In addition to formal fees, applicants usually paid for the services of someone who helped them fill out the forms, translate documents, arrange for fingerprinting, and so on. Given the high costs of the entire application procedure, service providers believe that a large number of eligible Salvadorans did not apply (Frelick and Kohnen 1994).

15. Newspapers in San Francisco regularly featured articles containing expert advice on how to weather the crisis. Mindful of the high-salaried professionals' consumer patterns, they offered information about gourmet dishes with cheaper ingredients, fixed-price meals, and price reductions in menus (see Fong-Torres 1991; Hall 1991; Minton 1991).

16. As Taylor (1992) points out in his study of farmworkers, controlling for the selection process, undocumented workers were more likely to be placed in low-wage, low-skill jobs than otherwise similar legal workers.

17. Salvadorans in other cities, particularly in Los Angeles, might have faced similar conditions during this period. According to a survey of Salvadorans in Los Angeles conducted by the Rand Corporation, the median

weekly salary for this group in 1991 was $165, with 80 percent of the inform-
ants earning less than $300 per week, and the reported median family income
was $11,250 (DaVanzo et al. 1994).

18. This image of the Salvadoran work ethic has been used extensively by
entrepreneurs to attract investment to El Salvador. For instance, in the
August 1991 issue of *Bobbin* magazine there is an advertisement that reads:
"Quality, Industriousness and Reliability Is What El Salvador Offers You!"
The caption of a picture of a woman sewing clothes says, "Rosa Martinez pro-
duces apparel for U.S. markets on her sewing machine in El Salvador. *You*
can hire her for 33 cents an hour. Rosa is more than colorful. She and her
coworkers are known for their industriousness, reliability and quick learning.
They make El Salvador one of the best buys."

19. The need for Salvadoran immigrants' remittances is so acute that it has
placed at least two Salvadoran presidents, José Napoleón Duarte and Alfredo
Cristiani, in compromising situations when they asked the U.S. government
not to deport any Salvadorans. Although Duarte and Cristiani argued "economic" reasons for such pleas (e.g., that the Salvadoran economy was not
strong enough to absorb a large influx of returnees), by asking another government to take care of Salvadoran citizens, they implied that their government was not capable of protecting its people.

20. It should be noted that although in general Salvadorans remit substantial amounts of money, not everyone does so at the same level. For
instance, at the Salvadoran Procuraduría General de Pobres (Attorney
General's Office for the Poor) there is a long list of absent fathers (who are
in the United States) who do not send a cent to their wives and children.
These mothers have petitioned the Office of the Attorney General to take
some action; unfortunately, there is not much that this office can do for
them.

21. By 1997 the median price of a house in San Francisco was more than
$300,000.

22. Increasingly more commercial and residential space in the Mission is
being gentrified, which has been pushing rents up at an accelerated pace. For
instance, a one-bedroom apartment that cost $750 in 1991 rented for $1,300
seven years later.

23. High housing costs, particularly in light of these immigrants' means,
led to frequent moves, as some were evicted because it became impossible to
pay rent. One informant mentioned that in the three years he has been living
in the United States, he has moved ten times, and another said that he has
moved five times in three years.

24. Some of these organizations are now switching strategies to concentrate on longer-term issues of settlement, and to reflect their new objectives,
they have changed their names. In some cases they have substituted the word
"refugee" — which they felt conveyed the temporary nature of this migra-

tion — for "immigrant" — which expresses the more permanent presence of these people.

25. For instance, the National Refugee Rights Project of the San Francisco Lawyers Committee for Urban Affairs filed a class action suit against the INS, charging that the fees demanded for Salvadorans applying for Temporary Protected Status were far too high for their means. In addition, the suit contended that they were unfairly denied fee waivers (in one case a Salvadoran man who earned $50 a month was denied a waiver). It was largely through the efforts of similar groups across the country that Salvadorans obtained TPS.

26. By this I mean what a community worker told me (and an informant echoed): "We are not fashionable anymore; since there is no more headline news about the war, people think that, oh, they are doing fine now." However, the end of the war has not meant an end to violence in El Salvador, and Salvadorans may continue to migrate to the United States. From the proliferation and activity of "travel agencies" (organized group trips led by coyotes) throughout El Salvador, one may surmise that this flow does not show signs of decreasing in the near future.

27. Erdmans (1998, 3–5) observes that we tend to homogenize communities, glossing over internal differences so as to make comparisons across groups. In doing so, we concentrate on identifying borders between, rather than within, groups, denying the internal fault lines along which groups collide and identities emerge.

28. These divisions may not be observed among other immigrants coming from politically conflictive contexts (e.g., Vietnamese, Cubans) because those refugee groups, who are usually officially recognized, tend to be ideologically more homogeneous.

29. Often the longtime Salvadoran residents' nationality goes unnoticed and they "pass" as, or are mistaken for, Mexicans or even Anglos.

30. My informants observed that the notaries are sure they will collect their fees because the informants are aware that if they do not pay up, they run the risk that the notaries will use the information they have gathered to denounce them to the INS.

31. Even though the immigrants who frequented community (refugee) organizations in search of help often personalized their relations with the community workers, these relations were more akin to patron-client relationships, with a hierarchical difference between those in charge of providing the services and those receiving them. In the case of the organizations described in this section, the relationships were of friendship and mutual trust based on relative equality of the members involved (see Eisenstadt and Roniger 1984 for a discussion of this difference).

32. There are now more of these "hometown" associations than at the time I was conducting this research. This reflects, in part, the fact that as these

immigrants begin to settle, they also begin to strengthen broader links to their country, not just to their own families. Belonging to hometown associations seems to be more commonplace among people who are more settled and, importantly, have documents.

33. By no means is this view shared by all members of such groups. This person might have made this point to emphasize the sharp contrast between their philosophy and that of the refugee organizations. On the other hand, workers in community organizations often said that it was their duty to impart a measure of political consciousness to the people who were requesting their services.

34. Those centered on political activities often work in conjunction with community organizations.

35. An example was provided by Governor Pete Wilson of California, who made headline news by blaming immigrants' and refugees' social service costs for the deep financial crisis of his state. Even with a generous policy of government reception, refugees who enter in a period of economic contraction may not encounter the welcome reception that one might expect.

36. An event that occurred while I was doing fieldwork disturbed many immigrants and community workers. The church where the food distribution took place was burned to the ground, so the distribution had to be moved to a different location — another church. Because residents of the area had started to complain to the city about the concentration of immigrants in their streets on the days when food was distributed, arson was suspected.

37. Mireya, the community worker who had earlier mentioned that it was difficult to organize among Salvadorans, told me that the anti-immigrant movement that had sparked the passage of Proposition 187 had caught them unprepared. They had for so long concentrated on fighting for basic rights that they had not worked hard enough to organize for achieving more long-term political objectives. In an effort to respond to the backlash, these community workers now have expanded their activities to include areas with longer-term objectives.

38. There have been other controversial initiatives in San Francisco that speak to the changing political climate in this city. For instance, when Army Street was renamed Cesar Chavez Street, there was considerable opposition. Voters had to decide whether to revert to the old name or keep the new one; keeping the new name won approval by a very slim margin.

39. The proposition's sponsors appealed the decision to dismiss the measures. Governor Davis has indicated that he will not implement the provision that denies education to undocumented children, but he cannot ignore the 60 percent of California voters who approved the proposition. So he has been seeking a "middle path" between opponents and supporters.

40. The Salvadoran government openly condemned the vote as a violation of the immigrants' human rights. But El Salvador's record in the area of

human rights is less than exemplary, and the government may well have been more concerned about the consequences of anti-immigrant sentiment for El Salvador — a decrease in remittances and an increase in deportees who may demand social services and jobs.

41. I do not mean to homogenize reactions to immigrants, for this would miss important nuances of the debate (see Clark 1998). Reactions vary greatly according to ethnic status, socioeconomic standing, educational level, and even region.

42. Of course, this conflict is not about nationalities per se but about the position of these groups vis-à-vis the unequal distribution of goods in society. Such tension may arise between groups that live in close proximity and compete for the same meager resources.

Chapter 5. The Dynamics of Social Networks

1. This point parallels an observation that Roberts (1973, 190) made about social networks among the Guatemalan poor: "Most relationships they use to cope with urban life are not based on the neighbourhood. . . . [T]he relationships they do maintain are not well integrated; people known in one situation are not often associates in other situations. . . . Instead, most families maintain relationships with dispersed sets of kin, friends, and possible patrons."

2. In this context it is difficult to categorize these ties into "nuclear" or "extended" families because these terms are situational; depending on the circumstances, individuals may regard distant relatives as members of their immediate family and vice versa. Thus I will limit myself to a broad characterization of these ties, and when it is not an immediate one, such as a sibling or a parent, I will only indicate if it is a cousin, an uncle, and so on. The main difference will be between relatives and friends, and when appropriate, I will note the degree of proximity. As noted earlier, the institution of compadrazgo is not as central in the Salvadoran context as it is in the Mexican one; therefore, expectations and assistance based on compadrazgo do not assume the level of family that is commonly observed among groups in which this institution is stronger.

3. Here I will limit the discussion to the three forms of help that I saw most frequently being exchanged, that is, financial and material, informational, and emotional or moral.

4. The importance of reciprocity is, of course, not limited to these few authors. The list of scholars who have written about this is long, and I do not intend to present an exhaustive review here.

5. I do not intend to paint a black-and-white picture of people who help one another and others who do not, for the situation is more complex. As Wellman (1981, 173) rightly points out, to portray support networks as either

supportive or not deemphasizes the multifaceted, complex nature of social ties. However, the point of contrast here is a valid one, since it evinces the importance of dissimilar contexts of reception at different historical periods, which leads to accessing qualitatively and quantitatively different resources, a point I develop in more detail elsewhere (Menjívar 1997a).

6. Once I tried to talk with the Salvadoran employees of a Salvadoran business owner. The business owner, however, refused to let me talk with them (in spite of the fact that she knew me well and that I needed this information for my "school work," as she put it). She jokingly said that I would "get things into their heads, and pretty soon they'll start demanding more than they deserve, like it's happening with those lazy terrorists in El Salvador, who want to become rich by force."

7. Both of these countries have sizable Salvadoran communities that were formed when Salvadorans migrated there during the civil war in El Salvador in the 1980s.

8. It must be noted that what Mauricio and Paula needed were two very dissimilar things and, consequently, the absence of help to obtain these was perceived quite differently. For Mauricio, it was something necessary but extra. Paula, in contrast, needed help to survive — food and shelter. Her deflated expectations that her siblings would provide these soured their relationship.

9. Some of my informants used the language of family unity when speaking about assistance. Interestingly, however, there was often a gap between what they said should (or was expected to) happen and what actually occurred. This point has been observed in other contexts, particularly where ethnographic methodologies — that allow one to observe the difference — have been used. Roschelle (1997a) found that among Puerto Rican women there was a substantial discrepancy between the *belief* that there were child care networks available and women *actually using* them. Among Mexicans, Rouse (1989) discusses in depth the differences between perception and the reality of family unity.

10. Once, while I was on a bus with Marcela Q., she intended to introduce me to people so that I could talk with them. Her strategy, however, proved somewhat embarrassing for me. She called on acquaintances sitting in the back and, as loud as possible, informed them (and the rest of the bus) that I was a Salvadoran doing a study about Salvadorans, at the "university."

11. A study of Filipinos' psychological adjustment in Chicago (Quisumbing 1982) found the opposite: less coethnic interaction in their social networks led to better adjustment.

12. Many of my informants complained of *nervios*, described by Guarnaccia and Farias (1988, 1223) as a "powerful idiom of distress used by Latinos from a variety of Caribbean, Central and South American countries. It expresses concerns about physical symptoms, emotional states, and

changes both in the family and in the broader society." To treat this condition some of my informants would drink herbal teas or take walks, but in some cases they would take medications — unsupervised — brought from either Mexico or Central America, which they could obtain locally without prescription in *botánicas* (stores that sell healing products of different sorts).

13. Some scholars (see Edwards and Foley 1997) find that Coleman's functional definition of social capital (e.g., what facilitates individual or collective action) mixes what it is and what it does, which has important implications for contemporary debates on social capital formation.

14. This conceptualization is somewhat similar to Wilson's (1987) with regard to "social isolation" in the inner city. Wilson (1987, 60) observes that residents of neighborhoods with high concentrations of poverty do not interact as frequently with friends and relatives in the more stable areas of the city or in the suburbs. One result of this isolation is that it is much more difficult for residents of impoverished neighborhoods to be tied into appropriate job networks. In the same vein, Laumann (1966) observes that because a person's position is similar to that of his or her contacts, a higher social position has advantage because it connects one to other similar positions.

15. The quality — in contrast to the quantity — of one's informal networks is crucial. For instance, in their research on occupational status, Lin, Ensel, and Vaughn (1981) found a significant and positive association between the kinds of social resources that a job seeker evokes and the status of the job he or she attains.

Chapter 6. Gendered Networks

1. Although gossip has received attention as a form of women's communication (Jones 1980), it is not limited only to women (Harper 1996). However, Harper (1996, 135) observes, "women seek and provide useful information through [this] communicative form." What is relevant here is that gossip serves as a form of social control, particularly for women, with repercussions for their networks of support. In its destructive form, gossip does not have to be verbal, for a woman's reputation (and her life) could be ruined simply by dressing "provocatively," that is, in a way that is not culturally accepted for a "decent" woman. Similar observations have been made elsewhere, for instance, in a study of Filipina domestic workers in Hong Kong (McAllister Groves and Chang 1993).

2. See my own experience as a woman doing research in this milieu in Appendix A.

3. There is a reason why I do not refer to them equally. Don David was in his seventies, so, like everyone else, I called him Don David out of respect. At first I started addressing Chentía either as *niña* (the colloquial Salvadoran to convey respect for a woman of any age) or "Doña." But Chentía did not

want me to, because she said that she was "young, not old like him." As their relationship deteriorated, she emphasized their substantial age difference more and more and often used it to get back at him, and it was an area in which Chentía could "win." Don David, for his part, made snide remarks about her "youth."

4. Salvadoran women have a long history of labor force participation (Nieves 1979; Ministerio Público 1983; Carter et al. 1989). Their labor force participation in formal activities reached 37 percent in 1988, and it was projected to reach 40 percent in 1990 (García and Gomáriz 1989, 115). García and Gomáriz note that Salvadoran women's participation in the informal sector is substantial as well, and in some cases it even surpasses that of men.

5. Men agreed that women's rights in the United States do have an influence on their actions. For instance, when I attended Amparo A.'s wedding to the father of her third child, I had the opportunity to chat about these issues with the men who were sitting at the table. Amid jokes, teasing, and laughter, they all pointed to the fact that women can call the police or have advocates for their rights, which makes them think twice about "misbehaving at home," as one of them put it. The women at the table also agreed that this is an important aspect of life in the United States that has affected relations at home. As one of Amparo's aunts said, "Here we don't have to *aguantar* [put up with] men if we don't want to. The law protects us." This does not imply that these men do not engage in domestic violence, for instance. But at least they think about the consequences of their actions, which may have an effect on what they do.

6. Zavella (1985) makes the important distinction between kin-based and work-related or work-based networks for women, though often when women work with kin this distinction gets blurred. But, according to Zavella, such a distinction only adds to these networks' cohesiveness.

7. Employers also preferred to hire women who were personally recommended, especially by a former employee whom they considered "very good" (this usually meant that the woman did much more than she was paid to do).

8. During a discussion of this point, Sang-Hea Kil observed that sometimes gossip is used to prevent people from getting ahead of the rest, very much like crabs in a barrel. In these cases, however, gossip was more general, and, at least to me, it did not seem as if it was used for that purpose.

9. Other researchers have found similar patterns (see Goldring 1996; Hondagneu-Sotelo 1994a).

10. This used to be a predominantly white neighborhood — whose composition is becoming increasingly Asian — where several of my informants worked.

11. Pleck (1983) found that immigrant wives and children often sought the protection of the law in dealing with child or wife abuse, which undermined traditional authority in the family.

12. Undoubtedly my gender, plus an interest in their lives and a willingness to listen, encouraged this personal disclosure.

13. This does not mean that all transactions between men were of this kind. There were cases in which men paid other men for a service that would otherwise be a favor. But the reasons for paying for services differed from men to women. For instance, while women did it mostly to avoid gossip, men would charge others for favors so as to make sure that other men were not just taking advantage of their kindness.

14. Transportation was vital for these immigrants, especially for the women who worked in more than one house. For instance, Lety R. purchased a used car for $1,500 with money that she had been saving for one year plus a loan from her sister. She said that it was critical for her to own a car because she could get more houses to clean that way, and also she said she wanted to be able to lend it to her sister and brother-in-law if they ever needed it.

15. This case illustrates the scarcity of jobs in San Francisco and the vulnerability of these immigrants when they are employed.

16. These unpaid "probationary periods" are not uncommon. Several of the men and women in this study had been given these "opportunities for work" for periods of up to two months.

17. The fact that Marcela, a legally married woman, cut off relations with her former in-laws when Rosa María, who had not been legally married to her partner, does not mean that the type of marriage had an effect on how postseparation relations would fare. Some legally married people did not break those ties; some people who were only cohabiting did.

Chapter 7. Informal Exchanges and Intergenerational Relations

1. When I discussed these issues with Tsun Kung, a Taiwanese student, he said that these concerns happen among his coethnics as well. In fact, he observed, back home there is a proverb, "America is heaven for the young, a battleground for the middle-aged, and a cemetery for the old."

2. Of course, it does not mean that older immigrants do not make any contributions. For instance, in a study of Nicaraguan elderly in San Francisco, Steven P. Wallace (1992) found that the elderly can make important contributions to their families and also build community.

3. My informants and people I came to know in organizations would comment on how dangerous the neighborhood has become. The woman in charge of the food distribution program was shot in the leg on her way to the program in broad daylight. The windows of a housing project right across the street from a building I used to visit regularly have been boarded up because of the many shootings lately.

4. This is important to note because, as we will see later, if they could gain knowledge of the wider sociocultural milieu, their prospects in the United States would improve. This case illustrates "segmented assimilation" (Portes and Zhou 1993), and it is related to Fernández-Kelly's (1994) observations about cultural capital in an African-American community and to Fernández-Kelly and Schauffler's (1994) findings on the socialization of immigrant children. As they correctly point out, what these children learn about becoming American hinges on what they see around them and the types of contacts they are able to establish.

5. This landlord's relations with the children were further complicated by the children's hanging out with friends on the steps of the building's main gate. He had had several confrontations with them, and whenever "el chino" (the Chinese, as these youngsters called him) would come by, they would deliberately antagonize him.

6. Several television commercials for mail-order English courses on the Spanish channels corroborate this point. To underscore the importance of learning English, they show images of worried parents with their mouths blurred, unable to understand their children, and advise parents that to be better able to communicate with the children they should learn English.

7. There is another unfortunate outcome for these children. Given their undocumented status, they are at risk of being deported to El Salvador. There they could potentially face problems communicating because of their lack of fluency in Spanish, or because the version of Spanish ("Spanglish") they are learning — for example, words with English roots and Spanish endings — will not be understood back home.

8. I am by no means arguing that the youngsters are fully responsible for their being cut off from the benefits of the larger society. This observation only speaks to the effects that language deficiency may have, as it contributes to their social marginalization, often reinforcing the already disadvantageous position from which these children start out.

9. Sometimes these youngsters assume adult roles so fully that, like adult immigrants, they feel responsible for relatives in El Salvador. For instance, Edwin M., a nineteen-year-old, told me that he misses his grandmother and often worries about her. He wants to get a job so that he can send remittances to her regularly and send her a plane ticket so that she can come to visit. When I asked Carolina and Ileana A. about their grandparents, with their eyes watery, they also expressed the wish to have them close and were concerned because they did not know how the grandparents were faring. When they started earning an income, they saved money to send to their grandparents for airfare so that they could come to the United States for a visit.

10. Their last child was born in the United States three years after Alicia and the other three children arrived.

11. Another alternative for girls was marriage and/or having a baby, as a couple of my informants' daughters had done.

12. Many of my informants continue to use language and have retained images commonly heard during the Salvadoran war. For instance, when Amparo A. and I were talking about a child that had been abducted in a shopping mall in Los Angeles, she commented, "Oh, God, they kidnapped her. Who knows what the parents are involved in." A child's disappearance in El Salvador during the war years usually meant that he or she had been kidnapped as a result of his or her parents' involvement with the wrong political side.

13. It has been noted that many Central American (mostly Salvadoran) children suffer from post-traumatic stress disorder, which hinders their ability to learn and thus their capacity to adapt (Espino 1991).

14. Many Salvadoran teenagers who were involved with gangs in the United States were either sent back to El Salvador by their parents to "straighten up" or deported. (In 1997 alone, according to the INS, 1,500 Salvadorans with criminal records were deported, a figure that excludes the "voluntary departures." Many of these deportees belonged to gangs [DeCesare 1998].) In the aftermath of the war these children have found fertile soil in El Salvador to re-create the very same gangs — with the same names — they were members of in the United States. This has contributed to driving the postwar Salvadoran per capita homicide rate to 150 per 100,000, the highest in the hemisphere, surpassing even Colombia's (Pan American Health Organization, cited in DeCesare 1998, 23).

15. Dinorah did not leave her house for good. She would leave for a couple of months and then come back, continuing with this pattern for some time.

16. This conceptualization parallels what Thomas and Znaniecki (1927) described as "social disorganization." According to these authors, one type of disorganization occurs when the young adopt the values of the new community instead of the parents' "old world" values, which simultaneously reduces parental control and communal ability to control the youngsters' behavior.

References

Adams, Richard N. 1976. *Cultural Surveys of Panama-Nicaragua-Guatemala-El Salvador-Honduras.* Pan American Sanitary Bureau, World Health Organization (1957 ed.). Detroit: Blaine Ethridge Books.

Aguayo, Sergio, with Agustín Aguilar Irigoyén and Miguel Ángel Velásquez, collaborators. 1985. *El éxodo centroamericano: Consequencias de un conflicto.* México: Secretaría de Educación Pública, Cultura, Foro 2000.

Aguayo, Sergio, and Patricia Weiss Fagen. 1988. *Central Americans in Mexico and the United States: Unilateral, Bilateral, and Regional Perspectives.* Washington, D.C.: Hemispheric Migration Project, Center for Immigration Policy and Refugee Assistance, Georgetown University.

Alvarenga, Patricia. 1996. *Cultura y ética de la violencia: El Salvador 1880–1932.* San José, Costa Rica: Editorial Universitaria Centroamericana-EDUCA.

American Friends Service Committee. 1988. *In the Shadow of Liberty: Central American Refugees in the United States.* Philadelphia: American Friends Service Committee.

Americas Watch. 1984. *El Salvador's Other Victims: The War on the Displaced.* New York: Lawyers Committee for International Human Rights and the Americas Watch.

Anderson, Thomas P. 1981. *The War of the Dispossessed: Honduras and El Salvador, 1969.* Lincoln: University of Nebraska Press.

———. 1992. *Matanza: The 1932 "Slaughter" That Traumatized a Nation, Shaping U.S.-Salvadoran Policy to This Day.* 2d ed. Willimantic, Conn.: Curbstone Press.

Aron, Adrianne, Shawn Corne, Anthea Fursland, and Barbara Zelwer. 1991. "The Gender-Specific Terror of El Salvador and Guatemala." *Women's Studies International Forum* 14 (1–2): 37–47.

Asimov, Nanette. 1992. "Poor Economy May Spell More Trouble for Schools." *San Francisco Chronicle,* March 10, A13.

Athey, Jean L., and Frederick L. Ahearn, Jr. 1991. "The Mental Health of Refugee Children: An Overview." In *Refugee Children: Theory, Research, and Services,* ed. Frederick L. Ahearn, Jr., and Jean L. Athey, 3–19. Baltimore: Johns Hopkins University Press.

Bach, Robert L., and Lisa A. Schraml. 1982. "Migration, Crisis, and Theoretical Conflict." *International Migration Review* 16 (2): 320–341.

Bailey, Adrian J., and Joshua G. Hane. 1995. "Population in Motion: Salvadorean Refugees and Circulation Migration." *Bulletin of Latin American Research* 14 (2): 171–200.

Baires, Sonia, Dilcia Marroquín, Clara Murguialday, Ruth Polanco, and Norma Vásquez. 1996. *Mami, mami, demanda la quota . . . la necesitamos: Un análisis feminista sobre la demanda de cuota alimenticia a la Procuraduría. Mujeres por la dignidad y la vida (Las Dignas).* San Salvador: Algier's Impresores.

Barnes, John A. 1954. "Class and Committees in a Norwegian Island Parish." *Human Relations* 7 (1): 39–58.

———. 1971. *Three Styles in the Study of Kinship.* Berkeley: University of California Press.

Barón-Castro, Rodolfo. 1978. *La población de El Salvador.* 2a ed. San Salvador: UCA Editores.

Barrera, Manuel, Jr. 1981. "Social Support in the Adjustment of Pregnant Adolescents: Assessment Issues." In *Social Networks and Social Support,* ed. Benjamin H. Gottlieb, 69–96. Beverly Hills, Calif.: Sage Publications.

Barry, Tom, and Deb Preusch. 1986. *The Central America Fact Book.* New York: Grove Press.

Bau, Ignatius. 1985. *The Ground Is Holy: Church Sanctuary and Central American Refugees.* Mahwah, N.J.: Paulist Press.

Becker, Howard. 1992. "Cases, Causes, Conjunctures, Stories, and Imagery." In *What Is a Case? Exploring the Foundations of Social Inquiry,* ed. Charles C. Ragin and Howard S. Becker, 205–216. New York: Cambridge University Press.

Belle, Deborah. 1982. "The Impact of Poverty on Social Networks and Supports." In *Ties That Bind: Men's and Women's Social Networks,* ed. Laura Lein and Marvin B. Sussman, 89–103. Marriage and Family Review 5. New York: Haworth Press.

Boissevain, Jeremy. 1974. *Friends of Friends: Networks, Manipulators and Coalitions.* New York: St. Martin's Press.

Borrero, Sarah Esther. 1992. "Hispanic Immigrant Mothers: Acculturation, Supports, and Stress." Ph.D. dissertation, University of Virginia.

Bott, Elizabeth. 1957. *Family and Social Network: Roles, Norms, and External Relationships in Ordinary Urban Families.* London: Tavistock.

Bourdieu, Pierre. 1982. "Les rites d'institution." *Actes de la Recherche en Sciences Sociales* 43: 58–63.

———. 1986. "The Forms of Capital." In *Handbook of Theory and Research of the Sociology of Education,* ed. John C. Richardson, 241–258. New York: Greenwood Press.

Boyd, Monica. 1989. "Family and Personal Networks in International

Migration: Recent Developments and New Agendas." *International Migration Review* 23 (3): 638–670.

Brewer, Toye Helena. 1983. "Women in El Salvador." In *Revolution in Central America,* ed. Stanford Central America Action Network, 400–407. Boulder, Colo.: Westview Press.

Browning, David. 1971. *El Salvador: Landscape and Society.* Oxford: Clarendon Press.

———. 1984. "Conflicts in El Salvador." *Conflict Studies,* no. 168. London: Institute for the Study of Conflict.

Burawoy, Michael. 1976. "The Functions and Reproduction of Migrant Labor: Comparative Material from Southern Africa and the United States." *American Journal of Sociology* 81 (5): 1050–1087.

———. 1991. Introduction to *Ethnography Unbound: Power and Resistance in the Modern Metropolis,* ed. Michael Burawoy, Alice Burton, Ann Arnett Ferguson, Kathryn J. Fox, Joshua Gamson, Nadine Gartrell, Leslie Hurst, Charles Kurzman, Leslie Salzinger, Josepha Schiffman, and Shiari Ui, 1–7. Berkeley: University of California Press.

Burdman, Pamela. 1992. "Holiday Food for Poor in Short Supply." *San Francisco Chronicle,* November 25, A15.

———. 1994. "Grass-Roots Anger Takes Hold: Frustration over Immigration Draws Thousands into Movement." *San Francisco Chronicle,* March 30, A1.

Buriel, Raymond, and Terri De Ment. 1997. "Immigration and Sociocultural Change in Mexican, Chinese, and Vietnamese American Families." In *Immigration and the Family: Research and Policy on U.S. Immigrants,* ed. Alan Booth, Ann C. Crouter, and Nancy Landale, 165–200. Mahwah, N.J.: Lawrence Erlbaum Associates.

Cabarrús P., Carlos Rafael. 1983. *Génesis de una revolución: Análisis del surgimiento y desarrollo de la organización campesina en El Salvador.* México: Ediciones de la Casa Chata.

Calderón, Ricardo. 1992. *Situación socio-económica de la communidad salvadoreña en el área de la Bahia de San Francisco.* San Francisco: Centro para Refugiados Centroamericanos/Asociación de Salvadoreños.

Cardoso, Fernando Henrique, and Enzo Faletto. 1979. *Dependency and Development in Latin America.* Berkeley: University of California Press.

Carter, Brenda, Kevan Insko, David Loeb, and Marlene Tobias. 1989. *A Dream Compels Us: Voices of Salvadoran Women.* Boston: South End Press.

Castells, Manuel. 1975. "Immigrant Workers and Class Struggles in Advanced Capitalism: The Western European Experience." *Politics and Society* 5 (1): 33–66.

Castillo, Manuel Ángel. 1994. "La migración internacional y el problema de los refugiados." In *Políticas de población en Centroamérica, El Caribe y*

México, ed. Raúl Benítez Zenteno and Eva Gisela Ramírez Rodríguez, 185–199. México: INAP/IIS–UNAM PROLAP.

Cervantes, Richard C., Nelli Salgado de Snyder, and Amado M. Padilla. 1989. "Posttraumatic Stress in Immigrants from Central America and Mexico." *Hospital and Community Psychiatry* 40 (6): 615–619.

Chávez, Leo R. 1991. "Outside the Imagined Community: Undocumented Settlers and Experiences of Incorporation." *American Ethnologist* 18 (2): 257–278.

——. 1994. "The Power of the Imagined Community: The Settlement of Undocumented Mexicans and Central Americans in the United States." *American Anthropologist* 96 (1): 52–73.

Chávez, Leo R., Estevan T. Flores, and Marta López-Garza. 1989. "Migrants and Settlers: A Comparison of Undocumented Mexicans and Central Americans in the United States." *Frontera Norte* 1: 49–75.

Chen, Ingfel. 1991. "Foreign Tourists Deserting the Bay Area." *San Francisco Chronicle,* February 19, A3.

Chinchilla, Norma Stoltz, and Nora Hamilton. 1992. "Seeking Refuge in the City of Angels: The Central American Community." In *City of Angels,* ed. Gerry Riposa and Carolyn Deusch, 84–100. Dubuque: Kendall/Hunt.

Chinchilla, Norma, Nora Hamilton, and James Loucky. 1993. "Central Americans in Los Angeles: An Immigrant Community in Transition." In *In the Barrios: Latinos and the Underclass Debate,* ed. Joan Moore and Raquel Pinderhughes, 51–78. New York: Russell Sage Foundation.

Chinchilla, Norma Stoltz, Milton H. Jamail, and Nestor Rodríguez. 1986. "Central American Migration to the United States: A Preliminary Discussion." Paper presented at the conference, The United States and Central America: A Five-Year Assessment, Los Angeles, February 20–22.

Clark, William A. V. 1998. *The California Cauldron: Immigration and the Fortunes of Local Communities.* New York: Guilford Press.

Coates, Jennifer. 1989. "Gossip Revisited: Language in All-Female Groups." In *Women in Their Speech Communities: New Perspectives on Language and Sex,* ed. Jennifer Coates and Deborah Cameron, 94–122. London: Longman.

Coleman, James S. 1988. "Social Capital in the Creation of Human Capital." *American Journal of Sociology* 94: S95–120.

Córdova, Carlos B. 1987. "Undocumented El Salvadoreans in the San Francisco Bay Area: Migration and Adaptation Dynamics." *Journal of La Raza Studies* 1(1): 9–37.

Cornelius, Wayne. 1982. "Interviewing Undocumented Immigrants: Methodological Reflections Based on Fieldwork in Mexico and the U.S." *International Migration Review* 16 (2): 378–411.

Coutin, Susan Bibler. 1993. *The Culture of Protest: Religious Activism and the U.S. Sanctuary Movement.* Boulder, Colo.: Westview Press.

Dada Hirezi, Héctor. 1978. *La economía de El Salvador y la integración centroamericana, 1945–1960.* San Salvador: UCA Editores.

DaVanzo, Julie, Jennifer Hawes-Dawson, R. Burciaga Valdez, and Georges Vernez. 1994. *Surveying Immigrant Communities: Policy Imperatives and Technical Challenges.* Report MR247FF. Santa Monica, Calif.: Rand Corp.

DeCesare, Donna. 1998. "The Children of War: Street Gangs in El Salvador." *NACLA Report on the Americas* 22 (1): 21–43.

De Graaf, Nan Dirk, and Hendrik Derk Flap. 1988. "'With a Little Help from My Friends': Social Resources as an Explanation of Occupational Status and Income in West Germany, the Netherlands, and the United States." *Social Forces* 67 (2): 452–472.

di Leonardo, Micaela. 1987. "The Female World of Cards and Holidays: Women, Families, and the Work of Kinship." *Signs* 12 (3): 440–453.

Diner, Hasia R. 1983. *Erin's Daughters in America: Irish Immigrant Women in the Nineteenth Century.* Baltimore: Johns Hopkins University Press.

Dorrington, Claudia, Ruth E. Zambrana, and Georges Sabagh. 1991. "Salvadorans in the United States: Immigrants and Refugees." Paper presented at the annual meeting of the Pacific Sociological Association, Irvine, Calif., April 11–14.

Dunkerley, James. 1988. *Power in the Isthmus: A Political History of Modern Central America.* London: Verso.

Durham, William. 1979. *Scarcity and Survival in Central America: Ecological Origins of the Soccer War.* Stanford: Stanford University Press.

Edwards, Bob, and Michael W. Foley. 1997. "Social Capital and the Political Economy of Our Discontent." *American Behavioral Scientist* 40 (5): 669–678.

Eggebeen, David J., and Dennis P. Hogan. 1990. "Giving between Generations in American Families." *Human Nature* 1 (3): 211–232.

Eisenstadt, S. N., and L. Roniger. 1984. *Patrons, Clients, and Friends: Interpersonal Relations and the Structure of Trust in Society.* Cambridge: Cambridge University Press.

Employment Development Department. 1993. *Annual Planning Information.* State of California: Health and Welfare Agency, San Francisco City and County. Employment Development Department/ Labor Market Information Division.

Epstein, Arnold L. 1969. "The Network and Urban Social Organization." In *Social Networks in Urban Situations: Analyses of Personal Relationships in Central African Towns,* ed. J. Clyde Mitchell, 77–116. Manchester: Manchester University Press for the Institute for Social Research, University of Zambia.

Erdmans, Mary Patrice. 1995. "Immigrants and Ethnics: Conflict and Identity in Chicago Polonia." *Sociological Quarterly* 36 (1): 175–195.

———. 1998. *Opposite Poles: Immigrants and Ethnics in Polish Chicago, 1976–1990.* University Park: Pennsylvania State University Press.

Eschbach, Karl, Jacqueline Hagan, Nestor Rodríguez, Rubén Hernández Leon, and Stanley Bailey. 1999. "Death at the Border." *International Migration Review* 23 (2): 430–454.

Espino, Conchita M. 1991. "Trauma and Adaptation: The Case of Central American Children." In *Refugee Children: Theory, Research, and Services,* ed. Frederick L. Ahearn, Jr., and Jean L. Athey, 106–124. Baltimore: Johns Hopkins University Press.

Espinosa, Kristin E. 1995. "The Effects of Social Networks for Mexican Migrants in the United States." Paper presented at the annual meeting of the Population Association of America, San Francisco, April 6–8.

Evenson, Laura. 1991. "Foreclosures Expected to Climb." *San Francisco Chronicle,* February 7, C1.

Facio, Elisa. 1996. *Understanding Older Chicanas: Sociological and Policy Perspectives.* Series on Race and Ethnic Relations, vol. 14. Thousand Oaks, Calif.: Sage Publications.

Fawcett, James T. 1989. "Networks, Linkages and Migration Systems." *International Migration Review* 23 (3): 671–680.

Fernández-Kelly, M. Patricia. 1990. "Delicate Transactions: Gender, Home, and Employment among Hispanic Women." In *Uncertain Terms: Negotiating Gender in American Culture,* ed. Faye Ginsburg and Anna Lowenhaupt Tsing, 183–195. Boston: Beacon Press.

———. 1994. "Towanda's Triumph: Social and Cultural Capital in the Transition to Adulthood in the Urban Ghetto." *International Journal of Urban and Regional Research* 18 (1): 88–111.

———. 1995. "Social and Cultural Capital in the Urban Ghetto: Implications for the Economic Sociology of Immigration." In *The Economic Sociology of Immigration: Essays on Networks, Ethnicity, and Entrepreneurship,* ed. Alejandro Portes, 213–247. New York: Russell Sage Foundation.

Fernández-Kelly, M. Patricia, and Anna M. García. 1990. "Power Surrendered, Power Restored: The Politics of Work and Family among Hispanic Garment Workers in California and Florida." In *Women, Politics, and Change,* ed. Louise A. Tilly and Patricia Gurin, 130–149. New York: Russell Sage Foundation.

Fernández-Kelly, M. Patricia, and Richard Schauffler. 1994. "Divided Fates: Immigrant Children in a Restructured U.S. Economy." *International Migration Review* 28 (4): 662–689.

Fischer, Claude. 1982. *To Dwell among Friends: Personal Networks in Town and City.* Chicago: University of Chicago Press.

Fong-Torres, Ben. 1991. "Surviving When You Get the Axe." *San Francisco Chronicle,* April 1, D3.

Frelick, Bill, and Barbara Kohnen. 1994. *Filling the Gap: Temporary Protected Status*. Washington, D.C.: U.S. Committee on Refugees.

FUNDASAL (Fundación Salvadoreña de Desarrollo y Vivienda Mínima). 1979. *Análisis del proceso evaluativo y las soluciones autónomas en proyectos de lotes y servicios*. Tomo 2. San Salvador: FUNDASAL.

Funkhouser, Edward. 1992. "Mass Emigration, Remittances, and Economic Adjustment: The Case of El Salvador in the 1980s." In *Immigration and the Workforce: Economic Consequences for the United States and Source Areas*, ed. George Borjas and Richard B. Freeman, 135–175. Chicago: University of Chicago Press.

Gamio, Manuel. 1930. *Mexican Immigration to the United States: A Study of Human Migration and Adjustment*. Chicago: University of Chicago Press.

García, Ana Isabel, and Enrique Gomáriz. 1989. *Mujeres centroamericanas: Ante la crisis, la guerra y el proceso de paz*. Tomo I, *Tendencias Estructurales*. San José, Costa Rica: FLACSO.

Garcia, Dawn, and L. A. Chung. 1990. "Many Hispanics Fear Mission District Is Losing Latin Flavor." *San Francisco Chronicle*, December 3, A4.

Georges, Eugenia. 1990. *The Making of a Transnational Community: Migration, Development, and Cultural Change in the Dominican Republic*. New York: Columbia University Press.

Gibney, Mark. 1991. "U.S. Foreign Policy and the Creation of Refugee Flows." In *Refugee Policy: Canada and the United States*, ed. Howard Adelman, 81–111. Toronto: York Lanes Press.

Gibney, Mark, and Michael Stohl. 1988. "Human Rights and U.S. Refugee Policy." In *Open Borders? Closed Societies? The Ethical and Political Issues*, ed. Mark Gibney, 151–183. New York: Greenwood Press.

Godfrey, Brian. 1988. *Neighborhoods in Transition: The Making of San Francisco's Ethnic and Nonconformist Communities*. Publications in Geography, vol. 27. Berkeley: University of California Press.

Gold, Steven J. 1992. *Refugee Communities: A Comparative Field Study*. Newbury Park, Calif.: Sage Publications.

Golden, Renny, and Michael McConnell. 1986. *Sanctuary: The New Underground Railroad*. Maryknoll, N.Y.: Orbis Books.

Goldring, Luin. 1996. "Gendered Memory: Constructions of Rurality among Mexican Transnational Migrants." In *Creating the Countryside: The Politics of Rural and Environmental Discourse*, ed. E. Melanie Dupuis and Peter Vandergeest, 303–329. Philadelphia: Temple University Press.

González de la Rocha, Mercedes. 1994. *The Resources of Poverty: Women and Survival in a Mexican City*. Oxford: Blackwell.

Gorostiaga, Xavier, and Peter Marchetti. 1988. "The Central American Economy: Conflict and Crisis." In *Crisis in Central America: Regional Dynamics and U.S. Policy in the 1980s*, ed. Nora Hamilton, Jeffry A.

Frieden, Linda Fuller, and Manuel Pastor, Jr., 119–135. Boulder, Colo.: Westview Press.

Gouldner, Alvin W. 1960. "The Norm of Reciprocity: A Preliminary Statement." *American Sociological Review* 25 (2): 161–178.

Granovetter, Mark S. 1995. *Getting a Job: A Study of Contacts and Careers.* 2d ed. Chicago: University of Chicago Press.

Grasmuck, Sherri, and Patricia R. Pessar. 1991. *Between Two Islands: Dominican International Migration.* Berkeley: University of California Press.

Guarnaccia, Peter J., and Pablo Farias. 1988. "The Social Meanings of Nervios: A Case Study of a Central American Woman." *Social Science and Medicine* 26: 1223–1231.

Gulliver, P. H. 1971. *Neighbours and Networks: The Idiom of Kinship in Social Action among the Ndendeuli of Tanzania.* Berkeley: University of California Press.

Hagan, Jacqueline Maria. 1994. *Deciding to Be Legal: A Maya Community in Houston.* Philadelphia: Temple University Press.

———. 1998. "Social Networks, Gender, and Immigrant Incorporation: Resources and Constraints." *American Sociological Review* 63: 55–67.

Haggerty, Richard A. 1990. *El Salvador: A Country Study.* Washington, D.C.: United States Government (Secretary of the Army): Federal Research Division, Library of Congress.

Hall, Carl T. 1991. "Getting in Shape for a Possible Layoff." *San Francisco Chronicle,* February 4, D2.

Hamilton, Nora, and Norma Stoltz Chinchilla. 1984. "Characteristics of Central American Migration to Southern California." Paper presented at the eighth annual meeting of the Illinois Conference of Latin Americanists, Chicago, November 15–17.

———. 1991. "Central American Migration: A Framework for Analysis." *Latin American Research Review* 26 (1): 75–110.

Hansen, Gladys. 1980. *San Francisco Almanac: Everything You Want to Know about the City.* San Rafael, Calif.: Presidio Press.

Harper, Anneliese Marie. 1996. "The Impact of Immigration on Rural Guatemalan Women's Ways of Speaking." Ph.D. dissertation, Arizona State University.

Hirsch, Barton J. 1979. "Psychological Dimensions of Social Networks: A Multimethod Analysis." *American Journal of Community Psychology* 7 (3): 263–277.

Ho, Christine. 1993. "The Internationalization of Kinship and the Feminization of Caribbean Migration: The Case of Afro-Trinidadian Immigrants in Los Angeles." *Human Organization* 25 (1): 32–40.

Hobhouse, L. T. 1951. *Morals in Evolution: A Study in Comparative Ethics.* London: Chapman and Hall.

Hogan, Dennis P., David J. Eggebeen, and Clifford C. Clogg. 1993. "The Structure of Intergenerational Exchanges in American Families." *American Journal of Sociology* 98: 1428–1458.

Hondagneu-Sotelo, Pierrette. 1994a. *Gendered Transitions: Mexican Experiences of Immigration.* Berkeley: University of California Press.

———. 1994b. "Regulating the Unregulated? Domestic Workers' Social Networks." *Social Problems* 41: 50–64.

Hondagneu-Sotelo, Pierrette, and Ernestine Avila. 1997. "I'm Here, but I'm There: The Meanings of Latina Transnational Motherhood." *Gender & Society* 11 (5): 548–571.

Huang, Larke Nahme. 1989. "Southeast Asian Refugee Children and Adolescents." In *Children of Color: Psychological Interventions with Minority Youth,* ed. Jewelle Taylor Gibbs, Larke Nahme Huang, and assoc., 278–321. San Francisco: Jossey-Bass.

Jones, Deborah. 1980. "Gossip: Notes on Women's Oral Culture." *Women's Studies International Quarterly* 3 (2–3): 193–198.

Jones, Richard C. 1989. "Causes of Salvadoran Migration to the United States." *Geographical Review* 79 (2): 183–194.

Joseph, Suad. 1983. "Working-Class Women's Networks in a Sectarian State: A Political Paradox." *American Ethnologist* 10 (1): 1–22.

Kearney, Michael. 1991. "Borders and Boundaries of State and Self at the End of the Empire." *Journal of Historical Sociology* 4 (1): 52–74.

Keefe, Susan Emley. 1979. "Urbanization, Acculturation, and Extended Family Ties: Mexican Americans in Cities." *American Ethnologist* 6 (2): 349–365.

Kibria, Nazli. 1993. *Family Tightrope: The Changing Lives of Vietnamese Americans.* Princeton: Princeton University Press.

———. 1994. "Household Structure and Family Ideologies: The Dynamics of Immigrant Economic Adaptation among Vietnamese Refugees." *Social Problems* 41 (1): 81–96.

———. 1997. "The Concept of 'Bicultural' Families and Its Implications for Research on Immigrant and Ethnic Families." In *Immigration and the Family: Research and Policy on U.S. Immigrants,* ed. Alan Booth, Ann C. Crouter, and Nancy Landale, 205–210. Mahwah, N.J.: Lawrence Erlbaum Associates.

Kossoudji, Sherrie A., and Susan I. Ranney. 1984. "The Labor Market Experience of Female Migrants: The Case of Contemporary Mexican Migration to the U.S." *International Migration Review* 18 (4): 1120–1143.

Kudat, Ayse. 1982. "Personal, Familial and Societal Impacts of Turkish Women's Migration to Europe." In *Living in Two Cultures: The Sociocultural Situation of Migrant Workers and Their Families,* ed. R. G. Parris, 291–305. New York: Gower and UNESCO Press.

Kulis, Stephen S. 1992. *Why Honor Thy Father and Mother? Class, Mobility, and Family Ties in Later Life.* New York: Garland.

Kury, Félix S. 1987. "Torture Syndrome as a Specific Case of Post-traumatic Stress Disorder in El Salvadoran Refugees." *Journal of La Raza Studies* 1 (1): 38–42.

Lacey, Marilyn. 1987. "A Case Study in International Refugee Policy: Lowland Lao Refugees." In *People in Upheaval,* ed. Scott M. Morgan and Elizabeth Colson, 17–33. New York: Center for Migration Studies.

LaFeber, Walter. 1984. *Inevitable Revolutions: The United States in Central America.* New York: Norton.

Lamphere, Louise. 1986. "Working Mothers and Family Strategies: Portuguese and Colombian Women in a New England Community." In *International Migration: The Female Experience,* ed. Rita James Simon and Caroline B. Brettell, 266–283. Totowa, N.J.: Rowman and Allanheld.

———. 1987. *From Working Daughters to Working Mothers: Immigrant Women in a New England Industrial Community.* Ithaca: Cornell University Press.

Lamphere, Louise, Filomena M. Silva, and John P. Sousa. 1980. "Kin Networks and Family Strategies: Working-Class Portuguese Families in New England." In *The Versatility of Kinship,* ed. Linda S. Cordell and Stephen Beckerman, 219–249. New York: Academic Press.

Lamphere, Louise, Patricia Zavella, and Felipe Gonzales, with Peter B. Evans. 1993. *Sunbelt Working Mothers: Reconciling Family and Factory.* Ithaca: Cornell University Press.

Landolt, Patricia. 1997. "Salvadoran Transnationalism: Toward the Redefinition of the National Community." Paper presented at the annual meeting of the American Sociological Association, Toronto, August 9–13.

Larner, Mary. 1990. "Changes in Network Resources and Relationships over Time." In *Extending Families: The Social Networks of Parents and Their Children,* ed. Moncrieff Cochran, Mary Larner, David Riley, Lars Gunnarsson, and Charles R. Henderson, 181–204. Cambridge: Cambridge University Press.

Laumann, Edward O. 1966. *Prestige and Association in an Urban Community: An Analysis of an Urban Stratification System.* Indianapolis: Bobbs-Merrill.

Leslie, Leigh A. 1992. "The Role of Informal Support Networks in the Adjustment of Central American Immigrant Families." *Journal of Community Psychology* 20 (3): 243–256.

———. 1993. "Families Fleeing War: The Case of Central Americans." *Marriage and Family Review* 19 (1–2): 193–205.

Leslie, Leigh A., and M. Laurie Leitch. 1989. "A Demographic Profile of Recent Central American Immigrants: Clinical and Service Implications." *Hispanic Journal of Behavioral Sciences* 11 (4): 315–329.

Li, Peter S. 1977. "Occupational Achievement and Kinship Assistance among Chinese Immigrants in Chicago." *Sociological Quarterly* 18: 478–489.

Lin, Nan, Walter M. Ensel, and John C. Vaughn. 1981. "Social Resources and Strength of Ties: Structural Factors in Occupational Status Attainment." *American Sociological Review* 46 (4): 393–405.

Lindo-Fuentes, Héctor. 1990. *Weak Foundations: The Economy of El Salvador in the Nineteenth Century.* Berkeley: University of California Press.

Lindstrom, David P. 1996. "Migration from El Salvador, Guatemala, and Nicaragua to the United States in the 1980s: Voluntary or Involuntary?" Paper presented at the annual meeting of the Population Association of America, New Orleans, May 9–11.

Lindström-Best, Varpu. 1988. *Defiant Sisters: A Social History of Finnish Immigrant Women in Canada.* Toronto: Multicultural History Society of Ontario.

Loescher, Gil, and John A. Scanlan. 1986. *Calculated Kindness: Refugees and America's Half-Open Door, 1945 to the Present.* New York: Free Press.

Lomnitz, Larissa. 1978. "Mechanisms of Articulation between Shantytown Settlers and the Urban System." *Urban Anthropology* 7 (2): 185–205.

———. 1985. *Cómo sobreviven los marginados.* 9a ed. México: Siglo Veintiuno Editores.

———. 1988. "Informal Exchange Networks in Formal Systems: A Theoretical Model." *American Anthropologist* 90 (1): 42–55.

Long, Thomas. 1992. "Will U.S. Abandon War-ravaged Salvador?" *San Francisco Chronicle,* February 2, A1.

Lopata, Helena Znaniecka. 1979. *Women as Widows: Support Systems.* New York: Elsevier.

Lopez, David E., Eric Popkin, and Edward Telles. 1996. "Central Americans: At the Bottom, Struggling to Get Ahead." In *Ethnic Los Angeles,* ed. Roger Waldinger and Mehdi Bozorgmehr, 279–304. New York: Russell Sage Foundation.

Lucas, Greg. 1993. "Governor Signs Immigration Bills." *San Francisco Chronicle,* October 5, A17.

Luker, Kristin. 1996. *Dubious Conceptions: The Politics of Teenage Pregnancy.* Cambridge, Mass.: Harvard University Press.

MacDonald, John S., and Leatrice D. MacDonald. 1964. "Chain Migration, Ethnic Neighbourhood Formation and Social Networks." *Milbank Memorial Fund Quarterly* 24: 82–97.

Mahler, Sarah J. 1995a. *American Dreaming: Immigrant Life on the Margins.* Princeton: Princeton University Press.

———. 1995b. *Salvadorans in Suburbia: Symbiosis and Conflict.* Boston: Allyn and Bacon.

Marshall, Jonathan. 1991. "Bay Area Tightens Belt Out of Fear of Recession." *San Francisco Chronicle,* February 4, A1.

Martín-Baró, Ignacio. 1990a. "Political Violence and War as Causes of Psychosocial Trauma in El Salvador." *International Journal of Mental Health* 18 (1): 3–20.

———. 1990b. "Religion as an Instrument of Psychological Warfare." *Journal of Social Issues* 46 (3): 93–107.

Mason, T. David. 1992. "Women's Participation in Central American Revolutions: A Theoretical Perspective." *Comparative Political Studies* 25 (1): 63–89.

Massey, Douglas S., Rafael Alarcón, Jorge Durand, and Humberto González. 1987. *Return to Aztlan: The Social Process of International Migration from Western Mexico.* Berkeley: University of California Press.

Massey, Douglas S., Joaquín Arango, Graeme Hugo, Ali Kouaouci, Adela Pellegrino, and J. Edward Taylor. 1993. "Theories of International Migration: A Review and Appraisal." *Population and Development Review* 19 (3): 431–466.

Massey, Douglas S., and Kristin E. Espinosa. 1997. "What's Driving Mexico-U.S. Migration: A Theoretical, Empirical, and Policy Analysis." *American Journal of Sociology* 102: 939–999.

Matute-Bianchi, María Eugenia. 1986. "Ethnic Identities and Patterns of School Success and Failure among Mexican-Descent and Japanese-American Students in a California High School: An Ethnographic Analysis." *American Journal of Education* 95 (1): 233–255.

Mayer, Philip. 1961. *Townsmen or Tribesmen: Conservatism and the Process of Urbanization in a South African City.* Cape Town: Oxford University Press.

McAllister Groves, Julian, and Kimberly A. Chang. 1993. "Culture and Control: The Making of the Filipina Maid Community in Hong Kong." Division of Social Science, Hong Kong University of Science and Technology.

McLanahan, Sara S. 1997. "Parent Absence or Poverty: Which Matters More?" In *Consequences of Growing Up Poor,* ed. Greg J. Duncan and Jeanne Brooks-Gunn, 35–48. New York: Russell Sage Foundation.

McLeod, Ramon G. 1992a. "Bay White-Collar Jobs Rise as Blue-Collar Fields Decline." *San Francisco Chronicle,* May 26, A1.

———. 1992b. "Why So Many San Francisco Poor Have Become Homeless." *San Francisco Chronicle,* November 12, A1.

Meillassoux, Claude. 1981. *Maidens, Meal, and Money: Capitalism and the Domestic Community.* New York: Cambridge University Press.

Menjívar, Cecilia. 1987. "The Political Economy of Development: Costa Rica and El Salvador in Historical Perspective." Unpublished manuscript.

———. 1992. "Salvadorean Migration to the United States: The Dynamics of Social Networks in International Migration." Ph.D. dissertation, University of California, Davis.

———. 1993. "History, Economy and Politics: Macro and Micro-level Factors in Recent Salvadorean Migration to the U.S." *Journal of Refugee Studies* 6 (4): 350–371.

———. 1994a. "Immigrant Social Networks: Implications and Lessons for Policy." *Harvard Journal of Hispanic Policy* 8: 35–59.

———. 1994b. "Salvadorean Migration to the United States in the 1980s: What Can We Learn *About* It and *From* It?" *International Migration* 32 (3): 371–401.

———. 1995. "Kinship Networks among Immigrants: Lessons from a Qualitative Comparative Approach." *International Journal of Comparative Sociology* 36 (3–4): 219–232.

———. 1996. "Continuidad, transformación o ruptura: Las experiencias de refugiadas salvadoreñas en Estados Unidos de América." *Revista Mundial de Sociología* 2: 51–84.

———. 1997a. "Immigrant Kinship Networks and the Impact of the Receiving Context: Salvadorans in San Francisco in the Early 1990s." *Social Problems* 44 (1): 104–123.

———. 1997b. "Immigrant Kinship Networks: The Case of Vietnamese, Salvadoreans, and Mexicans in Comparative Perspective." *Journal of Comparative Family Studies* 28 (1): 1–24.

———. 1999a. "The Intersection of Work and Gender: Central American Immigrant Women and Employment in California." *American Behavioral Scientist* 42 (4): 595–621.

———. 1999b. "Religious Institutions and Transnationalism: A Case Study of Catholic and Evangelical Salvadoran Immigrants." *International Journal of Politics, Culture, and Society* 12 (4): 589–612.

Menjívar, Cecilia, Julie DaVanzo, Lisa Greenwell, and R. Burciaga Valdez. 1998. "Remittance Behavior of Filipino and Salvadoran Immigrants in Los Angeles." *International Migration Review* 32 (1): 99–128.

Menjívar, Rafael L. 1980. *Acumulación originaria y desarrollo del capitalismo en El Salvador.* San José, Costa Rica: Editorial Universitaria Centroamericana.

Milardo, Robert M. 1988. "Families and Social Networks: An Overview of Theory and Methodology." In *Families and Social Networks,* ed. Robert M. Milardo, 13–47. Newbury Park, Calif.: Sage Publications.

Mines, Richard. 1981. "Developing a Community Tradition of Migration: A Field Study in Rural Zacatecas, Mexico, and California Settlement Areas." Monographs in U.S.-Mexican Studies no. 3. La Jolla, Calif.: Program in United States–Mexican Studies, University of California at San Diego.

Ministerio Público de El Salvador. 1983. *Procuraduría general de pobres, Oficina de la Mujer. Primera Jornada de Trabajo de la Oficina de la Mujer, tema: El empleo.* San Salvador.

Minkler, Meredith, Kathleen M. Roe, and Relda J. Robertson-Beckley.

———. 1994. "Raising Grandchildren from Crack-Cocaine Households: Effects on Family and Friendship Ties of African-American Women." *American Journal of Orthopsychiatry* 64 (1): 20–29.

Minton, Torri. 1991. "Cheaper Dining at Restaurants." *San Francisco Chronicle*, April 2, A1.

Mitchell, J. Clyde. 1974. "Social Networks." *Annual Review of Anthropology* 3: 279–299.

———. 1987. *Cities, Society, and Social Perception: A Central African Perspective*. Oxford: Clarendon Press.

Montes, Segundo. 1987a. *El compadrazgo: Una estructura de poder en El Salvador*. San Salvador: UCA Editores.

———. 1987b. *El Salvador 1987: Salvadoreños refugiados en los Estados Unidos*. San Salvador: Instituto de Investigaciones e Instituto de Derechos Humanos de la Universidad Centroamericana de El Salvador "José Simeón Cañas."

———. 1988. "Los Salvadoreños en Estados Unidos y la nueva ley de migración." *Estudios Centroamericanos* 459–460 (Marzo): 102–104.

Montes, Segundo, and Juan José García Vasquez. 1988. "Salvadoran Migration to the United States: An Exploratory Study." Washington, D.C.: Hemispheric Migration Project, Center for Immigration Policy and Refugee Assistance, Georgetown University.

Montgomery, Tommie Sue. 1982. *Revolution in El Salvador: Origins and Evolution*. Boulder, Colo.: Westview Press.

Morales Velado, Oscar Armando. 1994. La modificación y el cambio cultural de la familia en El Salvador. In *Cultura y desarrollo en El Salvador*, ed. Stefan Roggenbuck, 211–253. San Salvador: Imprenta Criterio.

Muir, Karen L. S. 1988. *The Strongest Part of the Family: A Study of Lao Refugee Women in Columbus, Ohio*. New York: AMS Press.

Murphy, Gregory J. 1999. *Strange Bedfellows: Democratic America and Totalitarian El Salvador in the Era of Roosevelt and Martínez (1933–45)*. Paper presented at the Conference on Inter-American Relations, Arizona State University, February 11–12.

Naciones Unidas. n.d. *De la locura a la esperanza: La guerra de 12 años en El Salvador*. San Salvador: Informe de la Comisión de la Verdad para El Salvador.

National Association of Latino Elected and Appointed Officials Educational Fund (NALEO). 1998. *America's Newest Voices: Colombians, Dominicans, Guatemalans and Salvadorans in the United States Examine Their Public Policy Needs*. Claremont, Calif.: Tomas Rivera Policy Institute.

National Asylum Study Project. 1992. *An Interim Assessment of the Asylum Process of the Immigration and Naturalization Service. Immigration and Refugee Program, Program on the Legal Profession*. Cambridge, Mass.: Harvard Law School.

Nelson, Nici. 1978–1979. "Female-centered Families: Changing Patterns of Marriage and Family among Buzaa Brewers of Mathare Valley." *Urban African Studies* 3: 85–104.

Nguyen, Nga Anh, and Harold L. Williams. 1989. "Transition from East to West: Vietnamese Adolescents and Their Parents." *Journal of the American Academy of Child and Adolescent Psychiatry* 28 (4): 505–515.

Nieves, Isabel. 1979. "Household Arrangements and Multiple Jobs in San Salvador." *Signs* 5 (1): 134–142.

Norris, William P. 1985. "The Social Networks of Impoverished Brazilian Women: Work Patterns and Household Structure in an Urban Squatter Settlement." Working Paper no. 84, Oberlin College.

Obbo, Christine. 1980. *African Women: Their Struggle for Economic Independence.* London: Zed Press.

O'Connor, Mary I. 1990. "Women's Networks and The Social Needs of Mexican Immigrants." *Urban Anthropology* 19 (1–2): 81–98.

O'Dogherty, Laura. 1989. *Central Americans in Mexico City: Uprooted and Silenced.* Washington, D.C.: Hemispheric Migration Project, Center for Immigration Policy and Refugee Assistance, Georgetown University.

Office of Refugee Resettlement. 1985. *Refugee Resettlement Program.* Report to Congress, Appendix A (Tables 7 and 8), January 31. Washington, D.C.: U.S. Department of Health and Human Services.

———. 1988. *Refugee Resettlement Program.* Report to Congress, January. Washington, D.C.: U.S. Department of Health and Human Services.

Paulston, Christine Bratt. 1978. "Education in a Bi/Multilingual Setting." *International Review of Education* 24 (3): 309–328.

Pedraza, Silvia. 1991. "Women and Migration: The Social Consequences of Gender." *Annual Review of Sociology* 17: 303–325.

Pedraza-Bailey, Silvia. 1990. "Immigration Research: A Conceptual Map." *Social Science History* 14 (1): 23–67.

Pessar, Patricia R. 1995. "On the Homefront and in the Workplace: Integrating Immigrant Women into Feminist Discourse." *Anthropological Quarterly* 68 (1): 37–47.

Petuchowski, Silvia Rita Chepal. 1988. "Psychological Adjustment Problems of War Refugees from El Salvador." Ph.D. dissertation, University of Maryland, College Park.

Pleck, Elizabeth H. 1983. "Challenges to Traditional Authority in Immigrant Families." In *The American Family in Social-Historical Perspective,* ed. Michael Gordon, 505–517. 3d ed. New York: St. Martin's Press.

Popkin, Eric. 1995. "Guatemalan Hometown Associations in Los Angeles." Occasional Papers, Monograph no. 1. Los Angeles: University of Southern California, Center for Multiethnic and Transnational Studies.

Porter Benson, Susan. 1983. "The Customers Ain't God: The Work Culture of Department Store Saleswomen, 1890–1940." In *Working-Class America:*

Essays on Labor, Community, and American Society, ed. Michael H. Frisch and Daniel J. Walkowitz, 185–211. Urbana: University of Illinois Press.

Portes, Alejandro. 1995. "Children of Immigrants: Segmented Assimilation and Its Determinants." In *The Economic Sociology of Immigration: Essays on Networks, Ethnicity, and Entrepreneurship,* ed. Alejandro Portes, 248–279. New York: Russell Sage Foundation.

Portes, Alejandro, and József Böröcz. 1989. "Contemporary Immigration: Theoretical Perspectives on Its Determinants and Modes of Incorporation." *International Migration Review* 23 (3): 606–630.

Portes, Alejandro, and Leif Jensen. 1989. "The Enclave and the Entrants: Patterns of Ethnic Enterprise in Miami Before and After Mariel." *American Sociological Review* 54 (6): 929–949.

Portes, Alejandro, and Rubén G. Rumbaut. 1996. *Immigrant America: A Portrait.* 2d ed. Berkeley: University of California Press.

Portes, Alejandro, and Richard Schauffler. 1994. "Language and the Second Generation: Bilingualism Yesterday and Today." *International Migration Review* 28 (4): 640–661.

Portes, Alejandro, and Julia Sensenbrenner. 1993. "Embeddedness and Immigration: Notes on the Social Determinants of Economic Action." *American Journal of Sociology* 98 (6): 1320–1350.

Portes, Alejandro, and John Walton. 1981. *Labor, Class, and the International System.* New York: Academic Press.

Portes, Alejandro, and Min Zhou. 1993. "The New Second Generation: Segmented Assimilation and Its Variants." *Annals of the American Academy of Political and Social Sciences* 530: 74–96.

Prieto, Yolanda. 1992. "Cuban Women in New Jersey: Gender Relations and Change." In *Seeking Common Ground: Multidisciplinary Studies of Immigrant Women in the United States,* ed. Donna Gabaccia, 185–201. Westport, Conn.: Greenwood Press.

Quisumbing, Maria Socorro. 1982. "Life Events, Social Support, and Personality: Their Impact on Filipino Psychological Adjustment." Ph.D. dissertation, University of Chicago.

Reichert, Josh, and Douglas S. Massey. 1979. "Patterns of U.S. Migration from a Mexican Sending Community: A Comparison of Legal and Illegal Migrants." *International Migration Review* 13 (4): 599–623.

Repak, Terry A. 1995. *Waiting on Washington: Central American Workers in the Nation's Capital.* Philadelphia: Temple University Press.

Ritchie, P. Neal. 1976. "Explanations of Migration." *Annual Review of Sociology* 2: 363–404.

Roberts, Bryan R. 1973. *Organizing Strangers: Poor Families in Guatemala City.* Austin: University of Texas Press.

———. 1995. "Socially Expected Durations and the Economic Adjustment of

Immigrants." In *The Economic Sociology of Immigration: Essays on Networks, Ethnicity, and Entrepreneurship,* ed. Alejandro Portes, 42–86. New York: Russell Sage Foundation.

Rodríguez, Néstor P. 1987. "Undocumented Central Americans in Houston: Diverse Populations." *International Migration Review* 21 (1): 4–26.

Rodríguez, Néstor P., and Jacqueline M. Hagan. 1992. "Apartment Restructuring and Latino Immigrant Tenant Struggles: A Case Study of Human Agency." *Comparative Urban and Community Research* 4: 164–180.

Rodríguez, Néstor P., and Ximena Urrutia-Rojas. 1990. "Impact of Recent Refugee Migration to Texas: A Comparison of Southeast Asian and Central American Newcomers." In *Mental Health of Immigrants and Refugees,* ed. Wayne H. Holtzman and Thomas H. Bornemann, 263–278. Austin: Hogg Foundation for Mental Health.

Rosaldo, Renato. 1989. *Culture and Truth: The Remaking of Social Analysis.* Boston: Beacon Press.

Roschelle, Anne R. 1997a. "Declining Networks of Care: Ethnicity, Migration, and Poverty in a Puerto Rican Community." *Race, Gender and Class* 4 (2): 107–125.

———. 1997b. *No More Kin: Exploring Race, Class, and Gender in Family Networks.* Thousand Oaks, Calif.: Sage Publications.

Rossi, Alice S., and Peter H. Rossi. 1990. *Of Human Bonding: Parent-Child Relations across the Life Course.* New York: Aldine de Gruyter.

Rouse, Roger. 1989. "Mexican Migration to the United States: Family Relations in the Development of a Transnational Migrant Circuit." Ph.D. dissertation, Stanford University.

Ruggles, Patricia, and Michael M. Fix. 1985. *Impacts and Potential Impacts of Central American Migrants on HHS and Related Programs of Assistance.* Washington, D.C.: Urban Institute.

Ruggles, Patricia, Michael M. Fix, and Kathleen M. Thomas. 1985. "Profile of the Central American in the United States." Resource Paper no. 3. Washington, D.C.: Urban Institute.

Rumbaut, Rubén G. 1989. "The Structure of Refuge: Southeast Asian Refugees in the U.S., 1975–1985." *International Review of Comparative Public Policy* 1: 97–129.

———. 1994a. "Origins and Destinies: Immigration to the United States since World War II." *Sociological Forum* 9 (4): 583–621.

———. 1994b. "The Crucible Within: Ethnic Identity, Self-Esteem, and Segmented Assimilation among Children of Immigrants." *International Migration Review* 28 (4): 748–794.

Salgado de Snyder, Nelly V., Richard C. Cervantes, and Amado M. Padilla. 1990. "Gender and Ethnic Differences in Psychosocial Stress and Generalized Distress among Hispanics." *Sex Roles* 22 (7–8): 441–453.

Salzinger, Leslie. 1991. "A Maid by Any Other Name: The Transformation of 'Dirty Work' by Central American Immigrants." In *Ethnography Unbound: Power and Resistance in the Modern Metropolis,* ed. Michael Burawoy, Alice Burton, Ann Arnett Ferguson, Kathryn J. Fox, Joshua Gamson, Nadine Gartrell, Leslie Hurst, Charles Kurzman, Leslie Salzinger, Josepha Schiffman, and Shiari Ui, 139–160. Berkeley: University of California Press.

Sandalow, Marc. 1993. "INS Chief Says Illegals' Goal Isn't Welfare." *San Francisco Chronicle,* October 30, A1.

Sassen, Saskia. 1988. *The Mobility of Labor and Capital: A Study in International Investment and Labor Flow.* Cambridge: Cambridge University Press.

———. 1991. *The Global City: New York, London, Tokyo.* Princeton: Princeton University Press.

Sassen-Koob, Saskia. 1984. "Notes on the Incorporation of Third World Women into Wage-Labor through Immigration and Off-Shore Production." *International Migration Review* 18 (4): 1144–1167.

Simmel, Georg. 1950. *The Sociology of Georg Simmel.* Trans. and ed. Kurt H. Wolff. Glencoe, Ill.: Free Press.

Singer, Audrey, and Douglas S. Massey. 1998. "The Social Process of Undocumented Border Crossing among Mexican Migrants." *International Migration Review* 32 (3): 561–592.

Smith, Michael P., and Bernadette Tarallo. 1992. *California's Changing Faces: New Immigrant Survival Strategies and State Policy.* Berkeley, Calif.: California Policy Seminar.

Stack, Carol B. 1974. *All Our Kin: Strategies for Survival in a Black Community.* New York: Harper & Row.

———. 1979. "The Kindred of Viola Jackson: Residence and Family Organization of an Urban Black American Family." In *A Heritage of Her Own: Toward a New Social History of American Women,* ed. Nancy F. Cott and Elizabeth H. Pleck, 542–554. New York: Simon & Schuster.

Stack, Carol B., and Linda M. Burton. 1993. "Kinscripts." *Journal of Comparative Family Studies* 24 (2):157–170.

Stanley, William. 1987. "Economic Migrants or Refugees from Violence? A Time-Series Analysis of Salvadoran Migration to the United States." *Latin American Research Review* 22 (1): 132–154.

Stanton-Salazar, Ricardo D. 1997. "A Social Capital Framework for Understanding the Socialization of Racial Minority Children and Adults." *Harvard Educational Review* 67 (1): 1–40.

Stark, Oded. 1991. *The Migration of Labor.* Cambridge, Mass.: Basil Blackwell.

Suarez-Orozco, Marcelo M. 1989. *Central American Refugees and U.S. High*

Schools: A Psychosocial Study of Motivation and Achievement. Stanford: Stanford University Press.

Taylor, Edward. 1986. "Differential Migration, Networks, Information, and Risk." *Research in Human Capital and Development: Migration, Human Capital, and Development* 4: 147–171.

———. 1992. "Earnings and Mobility of Legal and Illegal Immigrant Workers in Agriculture." *American Journal of Agricultural Economics* 74 (4): 889–896.

Thomas, William I., and Florian Znaniecki. 1927. *The Polish Peasant in Europe and America.* New York: Alfred Knopf.

Thomson, Marilyn. 1986. *Women of El Salvador: The Price of Freedom.* London: Zed Press.

Tietjen, Anne Marie. 1980. "Integrating Formal and Informal Support Systems: The Swedish Experience." In *Protecting the Children from Abuse and Neglect: Developing and Maintaining Effective Support Systems for Families,* ed. James Garbarino, S. Holly Stocking, and assoc., 15–36. San Francisco: Jossey-Bass.

Torres-Rivas, Edelberto, and Dina Jiménez. 1985. "Informe sobre el estado de las migraciones en Centro América." *Anuario de Estudios Centroamericanos* 11 (2): 25–66.

Torrez, Diana J. 1997. "The Role of Gender and Race in the Older Latina's Economic Well-Being." *Race, Gender and Class* 4 (20): 73–90.

Trager, Louis. 1991. "Blue Collar Blues." *San Francisco Chronicle,* June 2, D1.

Tuller, David. 1994. "Bay Poll Backs Ballot Measure on Immigration." *San Francisco Chronicle,* May 9, A1.

Ulloa, Roxana Elizabeth. 1998. *De indocumentados a ciudadanos: Características de los salvadoreños legalizados en Estados Unidos.* San Salvador: FLACSO.

UNESCO. 1995. *Statistical Yearbook.* New York: UNESCO Publishing and Bernan Press.

United Nations. 1996. *1994 Demographic Yearbook.* New York: United Nations, Department for Economic and Social Information and Policy Analysis, Statistics Division.

Urrutia-Rojas, Ximena, and Néstor P. Rodríguez. 1997. "Unaccompanied Migrant Children from Central America: Sociodemographic Characteristics and Experiences with Potentially Traumatic Events." In *Health and Social Services among International Labor Migrants: A Comparative Perspective,* ed. Antonio Ugalde and Gilberto Cárdenas, 151–166. Austin: University of Texas Press, Center for Mexican American Studies.

U.S. Bureau of the Census. 1980. *Foreign Born Immigrants in the United States.* Washington, D.C.: Bureau of the Census.

———. 1993. *Census of Population and Housing, 1990.* Summary Tape File 4 (California) [machine readable data files], prepared by the Bureau of the Census. Washington, D.C.: Bureau of the Census.

U.S. Department of State. 1982. *Country Reports on Human Rights Practices for 1981.* Washington, D.C.: Government Printing Office.

U.S. Immigration and Naturalization Service. 1978. *Annual Report.* Washington, D.C.: Government Printing Office.

———. 1981. *Statistical Yearbook of the Immigration and Naturalization Service.* Washington, D.C.: U.S. Department of Justice.

———. 1995. *Statistical Yearbook of the Immigration and Naturalization Service.* Washington, D.C.: U.S. Department of Justice.

———. 1997a. "INS Releases Updated Estimates of U.S. Illegal Population." News release. Washington, D.C.: U.S. Department of Justice.

———. 1997b. *Statistical Yearbook of the Immigration and Naturalization Service, 1996.* Washington, D.C.: Government Printing Office.

———. 1998. *Nicaraguan Adjustment and Central American Relief Act, 1997.* Washington, D.C.: U.S. Department of Justice.

Vaa, Mariken, Sally E. Findley, and Assitan Diallo. 1989. "The Gift Economy: A Study of Women Migrant Survival Strategies in a Low-Income Bamako Neighborhood." *Labour, Capital, and Society* 22 (2): 234–260.

Vaux, Alan. 1988. *Social Support: Theory, Research, and Intervention.* New York: Praeger.

Wallace, Steven P. 1986. "Central American and Mexican Immigrant Characteristics and Incorporation in California." *International Migration Review* 20 (3): 657–671.

———. 1989. "The New Urban Latinos: Central Americans in a Mexican Immigrant Environment." *Urban Affairs Quarterly* 25 (2): 239–264.

———. 1992. "Community Formation as an Activity of Daily Living: The Case of Nicaraguan Immigrant Elderly." *Journal of Aging Studies* 6 (4): 365–383.

Walton, John. 1975. "Internal Colonialism: Problems of Definition and Measurement." In *Urbanization and Inequality: The Political Economy of Urban and Rural Development in Latin America,* ed. Wayne A. Cornelius and Felicity Trueblood, 29–50. Beverly Hills, Calif.: Sage Publications.

Ward, Thomas W. 1987. "The Price of Fear: Salvadoran Refugees in the City of Angels." Ph.D. dissertation, University of California, Los Angeles.

Warren, Robert. 1994. "Estimates of the Unauthorized Immigrant Population Residing in the United States, by Country of Origin and State of Residence: October 1992." Paper presented at the Conference on Immigration, Center for California Studies, Sacramento State University, April 29.

Waters, Mary C. 1997. "Immigrant Families at Risk: Factors That Undermine Chances for Success." In *Immigration and the Family:*

Research and Policy on U.S. Immigrants, ed. Alan Booth, Ann C. Crouter, and Nancy Landale, 79–87. Mahwah, N.J.: Lawrence Erlbaum Associates.

Wellman, Barry. 1981. "Applying Network Analysis to the Study of Support." In *Social Networks and Social Support,* ed. Benjamin H. Gottlieb, 171–200. Beverly Hills, Calif.: Sage Publications.

———. 1988. "Structural Analysis: From Method and Metaphor to Theory and Substance." In *Social Structures: A Network Approach,* ed. Barry Wellman and S. D. Berkowitz, 19–61. New York: Cambridge University Press.

Wellman, Barry, and Scot Wortley. 1989. "Brothers' Keepers: Situating Kinship Relations in Broader Networks of Social Support." *Sociological Perspectives* 32 (3): 273–306.

Wetherell, Charles, Andrejs Plakans, and Barry Wellman. 1994. "Social Networks, Kinship, and Community in Eastern Europe." *Journal of Interdisciplinary History* 24 (4): 639–663.

White, Lynn K., and Agnes Riedmann. 1992. "Ties among Adult Siblings." *Social Forces* 71 (1): 85–102.

Wilcox, Brian L. 1981. "Social Support, Life Stress, and Psychological Adjustment: A Test of the Buffering Hypothesis." *American Journal of Community Psychology* 9 (4): 371–386.

Wilson, William Julius. 1987. *The Truly Disadvantaged: The Inner City, the Underclass, and Public Policy.* Chicago: University of Chicago Press.

Yanagisako, Sylvia Junko. 1977. "Women-centered Kin Networks in Urban Bilateral Kinship." *American Ethnologist* 4 (2): 207–226.

Zaborowska, Magdalena J. 1995. *How We Found America: Reading Gender through East-European Immigrant Narratives.* Chapel Hill: University of North Carolina Press.

Zavella, Patricia. 1985. "'Abnormal Intimacy': The Varying Work Networks of Chicana Cannery Workers." *Feminist Studies* 11 (3): 541–557.

Zhou, Min. 1992. *Chinatown: The Socioeconomic Potential of an Urban Enclave.* Philadelphia: Temple University Press.

Zolberg, Aristide, Astri Suhrke, and Sergio Aguayo. 1989. *Escape from Violence: Conflict and the Refugee Crisis in the Developing World.* New York: Oxford University Press.

Zorbaugh, Harvey Warren. 1929. *The Gold Coast and the Slum: A Sociological Study of Chicago's Near North Side.* Chicago: University of Chicago Press.

Index

FRAGMENTED TIES